Woman, live a full life!

....

Everything you need to know to get your life back in control in just 30 days.
A complete plan to get out of the chaos.

·

Emily Kendall

Copyright © 2021 Emily Kendall
All rights reserved.

CONTENTS

Introduction	**5**
You're Not Alone	**5**
How to Complete This Guide	**8**
DAY 1: REPLACE YOUR PAPER PLANNER	13
DAY 2: ORGANIZE YOUR LIFE	25
DAY 3: YOUR LIFE JAR	35
DAY 4: DESIGN EFFECTIVE ROUTINES	43
DAY 5: MAKE TIME PART 1	55
DAY 6: MAKE TIME PART 2	69
DAY 7: STOP PUTTING YOURSELF LAST	87
DAY 8: THE ART OF SAYING "NO"	91
DAY 9: SOUL-CARE	99
DAY 10: AUTOMATE GROCERY SHOPPING	111
DAY 11: PLANNING & MAKING MEALS	119
DAY 12: LIVE WITHIN YOUR SEAMS	129
DAY 13: SET A CLEANING SCHEDULE	141
DAY 14: SHARE THE LOAD	151
DAY 15: MAINTAIN CLEANLINESS	165
DAY 16: SOLVE YOUR PAPERWORK PROBLEM	169
DAY 17: EMPTY YOUR SINK FULL OF DISHES	179
DAY 18: TACKLE YOUR MOUNTAIN OF DIRTY LAUNDRY	185
DAY 19: ELIMINATE A POINT OF TENSION	199
DAY 20: PAY YOUR BILLS	203
DAY 21: AVOID "DECLINED" EMBARRASSMENT	209
DAY 22: CUT EXPENSES PART 1	227
DAY 23: CUT EXPENSES PART 2	241
DAY 24: MAKE MORE MONEY & STICK TO YOUR BUDGET	255
DAY 25: TAKE PRIDE IN YOUR APPEARANCE PART 1	265
DAY 26: TAKE PRIDE IN YOUR APPEARANCE PART 2	275
DAY 27: DIGITAL DECLUTTER & TECHNOLOGY TROUBLES	283
DAY 28: CHRONICALLY LATE	293
DAY 29: LOSING YOUR KEYS & OTHER STUFF	297
DAY 30: A MESSY CAR & EMPTY TANK	301
Conclusion	**311**

Introduction

I'm so glad you're here because that means you took the first step towards transforming your life, admitting there's room for improvement! I'm super excited for you to begin your journey from being a hot mess gal to a refined woman.
I say "refined" because it's possible that even after these thirty days you may still be a hot mess. In fact, that's expected. You know why? Because being a little bit of a mess is normal.

Whether people want to admit it or not, no one has lived today yet. Everyone is just winging it!

We're all a little bit of a hot mess in one way or another, though I believe that some people are more prone to it and must work harder than others to not be. Thankfully, we have schedules, systems, and the tiny robot in our pocket to help us out. And now, you have something extra, a secret weapon that will help you take on the adulting world by storm, this guide!

Before we continue, let's briefly define the terms "hot mess" and "adulting," just so that we're on the same page. Adulting is defined by Oxford Languages as "the practice of behaving in a way characteristic of a responsible adult, especially the accomplishment of mundane but necessary tasks." Hot mess, on the other hand, seems to be quite the opposite of that. It is defined by Oxford Languages as "<u>a person or thing that is *spectacularly* unsuccessful or disordered</u>."

I'm going to choose to view their term "spectacularly" as a compliment. But that's no exaggeration when it comes to the cringe-worthy mishaps and hilarious shenanigans I've experienced and brought upon myself, some of which you're about to learn.

You're Not Alone
Right now, you might be feeling like you're the only one who doesn't have their stuff together. <u>Your world may seem out of control, but you're *not* alone in feeling that way.</u>
I was the same way a few years ago, and I too wondered how everyone else seemed to have their stuff together while I felt like I was *drowning* just trying to do the basics.
Growing up, I was always the "late friend," the "hot mess friend," the "running out of gas, bald tires, and no money in the bank" friend. And

when I moved out of my parents' house, things just got worse. On my own, I began learning the hard way just how *not* on top of it I really was.

Despite my parents not having a dishwasher, their dishes always got clean. Yet when I moved into an apartment, one that *had* a dishwasher, my dishes somehow never got done. They sat in the sink *way* longer than they should have, even growing mold a few times! And I was too grossed out to do anything about it, and too ashamed to ask for help to get them back under control.

Things were the same when it came to doing my laundry. I had a mountain of it that was literally the size of a Volkswagen beetle. How do I know? Because my beetle was parked in my garage right next to my laundry machine and giant pile of laundry! I went weeks, sometimes even a month, between completed loads. Instead of putting things away, everything just lived in my dryer. And I could never find what I wanted to wear as it was all lost, buried somewhere underneath all of the other clothes.

Paying the utilities was a new concept to me as well. My electricity and water were cut off many times simply because I forgot to pay them. One time, I had to carry my dogs' water bowl over to a neighbor's house and ask them for water because I couldn't fill it up myself. How *embarrassing!*

Worst of all, a few years ago I hit one of the lowest points in my life. I became depressed, anxious, and my hot messiness seemed to hit an all-new high. I felt completely out of control of my life!

I ended up being let go from my job, something that I thought was going to be my career for the next fifteen years. And I believe it was partly due to me being a hot mess. I think that if I knew the things I know now, things I'm going to teach you, it would have turned out differently.

I know these things may sound alarming to some. But to others, I hope that my open, albeit embarrassing transparency, helps you feel better about yourself and your situation.

Now I'll admit, things were not quite this hectic when I lived by myself. In fact, I feel like I was pretty on top of it, at least as far as cleanliness goes, as a single woman. However, things changed as a newlywed. Suddenly, I found myself in situations that I'd never been in before. So if you're single and living by yourself or with a roommate, are about to get married, or even if you've been married for a few years, <u>the program I've developed for you in the upcoming pages will help you navigate no matter what situation you're in.</u>

I've improved so much since that time in my life. I used the opportunity that I was gifted by being let go from my job to pursue my dreams. Now,

thanks to God's goodness, I get to spend my days making women's lives easier through my blog and boutique (which is perhaps where you found this guide). My laundry *always* gets done *and* put away. My sink stays empty. My electric bill hasn't been shut off in years, and so much more! Best of all, I remembered to call my mom on her birthday, something that I had missed the last *nine years* (bless her for putting up with me).
I can proudly say that I'm a refined woman, but that's not to say that I'm never a hot mess anymore. Heck, I still have many of those days where I feel like a chicken with my head cut off. This brings me to an important point that I'd like to make. The suggestions and ideas throughout this guide are all things I *try* to do. However, I do not do everything every day, and I don't expect you to either! But that doesn't mean that we can't aspire to be better versions of ourselves.

I know that these tips would have saved me a lot of headache and made my life *way* easier. So allow me to divulge my mistakes to you so that you can learn from them and laugh with me at them. My hope is that by sharing this compilation of tips with you, I'll prevent the same misfortunes that I encountered, and that this guide will truly make your life all the better. So know that I speak from a place of understanding, and again, that you're not alone in your struggle.

This guide, or written course as I'm considering it, is not just based on my own limited experience and viewpoints though. The tips, tricks, and suggestions that you'll find throughout the next thirty days are the result of countless hours of researching, interviewing, watching videos, reading books, and listening to podcasts. I called companies to get the inside scoop and tested out apps and systems to see which ones worked and would offer the most value to you. I spoke to strangers, mentors, and fellow hot messes to gather their opinions and secrets so that this guide would be the ultimate, well-rounded tool for you.

I'll link to the resources I gathered my information from so that if any topics interest you, you can dive into them further on your own. Disclaimer: Some of the things I link to may contain affiliate links. As an Amazon Associate, I may earn a small commission at *no extra cost to you* when you click my links and make a qualifying purchase. With that being said, it is important to me to never recommend something purely for the sake of earning a commission. So you will occasionally see me reference material or a product without a link because I do not endorse it, or because

I believe you can find the item cheaper in person, like at a thrift store for example.

While I'm disclaiming things, I'd like to be clear about the fact that <u>I do not have a degree in any of the subjects that I'll be covering.</u> The only degrees I have for the topics in this guide are the ones I received from the school of hard knocks. So <u>if you choose to partake in any of the activities, you do so at your own risk.</u> Please use your discretion.

Grab a Friend
"If you want to go fast, go alone. If you want to go far, go together." – African proverb

Before we get into how to complete this guide, why not grab a buddy to do it with you? While you certainly can complete it by yourself, <u>everything's better with a friend!</u> Plus, as this 30-day program can be pretty tough at times, it may help keep your motivation up to have someone else going through the same process. So consider inviting one of your girlfriends to order their own guide and join you on your journey, someone who you think could benefit from it, or someone who you know would be a great accountability partner. Please be aware that sharing any of the contents of this guide, including any downloadable content or spreadsheets, with anyone (other than your spouse) is strictly forbidden. All rights have been reserved. No portion may be reproduced in any form without our explicit permission, except as permitted by U.S. copyright law.

How to Complete This Guide
Although the program is thirty days, you do not need to wait until the beginning of a month to start it. You can start it at any time that best suits your needs. However, <u>I recommend that you do not start it when you have any big obligations coming up.</u> This is because it's going to require you to spend some time working on it daily, which you may not have time for if you're in the middle of a big event or trip.

Unfortunately, I can't just snap my fingers and improve your life for you. You, my little diamond in the rough, are going to have to sacrifice some of your valuable relaxation time and put in some work. Ugh! But isn't your future self worth it? So set aside time every day to work on this guide. You'll have a topic to read as well as an Action Plan, or your homework, to complete. Some days, you'll have a lot to read, and other days the chapters will be much shorter. Sometimes, you'll have a bunch of homework to do, and other times you might not have any if you already have all of the steps completed that are required of you. To get the most out of your experience, be sure to complete every activity fully, as they're all built complimenting and compounding on one another. With that being said though, there is a lot of material to cover. So <u>it's okay if you don't get to everything at first. Just make a plan to get back to the things you miss and address them another time</u>. If you find that the work asked of you each day is too much, slow down the pace at which you go through the guide by spreading out each day's work over the course of several.

I know it'll be tempting with some activities to think, "This doesn't apply to me" or "I don't like doing stuff that way so I'm going to do it how I normally do." But whatever you're currently doing isn't working. Right? That's why you're here. So I ask that you give the steps of this program a chance to work for you by following along with the prompts the way they've been designed, to be done in full. Plus, <u>it's only thirty days, so after that, you can go back to doing things how you like *if* you want to.</u>

Just like how I suggest you do *every* activity, it's best if you go through the guide *in order*, as it was created in a certain way to make things easier for you. If you instead go through the guide in whatever order you choose, some parts may be confusing as you won't understand the context. You'll also be behind on the Action Plans. So your homework may be harder, if not impossible, to complete.

Section 1: The Tools You'll Need

Day 1: Replace Your Paper Planner
Day 2: Organize Your Life

Section 2: Get a Grip on Life

Day 3: Your Life Jar
Day 4: Design Effective Routines
Day 5: "Make" Time Part 1
Day 6: "Make" Time Part 2
Day 7: Stop Putting Yourself Last
Day 8: The Art of Saying "No"
Day 9: Soul-Care

Section 3: Adulting Basics

Day 10: Automate Grocery Shopping
Day 11: Planning & Making Meals
Day 12: Live Within Your Seams
Day 13: Set a Cleaning Schedule
Day 14: Share the Load
Day 15: Maintain Cleanliness
Day 16: Solve Your Paperwork Problem
Day 17: Empty Your Sink Full of Dishes
Day 18: Tackle Your Mountain of Dirty Laundry
Day 19: Eliminate a Point of Tension
Day 20: Pay Your Bills
Day 21: Avoid "Declined" Embarrassment
Day 22: Cut Expenses Part 1
Day 23: Cut Expenses Part 2
Day 24: Make More Money & Stick to Your Budget
Day 25: Take Pride in Your Appearance Part 1
Day 26: Take Pride in Your Appearance Part 2

Section 4: Hot Mess Solutions

Day 27: Digital Declutter & Technology Troubles
Day 28: Chronically Late
Day 29: Losing Your Keys & Other Stuff
Day 30: A Messy Car & Empty Tank

DAY 1:
REPLACE YOUR PAPER PLANNER

You may recall how I mentioned in the Read First section that <u>you need to be open to doing things a new way because the old way you were doing things wasn't working for you</u>. Well, today will be your first real test of that, because I'm going to ask you to do something that may be very difficult. I'm going to ask you to give up paper. Why do I want you to switch from writing things manually to having everything be digital? I'll go over some big reasons shortly. But for now, I ask that you give this new way of doing things a try. Like I said before, after these thirty days are over you can go back to your old ways. That is to say, you can go back to using your paper planner *if* you still want to.

Now with that being said, <u>you may be on the opposite side of things and have been using Google Calendar and other digital software for years</u>, so giving up paper won't be a big deal. Maybe you're super organized when it comes to scheduling, but you picked up this guide because you need help in other areas. I ask that you <u>read through this chapter anyway</u> as it's always good to get a refresher. Plus, you may learn something new.

One last note before we jump in, I understand if you have an iPhone that you may want to use apps made for your device. But in this guide, I'll only be going over options available to everyone. So while you may prefer to use Apple's calendar and notes, we'll be going over Google's equivalents.

Why a Digital Planner Is Better

Let's begin with a real-life scenario so you can start to understand just how powerful a tool Google Calendar is.

Imagine that you have an appointment at the dentist's. While there, they want to schedule you for your next appointment. Because you always have your phone with you, you can check your schedule to confirm that you don't have anything planned. That time works for you, so you put it right into your calendar, complete with notifications that will alert and remind you when that date and time come up. You also help save a tree (or more like a twig) because you don't need to have a reminder slip printed out for you. You "write" down your dental appointment one time and then cross it off your mental checklist knowing that all devices you use will have that event synced up to them without any more work on your part. There will be no need for you to write the calendar event in multiple locations, or even write it a second time from a paper slip into a paper planner. In addition, because your spouse has access to your calendar, he can see when you have that appointment so he'll be able to plan his schedule accordingly.

As you can see, using Google Calendar would incorporate order and ease into your life. But if that scenario wasn't enough to convince you to give up your beloved spiral-bound planner, let's go over some reasons why you should switch.

You save time. I think one of the biggest benefits of switching from using a paper planner to a digital one is how much time you save. A digital planner allows you to <u>set events to repeat</u> without having to write recurring dates over and over again like you would with paper. It also eliminates those time "wasters" like adding stickers, pictures, notes, and little doodles with gel pens. I'm not denying that having a pretty planner is fun and that having something beautiful to admire and carry around can get you excited to write stuff in it, but that doesn't help you get organized. <u>A planner is to help you be productive, not to be a showcase of your art.</u>

Don't get me wrong. I like having an aesthetically pleasing schedule, but changing things digitally takes a few clicks. It's not going to suck up your time like trying to replicate a bullet journal with calligraphy lettering that you saw on Youtube. That's not practical nor time-efficient.

You'll always have it with you. Another great benefit to switching to a digital calendar is that <u>while you may occasionally forget to bring a planner, you'll most likely always have your phone, so you'll always be prepared to schedule something</u>. This will help you avoid trying to remember the important details of an event, only to completely space it. Or prevent you from having appointments on little pieces of paper that could potentially get lost. Instead, you'll be able to put things directly into your schedule, and even put notes in about them too, such as "Bring proof of insurance to the next dental appointment." We'll go over that more later.

It's less clutter. <u>Using a digital calendar helps eliminate both physical and mental clutter.</u>

Being surrounded by paper clutter, or clutter in general, can negatively affect your mood and quality of life. This is why we'll be spending an entire day going over how to Solve Your Paperwork Problem. But for now, you'll be able to clean off all those sticky notes from your desk and enjoy a clearer living space. And you'll be able to rest assured that all of your must-not-forgets on those sticky notes won't be forgotten because they'll be written down in a space designated just for them.

In addition to leading to less physical clutter, Google Calendar will reduce your mental clutter as well. <u>Its great notification system can send you reminders about events, giving you one less thing to think about and have to remember</u>. So you won't have to worry that you'll blow off your friend for a coffee date again because you forgot to check your schedule. Google Calendar will remind you.

You can't lose it. I feel that this point is especially important for us hot messes. I've personally misplaced my paper planner before and spent many agonizing days looking for it hoping I wasn't missing important events or appointments. You can do away with that problem altogether by eliminating your paper planner. Now you may be thinking, "What happens if I put my schedule on my phone and then I lose that?" Girlfriend, I've lost that too. But you know what I didn't lose? My calendar.

Everything is synched. Like I just mentioned, you can accidentally leave your paper planner somewhere, and then you're out of luck! But with Google Calendar <u>you won't lose important dates</u>, and you'll be able to pick back up wherever you left off. This is exactly what I did. Plus, having everything linked makes things so much easier. <u>Not only does Google have different devices sync to each other, but it also has its apps linked as well</u>. For instance, Gmail can be linked to Google Calendar.

Your information is backed up. Did you ever stay up late working on a paper for school only to have the power go off and hours of work be wasted because you forgot to save? Just me? Well, with Google Calendar that won't be a problem. At this time, <u>Google backs up calendars every 12 hours</u>, which means that twice a day your events and dates will be saved. However, if every 12 hours isn't good enough for you, they do have an option where you can manually download your calendar as well.

You can share events with others easily. This is <u>great for keeping everyone on the same page</u>. You can conveniently share calendars with your spouse and friends to make coordinating dates and avoiding schedule conflicts easier. Even better, you don't have to remind them of those events. You can let Google handle that for you.

An example of this would be scheduling activities for a wedding. If you were the Maid of Honor and had to wrangle a bunch of people to get to the bridal shower, bachelorette party, and dress rehearsal, you could invite everyone via Google Calendar. Then all the guests would know the dates, times, and where things would take place. You wouldn't have to reach out to every single person to tell them the details. And you could send a quick email update to all of them if one of the locations had to be changed due to inclement weather. People would even be able to RSVP to events you shared with them by responding with "Yes," "No," "Maybe," or "Yes, joining virtually." So you'd know which people wouldn't be able to get to the dress rehearsal and could plan accordingly.

It's environmentally friendly. According to the University of Southern Indiana, every year Americans use about 680 pounds of paper per person. Of that, 13,000 sheets of paper are thrown away per household. Switching to a digital calendar will help lessen this unnecessary waste that we sometimes thoughtlessly create.

It doesn't cost anything. I'm still dumbfounded that Google gives us access to all of their great software at no charge. So what have you got to lose by trying it? Free certainly beats forking out $60 for one of those fancy Erin Condren planners that cost so much you're scared to write in them.

How to Set Up Google Calendar

Now that you know why switching to a digital planner like Google Calendar is a better option than paper planners, let's set yours up!

Because you can access more while using a computer, I'm going to be walking you through how to use the majority of the features from a desktop. Be sure to download the "Google Calendar" app on your phone as well though, if it isn't already installed. This way, you can access your schedule anytime, anywhere.

After that step, and while you're still logged into your Google Account, pull up Google Calendar. To do this on your desktop, start at the Google homepage and click the nine little dots forming a square in the upper right of your screen to see Google's apps. Scroll down and click on "Calendar."

You could also simply type into the search bar "calendar.google.com" to immediately pull it up.

<u>Your Google Calendar will then be generated and a few different calendars will be created</u> which will consist of reminders, tasks, birthdays, holidays, and one for your general use.

How to Use Google Calendar

Let's next go over the basics of how to use your new calendar as well as a few good-to-know tips and tricks.

Adjust your settings. What date and time format do you want to use? What time zone do you want to be set as your primary? What day do you want your week to start on? These are all things that can be changed in the "General" settings. <u>Give this area a quick scan to make sure that everything is how you want it</u>. To do this, click on the "Settings menu," or the gear icon on the upper right, then on "Settings," and scroll through the first section you land on.

After you finish with the general settings, you can <u>edit the settings for specific calendars</u>. Scroll down on the left side and click on any calendar you want to edit. Here you can change the calendar's name and share it with other people, an option which we'll be going over shortly.

Create events. The most fundamental thing you'll need to know is how to create events. To do this, click the button in the upper left which says "Create," or just right-click on the day you want to make an event. Then fill out the details.

<u>If after you've created an event you decide you want to change the date or time</u>, you don't need to go back in to edit it. Simply <u>drag and drop the event to rearrange</u>.

Set alerts. By far the most useful, and what I feel is <u>the most crucial for us hot messes</u>, is the notification feature. Instead of wasting time repeatedly checking your schedule throughout the day, or worse, not checking it and missing something, you can set alerts.

To set them, click on "Add alert," or hit the bell symbol when making a new event. Then choose when you'd like to be notified. I recommend, depending upon the event, that you <u>set multiple reminders</u>.

If you wanted to set reminders for that dental appointment example from earlier, I'd suggest you <u>set a notification to alert you the day before, so you can make any necessary preparations</u> (ensuring you have transportation, paperwork you need to bring, etc). <u>Set a second alert for the day of, to remind you when to start getting ready to leave. And a third alert should be set for when it's time to head out the door</u>. Note how the final alert is NOT set for WHEN the appointment is scheduled, as by that time it would be too late.

I highly recommend that you also set multiple alerts for any special occasion where you need to *do* or *get* something for it. When you add someone's birthday to your calendar, today and in the future, <u>set an alert for that event three weeks in advance so you can buy them a gift. Set a 2nd alert two weeks out so you remember to put the gift in the mail. Then set a 3rd alert for the day of, to remind you to call or text that person</u> and wish them a happy birthday.

<u>If instead, you have an event that requires little to no preparation, one alarm may suffice</u>. An example of this would be when it's time for me to stop typing and go cook dinner.

Change colors. Another thing you could do <u>to make important events "pop" so you don't miss them</u>, besides setting an alert, is to <u>change their color</u>. I have my most important events set to a stark red, while the rest of my calendar is made up of light blues, greens, and pinks. To edit an event's color, pull up the event editing page by double-clicking on an event, or by single-clicking and tapping the pencil icon. Then open the color swatch drop-down menu.

<u>You can change a calendar's color as well</u> if you want it to reflect more of your personal style. On your Google Calendar's homepage, hover over the calendar you want to change which will be listed underneath "My calendars" on the left side. Click the three dots that appear, and then choose which color you'd like. Those will be the basic color options available to you, but we'll go over additional ways you can spruce things up later.

Get reminders. If you have something coming up and you're worried you might forget about it, have Google Calendar remind you. Doing so won't make a single event that can be forgotten about after that day passes. Instead, it'll create an "event" that carries over, day after day, until you mark it complete (or until you just delete it because you're never going to get to it).

Reminders default to being shown all day, but if you need to be reminded at a specific time you can set them to pop up then.

To make one, click on "Create." And instead of leaving the popup on "Event," which is the default, switch it to "Reminder." These will be stored in the default "Reminders" calendar that was generated for you. To see them, check or uncheck the box next to the calendar name on the lower left of the main page.

Repeat events. This feature is especially handy when it comes to things like birthdays and anniversaries, so take some time today when making your calendar to set all recurring dates to repeat yearly.

To make an event repeat, open the editing page how it was mentioned earlier. Then click on the drop-down menu underneath the dates at the top and choose how often you want it to repeat.

If you have an event that only repeats a limited number of times, you can still use this feature. If you want it to stop after a certain amount of occurrences click on "Custom..." You can then set it to "end after 5 occurrences," and after that time has passed the calendar will no longer show events for it without you needing to delete or stop it.

Duplicate events. This is a fast way to create *similar* events when you only want to make *minor* changes, like adding a new date and time. This is opposed to having to create a whole new event and needing to enter in all of the details again. It's particularly helpful if you have people invited to the event because duplicating it carries over the invitees, so you don't have to re-invite everyone again. To do this, single-click on an event, click the three dots, and then hit "Duplicate."

Keep track of locations. Because Google Maps is connected to Google Calendar, you can add locations to events! This way, you won't only know *when* an event is going to happen, but also *where* and *how* to get there.

To add an address, go to the event's editing page, find the location symbol inside of the "Event Details" section, and start typing the address or keyword of the place you're looking for. When it's time for that event, you can click "Directions" from inside your Google Calendar to be taken there.

"Write" and store pertinent information. The note's feature inside of an event is extremely useful for a few reasons, so I recommend taking advantage of it. Perhaps the most obvious is that you can "write" notes about an event, such as directions on how to find its entrance. You can quickly jot down your thoughts *during* that event for reference later. And best of all, you can add links, which offers a myriad of possibilities.

Say for instance that you're presenting a meeting for work. You could make an event for it on your calendar. Then you could put in the note's section a link to the Zoom meeting, the presentation you made for it, and a link to an article you need to read before it takes place. To take it a step further, you could also set an alert to go off so many minutes before the meeting, so you could read that article and have the information fresh in your mind.

Set up multiple calendars. You no longer need to carry around multiple planners or highlight everything in different colors to keep activities separate. Now you can just make a new calendar.

What calendars do you need? My husband and I both have our own calendars. I have a few extras for my business, and he has some additional ones for his work and volunteering. You may have ones for personal and work as well, and also have calendars for working out, bible study, and your hobby group. Can you think of any others?

To create a new calendar, hit the plus symbol next to where it says "Other calendars" on the lower left side of the main page. Click "Create new calendar," and enter the basic details. Once done, click on the calendar you just made to the left. This will open its settings and let you edit more details.

You may also consider adding one of Google's calendars of interest, such as holidays for different countries, holidays for different religions, moon phases, and sports teams. What a great way to know ahead of time when the Cowboys will be playing so you don't accidentally plan any activities for when your significant other will be glued to the tv.

To set this up, follow the same steps as before but choose "Browse calendars of interest." Pick one that piques your curiosity, and Google will populate your new calendar for you.

After you've created all the different calendars you need to keep your life organized, don't fret if your screen looks a bit cluttered or overwhelming. You can choose which calendars you want to view by either checking or unchecking their boxes to the left of the screen on the main page.

Google will make these new calendars different colors. I recommend you keep each calendar with its own unique color, so it's easier to differentiate between them at a glance.

Share calendars. If you're married, make sure to link your calendar and your spouse's. Having access to each other's schedules will make life that much easier for you both, especially if schedules tend to change or if there are a lot of balls in the air. This will also eliminate any unnecessary back and forth questioning about when one of you has something planned, which could lead to confusion and accidental double-booking.

If your significant other doesn't already have a Google calendar, now would be the perfect time for them to make one. Encourage them to do so by following the simple steps mentioned above, and if they so choose, to read the rest of this chapter and gain full insight into all of the benefits of having a digital calendar.

If you'd like to share your calendar, follow the steps mentioned earlier to open the calendar's settings. Scroll down on that page to where it says "Share with specific people," and enter in the email of whomever you'd like to have access to it.

If you'd like to receive access to someone else's calendar, look to the left of your screen on that same page. Click on "Add calendar," then "Subscribe to calendar," and enter in their email. It'll let them know you're requesting access so they can accept/approve it.

Sync Gmail. Instead of having to scroll through your emails to find dates and times, and then transferring the data into your calendar, you can sync the two together. Google Calendar can pull events from Gmail and set them up in your calendar automatically. It can do this for flights, hotel and restaurant reservations, and ticketed events like movies and concerts.

To enable this, go to Gmail and click "Settings," and then "See all settings." In the "General" tab scroll down to where it says "Smart features and personalization," and check the box. Back in Google Calendar go to "Settings," "Events from Gmail," and make sure the box is checked as well.

Use voice commands. You've probably noticed that Google Calendar can do a lot of stuff for you. Why not also have it <u>add, change or delete things using your voice</u>? It's audio compatible just like Siri and Alexa, so you can tell it to "Set a reminder," "Show my reminders," and "Make an event" for starters. For us hot mess gals who are always behind, I especially appreciate that you can say, "Send an email to my next meeting and tell them I'll be late" and it handles that for you while you rush to get there. You can't edit a lot of details with this audio feature, but you can have it do simple things such as changing a title or time or deleting an event.

<u>You'll need to have Google Assistant to use this</u>, which comes downloaded on Androids and can be added to iPhones. Read how to set up on either device if interested.

Set goals. This won't work for planning large, multi-step goals. But Google can make time slots for basic repeating ones, such as a goal to walk every day for thirty minutes. It'll check in with you to hold you accountable, and it'll even track your success! Of course, you could make these goals/events on your calendar yourself, but <u>this is a fun way to set your intentions. And it offers good prompts to help you set aside time for things that are important to you</u>.

For example, if you click on "Family & friends" it'll ask what you want to do. "Reach out to a friend." How often do you want to do that? "Twice a month." How long will you reach out? "30 minutes." And the best time of day for you to do this? "Evening." <u>It'll then create a repeating event for you based upon what you entered and when you have available in your schedule</u>.

At this time you can only create goals on a mobile device, but you can still edit them on a desktop. To create a goal, click on the plus icon on the bottom right of your screen. Choose "Goal," and then follow the intuitive prompts.

Recover deleted events. If you accidentally delete something, never fear. There is a recovery option! You don't have to deal with the embarrassment of asking someone when an event is happening, *again*. You can simply find and restore the event. To do this, click the "Settings" icon and then "Trash." Look for the event you want to restore, and click on the curved arrow to the right that will be next to the trash icon.

Add-Ons for Google Calendar

Here are some additional add-ons you can download if you'd like to further improve or personalize your experience.

GcalPlus This extension can <u>display full titles when you hover over an event</u>, which is helpful if you write long descriptive ones like I do. And <u>if you have a lot of events in a day, you can have your calendar display more of them</u>, instead of having some be cropped out causing you to forget that you had them scheduled in the first place. Watch this video for an overview and to learn what other minor modifications it offers.

Button for Google Calendar™ This Chrome extension is useful because it allows you to <u>quickly see your schedule without having to open up a new window</u> and wait for everything to load. Even better is that <u>it can show you how much time you have left until your next event</u>. And if you hover over the extension, you can see what that event is. This add-on also makes it slightly faster to create events as it takes you directly to a new event page when you click on its plus icon.

Custom Calendar Background Don't worry, I'm not going to take away all your fun of having an aesthetically pleasing planner. Use this Chrome extension to <u>add a pretty background</u> to replace the plain, boring white one.

First, download the extension. Second, find an image/s you like on Google. Right-click on the image/s and select "Copy image address." Back in Google Calendar click on "image" on the upper right near the search icon. Pick either "single image" if you want the background to stay the same, or choose "monthly images" if you want it to change every month. Paste the copied text into the "Image URL" section.

More Colors for Calendar! If the default color options don't offer enough variety, or if you'd like to personalize things even more, you can <u>add your own colors to events</u>. Begin by downloading the extension. Then visit www.htmlcolorcodes.com to choose a color and copy its HEX code. Go back to Google Calendar and double-click on an event you want to change the color of. Open the color drop-down menu and hit the plus sign. Next, paste the HEX code into the popup that'll appear. Your color of preference will then be added to the swatches you can choose from back in the color drop-down menu.

Action Plan

Today, set up a Google Account if you don't have one already. Next, set up your Google Calendar using that account, and be sure to download the app on your phone as well. Edit the settings and preferences how you see fit and add any of the Chrome extensions if you'd like.

Create one or multiple calendars depending upon if you want everything to be together or if you'd like to keep your things separate. If you're married, does your spouse have their own calendar? If not, would it be helpful for both of you if they made one today too? If they already have a Google calendar, give each other access to your schedules.

Finally, move all of the events/appointments you have in your paper planner into your Google Calendar. Don't forget to also add all of those that are on sticky notes and reminder slips. Most importantly, make sure you set alerts so you don't miss anything.

**DAY 2:
ORGANIZE YOUR LIFE**

You Can't Remember Everything

How many times have you thought, "I'll remember that" and then forgotten? Maybe you forgot where you parked your car, where you placed your sunglasses, what time your friend said to meet up, or signed up to do something or bring something somewhere and then totally spaced. We've all been there.

You have a million things on your mind, but <u>you don't have to keep them all locked up in there</u>. Trying to remember everything all the time will only lead to you dropping the ball at some point, perhaps even at the most inopportune time.

I experienced one of these cringe-worthy ball-dropping moments when I was first hired at a job I used to have. One of the head bosses had a habit of meeting up with all new employees. She did this to make sure new individuals were settling in well and to start building a relationship with them. The problem was, I completely forgot about the appointment and blew her off! This was *not* a good first impression and one that had negative rippling consequences. This affected how I was viewed and treated at that job for years, and it all started because I *thought* I would remember the appointment with her.

This example might make the most sense in reference to yesterday's topic. But this story still serves as a reminder that we can not remember *everything*, even the little things, even if we think we can and we will. "<u>Your mind is for having ideas, not holding them.</u>" – David Allen (a productivity consultant and author of *Getting Things Done*)

Attempting to keep it all up in your head just adds unnecessary stress when there are plenty of other surefire ways you can *ensure* things won't be forgotten or missed. Plus, <u>with the technology that's available to us nowadays, there's little room for excuses for failing to remember something</u>, especially when you could have just written it down.

Today, I'm going to introduce you to Google Keep, a digital note-taking software, where you'll be able to write down and keep track of all of those things you need to remember.

Why Google Keep

So why are we going to use Google Keep?

There are plenty of other apps out there that could provide you with the same services. However, as I mentioned yesterday, Google links and syncs their different software. This is particularly handy with Keep because you can take notes when you are out and about, and then reference them later through other applications or when using your computer. Plus, it's free! And as I want to make this guide as generally applicable to everyone, no matter their device or financial status, I've chosen to use this.

Once again, activities later in this guide depend upon you doing the activities earlier in this guide, in the order that I have laid them out for you. Two of the most foundational are yesterday's and today's. So follow along for the time being, even if there is something else that you'd prefer to use for note-taking. After you've finished the program, if you want to use something else, that is perfectly fine.

So what can Google Keep offer you? Simply put, a lot. Think of it as souped-up sticky notes. Not only can you jog down quick reminders and draw little sketches, but if you ever think of something you need to write down when you can't, the app can transcribe your speech into text for you. You can make your notes different colors, have them pop up at certain times to remind you of things, archive them for a clutter-free screen but still be able to reference them, and label or "pin" them so you can quickly find the information that is most important to you. Additionally, this digital equivalent takes up no room when compared to physical sticky notes and notebooks.

As you can see, Keep has lots of features that will make organizing your life that much easier. Let's get it downloaded so you can begin learning how to use it.

How to Set It Up

Just like yesterday, I'll be going over how to use Google's software on a desktop, but make sure you download Google Keep on your phone as well so that you can take notes wherever you are.

Since you set up your Google Account yesterday, today will be a cinch. Start from your Google homepage again and click the nine little dots forming a square in the upper right of your screen. Scroll down and click on "Keep." You could also just type "keep.google.com" into the search bar. Google will then generate your new Keep for you.

And that's it. Your setup is done.

How to Use It

Google Keep is pretty easy to understand and navigate intuitively, but feel free to watch this video if you want a visual walkthrough of its features and how to use them. As you'll be able to learn the majority of things through that video, I'm only going to cover a few aspects of the app which I think are most important for you to know.

Let's go over the most fundamental part. To add a note, open Keep and begin typing in the little box at the top of your screen where it says "Take a note…" You can then click "Close" or just click out of the box when done typing. There are other things that you can do as well, as I mentioned and which I'll go over shortly, but that's basically it. I told you this was easy!

Now that you know how to take notes, I want you to remove the phrase, "I'll remember that" from your mental vocabulary. As a refined hot mess, you're going to write down what you need to remember in your notes from now on, *no matter* how small.

Yes, taking the time to type "I parked in parking zone B11" or just "B11" might seem silly or insignificant. But when you walk out into the parking lot later and know exactly where your car is, you'll avoid the situation mentioned earlier. It's these simple, little things that will help your life become more structured and less chaotic.

Additionally, only use Google Keep to write down things that *aren't* date or time specific. This is because anything that *does* have a date or time should now be going directly into your calendar.

Keep things organized. At first, you might be able to get away with not adding titles or labels to your sticky notes. But eventually, you'll have a plethora of information on hundreds of different notes, and you won't be able to sort through them quickly or efficiently. To avoid this headache in the future, make things easier on yourself by labeling and titling everything from the get-go. Labeling things will allow you to search for and pull up all notes with a certain label. And titling things will, of course, help you know what the contents of that note are about. To add a title, click where it says "Title" when inside of a note. And to add a label, click the three dates and then "Add label". You can then type in a new name or choose from the list of premade names. An example of a label that you might create would be "Personal Growth." You could then have related sticky notes with that label such as "Books to Read" and "New Year's Resolutions." You could also store a bunch of recipes under the label "Food" or "Recipes."

Enhance your lists. When you're making lists, it's helpful to know what things are done and what things still need to be accomplished. You can do this through checkboxes.

To add these, click the three dots on the bottom of the note all the way to the right. Then click "Show checkboxes". When you check a box, Google will move that finished item down below into a completed section and cross it out for you. This way, it will still be visible but kept separate.

Pin important notes. If you want a note to remain towards the top of the list so that you can easily find it, put a "pin" in it. You can do this by clicking the little pin icon on the upper right when inside of a note. To unpin something from the top, click the pin button again.

Set notifications. This is something that I'm going to have you set up tomorrow and the day after for two of the downloadables/printables you get in this guide. Here is how you will do this: Down at the bottom and all the way to the left, you'll see a little bell icon that when you hover over it says, "Remind me". Click this anytime you want to be reminded about a specific note and have it pop up on your screen. You can set the note to pop up repeatedly by clicking "Pick a date & time" and then filling it out accordingly.

Share notes. The next button to the right, one that resembles a person with a plus mark, is for collaborating. This is good to know if you ever want to share information that you wrote down with someone else. Instead of having to take the time to copy and paste or retype your whole note, just share it through email.

Personalize. After that icon, there is one that resembles a paint pallet. Click this "Background options" button if you want to add color to your stickies. Google also provides themed images that you can choose from. This is a nice option for adding some color to your setup or to add another layer of organization.

For instance, if you love purple, you might make all of your sticky notes about your personal life purple. You could make all of your notes about work pink, and all of your notes about school blue, or however you want to set it up. Organizing your notes in this way will allow you to quickly skim them and find the category you're looking for. Plus, it's pretty. Include pictures. As a visual person, I love that you can add a photo to a note and then type in a little blurb about it. This is also something that I'm going to have you do tomorrow and the day after, so here is how to do it: Click on the little square that says "Add image" when you hover over it. If it's a new note, it'll say "New note with image". Then just upload the photo you want.

Make a copy. After you receive the downloadables/printables I mentioned, you're going to upload them onto Google Keep. After you've filled them out, you may wish to erase your work so that you can use them once more. Instead of just wiping them clean, however, I suggest that you instead make a copy of them, archive one set, and then remove any markings on the other. Doing this will allow you to keep a record of what you've done, so you can reference your work later on and see how far you've progressed. To do this, click on the three dots and then click "Make a copy".

Archive notes. Anytime that you're done with a note for the time being, hit the archive button. This is the one shaped like a square that has a downward-facing arrow. This will help you declutter your screen, but you'll still be able to access that note again later if you need to.

To find notes that you've archived, click on the three horizontal lines on the upper left of your screen. Look for the section called "Archive" and then find the note you want. You can then unarchive it, if you'd like, by hovering over the note and clicking the icon that says "Unarchive".

Archiving is different from deleting. When you are sure you are finished with a note and you won't be needing it again, click the three dots on the bottom of the note, and then the top option to delete it. Deleted notes will only be kept in the trash for seven days.

<u>Make a habit of periodically going through your notes and deleting ones you don't use or need any longer</u>. I recommend doing this on a monthly basis at least and adding this as a repeating event into your calendar.

Practical Application & Hot Mess Solutions

As I mentioned, I'm a bit of a hot mess. I'm also, much to my husband's annoyance, *extremely* forgetful. This is not to say that a forgetful person is always a hot mess and vice versa. But if you are similarly forgetful, and you continue to do nothing to mitigate the problem, then you run the risk of being perceived as a hot mess.

The following ideas are just a few examples of what I came up with for myself in order to try to manage on a somewhat more "normal" level. Give these suggestions a try, whether you have a hard time remembering things or not, and I hope they will work for you too.

Organize your recipes. <u>I've found Google Keep very helpful in bringing together various mediums</u> such as internet links, photos of physical recipes on 3x5 notecards, screenshots of recipes people have texted to me, and typed up recipes I've put together myself.

Storing your recipes like this will help you look up things faster than flipping through a book. It takes up less space than a cookbook, and it keeps everything in one place so that you won't be wondering which book or site you got a recipe from. Plus, you can add any additional notes you want to remember about a recipe to the note, such as "Use half of the amount of salt it calls for." Better still, grandma's secret biscuit recipe will be kept safe for generations to come, instead of being destroyed in an instant when you accidentally spill something on the only copy.

I highly recommend that if you haven't found a way of keeping track of recipes that works for you, you <u>compile a digital file using Google Keep</u>. I'll be going into this more in-depth in the chapter called Planning & Making Meals. I'll also be going over a few other options you have for saving recipes as well.

Keep track of gifts you buy. Have you ever found a great sale and bought a bunch of gifts because they were at a low price, put them away for Christmas, and then completely forgot about them? Then when December rolled around you most likely went out and bought more gifts, spending unnecessarily and breaking your gift budget, if you had one to begin with.

To help you keep track of what gifts you've bought, I suggest you make a Google Keep note specifically for this. You can do this for all of the events throughout the year or just for Christmas. Then, <u>whenever you purchase an item, write down what it is, who it's for, and the amount it cost you</u>. Also, very importantly, <u>markdown where you are going to store it</u> until it's time to be given away. This way, you can find it either in your attic, under your bed in a designated gift box, in the garage, etc. And you won't be tearing up your house trying to locate one item.

<u>Don't forget to label your note as well</u>. Something along the lines of "Gifts" or "Xmas gifts" should suffice.

Keep track of what things people like. Maybe you can usually remember that your brother-in-law loves anything that has to do with Star Wars. But when you're trying to do a million other things in combination with getting him a birthday present, you might forget. To save yourself from the embarrassment of having to ask someone what they like over and over, just keep track of it. Create a new note and <u>anytime someone mentions something they like, write it down</u>!

If someone prefers shopping at a specific store, you could write that place's name down and get them something from there. But an even easier option, and one preferable if they like a restaurant, is to get them a gift card. If you choose this option, I suggest you first ask them if they are okay with gift cards. If they are, and if the place they like is a well-known chain, you could just put, "Likes gift cards from Target" on your list.

If however, someone likes an obscure little-known place, find that store or restaurant's website and bookmark it. Put this bookmark into a designated bookmark folder specifically for gifts, and then mark who that website is for. Alternatively, you could <u>share a website's link directly to your Keep and then label that note as "Gifts."</u> Afterward, <u>open up that note and type in who that link is for. Then, on your main list of who likes what, put down "See saved website in bookmark folder" or "See saved website under 'Gifts' label"</u>

The cool thing about having all of this organized is that it lowers your stress when gift shopping and you can buy with confidence knowing that you're getting exactly what your friends and family like. This one tip might even improve your relationships. I mean if a person offhandedly mentions that they like this one thing, one time, and then months later you get it for them, <u>they are going to feel</u> *so* <u>loved and listened to!</u> They don't have to know that you didn't remember and just wrote it down, unless you want to tell them.

Here is a little side note for women who are in the military or whose spouse is currently serving. When you are constantly moving, this list of people you know and gift ideas is going to grow. Because of this, I don't recommend just putting a first or even just a last name down. After a few years, you run the risk of forgetting who is who. Instead, make a little note to yourself saying who someone is and where you knew them (I recommend doing this with your phone contacts as well). So on your list of gifts, instead of saying something like, "Sam - Likes orange chocolate," you could say, "Sam (neighbor in Atlanta, GA) - Likes orange chocolate."

<u>What other things do you need to keep track of</u>? What things do you find yourself repeatedly asking about because you forgot? Consider making notes for these things as well.

Brain Dump

Now that you're somewhat familiar with using Google Keep, you're going to create your first note.

As we went over earlier, trying to remember everything is not necessary. And having all of those mental lists of to-dos and must-not-forgets clogging your brain can really bog you down. Remember David Allen's quote? So we're going to uncork your poor, overwhelmed brain with this next exercise by doing a brain dump.

Write down (or rather type) everything that is on your mind into a note, everything you have to do, and everything you've been telling yourself not to forget. <u>Let your thoughts flow unhindered.</u> We'll make sense of this scramble of words later, but for now, just enjoy the sweet relief you feel when you stop thinking that you have to hold it in and remember it all!

After you've written everything down, go back through and put any activities or events into your calendar. As mentioned before, these things now have a designated place for them, so they do not need to be taking up any mental real estate.

Next, move anything that you want to/need to remember into a separate note. You'll now have two notes, one with things to remember and another with things to accomplish. We'll be breaking your note of things to accomplish down further another day. But for now, anytime you think of something that belongs in either category, write it down into it.

Action Plan

Today, set up your Google Keep and download its app onto your phone. Move the app to a location you can easily access, because from now on you're going to immediately write down anything you need to keep track of into it. Be sure to keep your notes organized as you go so you do not get overwhelmed by digital stickies. And if something hasn't been looked at in a while, archive it or delete it. How often will you choose to go through your list and delete notes you no longer use? <u>Add this as a recurring event into your calendar.</u> Do the brain dump exercise if you haven't already. Afterward, go through it and move anything time-bound into your calendar and anything you need to remember into a different note.

Something that we did not talk about today but that I recommend you do, is to consolidate all other notes, either physical sticky notes or notes from other apps, into this one location. After you do this, throw away your scrap paper and you'll be one step ahead for the chapter on paper clutter.

DAY 3:
YOUR LIFE JAR

Are You Living or Waiting to Die?

The original cover of this guide showed a woman walking through a field of sunflowers with the words, "Where you are a year from now is a reflection of the choices you make today." It served as a reminder that the actions you make right now will determine the life you lead in the future. So let me ask you a sobering question. If you continue doing what you're doing, where will you end up? Where will your current lifestyle take you in one year or five years? Are you *happy* with the future trajectory that your decisions are plotting out for you?

In her book, *The Top Five Regrets of the Dying*, Bronnie Ware reveals the lamentations she heard during her many years of working with those who were close to passing.

The following are the regrets that she heard most often:

I wish I'd had the courage to live a life true to myself, not the life others expected of me.

I wish I hadn't worked so much.

I wish I'd had the courage to express my feelings.

I wish I had stayed in touch with my friends.

I wish that I had let myself be happier.

Do any of these strike a chord with you? <u>If you feel a surge of emotion when reading one or more of these, how could you change this for yourself to avoid the same fate as those who said these things</u>? The good news is that you are in control of your actions. You can control your future, and you still have time to change things. It is not too late for you, compared to those who made these statements.

You Are Responsible

"You always do what you want to do... You may say that you had to do something, or that you were forced to, but actually, whatever you do, you do by choice." - W. Clement Stone

Put another way, at any given moment you are doing *exactly* what you want to do. When I first heard this, I thought it was profound for two reasons.

The first reason was that I thought it was a complete lie. Like everyone, I have gone through difficult times, and I certainly wouldn't have *chosen* to be in those situations. You may currently be in an unhealthy relationship, working at a job you despise, be unsatisfied with how you look, be going through a difficult season, or be unhappy with life in general.

The second reason I found it profound was that the longer I thought about it, the more I realized that I was, in fact, responsible for those things in at least *some* small way. I was the one who chose to *enter into* those positions/situations. And when things became difficult, I was the one who chose to *remain* and did very little, if anything, to try to change them. You have the capabilities at any point in time, to change who you are and where your life is headed. It is *never* too late to change the trajectory of your future.

You see, when you make excuses or blame others, your circumstances, or your environment, you *give away* your power. This quote reminds you of the control you have, but it also gives you responsibility. It gives you the responsibility to spend your time *wisely,* because you are responsible for what you are doing right now and where those actions will lead you, either to a life of fulfillment or regrets. So I ask...

What Are You Filling Your Life With?

Sometimes as hot messes we may get down on ourselves when we see other people doing so much, and we wonder how they manage to do it, while we struggle to do the little we are. Today, you're going to learn about prioritization in a very visual way that may finally help you grasp how others, and now you too, can do it "all." Of course, *no one* actually does *everything*, but what some people have figured out is the delicate balance of prioritization.

Watch this video before continuing with the rest of this chapter to learn how to balance your own life.

In the video, the jar symbolizes your time as well as your life. So you may see me referring to it interchangeably, as whatever you fill up your time with, you also fill up your life with. Now, take a look at your own life. Are some things of lesser importance taking more priority and being done before things of greater importance? <u>Are you filling your jar with sand and pebbles before putting in your rocks</u>?

You may find it fun to draw your own jar and fill it with the rocks, pebbles, and sand of your life at another time. But for now, let this just serve as food for thought. Whenever you're considering things that you will or won't do, or how much time you will or won't spend on something, consider where it would fall in your jar. Is the thing in question a rock or is it just a pebble? Remember, in your life, as it is in your jar, you only have so much you can fit in.

Define Your Goals

It is easy to get lost in caring for and tending to the rocks that you currently have in your life. These are, by your admittance, the most important things to you. But you must not lose sight of the future you want for yourself. That is why we're going to do a little exercise to help you figure out your goals so you can fill your jar not only with those things that are a priority *now* but also those things that will add up to build the future you want.

This activity is taken from Brian Tracy's book *Eat That Frog!*, which I'll discuss later in this guide. He calls this the Quick List Method because what he found through many years of working with people is that whether you have a lot of time or a little bit of time, your answers to the following exercise will usually be the same.

Set a timer for thirty seconds, and then write out your top three goals in life that you have right now. According to Tracy, in 80% of cases, people will usually write down a financial goal, a relationship goal, and a health goal. If you have time later, you can expand this exercise by repeating it to define your goals for your career, finances, family or relationships, health, personal and professional development, social and community, and your biggest concerns/problems.

Plan Out Your Path to Achieving Them

In order to get from Point A, where you are now, to Point B, where you want to go, you must have a set path. You must create a plan to reach your goals. If you do not, they will remain just a wish. <u>You can begin by further defining your goals</u> to make them SMART.

Make SMART goals:

S - Specific: The more specific the better.

M - Measurable: Is progress trackable?

A - Achievable: It is physically possible.

R - Relevant: Is it worthwhile? Does it align with your other life goals?

T - Time-Bound: Give it a deadline.

For example, you might have just written down a health goal such as "I want to be thinner." To make this a SMART goal you could rewrite it to say "In one year, I want to lose twelve pounds." This is specific. It can be measured by a scale. It's attainable, as this example gives a whole month to lose one pound. It's certainly worthwhile to be healthier or feel more confident in your own body. And lastly, this rewritten goal now has a deadline.

Now, it's your turn. Rewrite each of your goals to make them SMART. After you're done, put the deadlines that you gave each goal into your calendar.

Next, I want you to visualize these large, seemingly unattainable goals as boulders. Boulders can obviously not fit into a jar. But if you break them down into rocks, they will fit. Similarly, you can not eat a whole elephant in one swallow. However, as the saying goes, you can eat it one bite at a time. In other words, in order to achieve your goals, you must break them down into smaller, more manageable steps. Put these steps or "bites" in order of what must be accomplished first. Set *reasonable* deadlines for each of them, and then add them to your calendar.

Lastly, reserve time in your calendar to work on each of these small steps.

This is key! Anyone can make a resolution, but if you're to achieve what you're after, you need to make time to make it happen. <u>You need to make these rocks, the smaller pieces of your boulder, a priority.</u>

While you're looking at your calendar, consider the other things that are filling up your time. Do the things that are on your schedule align with the kind of woman you want to become? Do they support the future you want for yourself? <u>If you don't have room to work on your priorities in life, to work towards your goals, what things on your schedule can you move to accommodate? What things can you eliminate?</u>

You have now clearly defined your goals and created steps to reach them with set deadlines. All that's left to do is the work. This is, without a doubt, the hardest part.

The Power of a Small Action

As you begin and continue on your journey, do not grow discouraged by thinking that the little steps you're making now will not amount to much, or that you're not reaching your goals fast enough. Don't focus on *progress*. Focus on *persistence*.

Consider the images below that show a mortarless wall that is built on top of a single book.

Although it seems to make little difference at first, the book's effect on the wall becomes more apparent when looking at its compound effect. This one small object interrupts the wall's alignment, creating waves with the bricks which eventually fan out and lead to a noticeable bulge.

This artwork, titled *The Castle* by Jorge Méndez Blake, represents the notion that small ideas can have a big impact. I believe that it also serves as a visual reminder that <u>small *actions*, stacked together, can have a big impact</u> as well.

In *Atomic Habits*, another book which I'll mention again later in this guide, the author James Clear says that by only improving 1% per day you'll amass a thirty-seven times improvement by the end of a year. He claims that tiny but consistent gains will add up to significant results. <u>You just need to *keep going*.</u>

At times, you may feel that working on your rocks is slow going and that nothing is improving. As Clear says, "... <u>improving by just 1 percent isn't notable (and sometimes it isn't even *noticeable*). But it can be just as meaningful, especially in the long run.</u>"

My challenge to you is to show up persistently, hit each of your deadlines for your smaller steps, and never stop striving until you reach your goals.

The regrets of the dying may not tie in to your goals at all, but my guess is that they probably do in some way. <u>Keep them in mind when you grow tired of pursuing your resolutions</u>. Let them serve as an encouragement to live the life you want to live and become the woman you want to become. It would be a tragedy to reach the end of your life and be left with such great remorse.

Track Your Progress

I've created a special downloadable/printable for you that will help serve as encouragement for you to keep pursuing your goals. My hope is that you'll feel motivated to continue your momentum when you build a streak of checked-off boxes and that you'll feel inspired when you can look back at previous months and see how far you've come.

Use this to measure your progress towards your big goals as well as any other smaller things you'd like to get better at during the month. <u>These smaller things are what you'd like to eventually build into new habits for yourself</u>. They might include something like "Make my bed each morning" or "Put all of my laundry into the hamper and not on the floor."

Download the Monthly Goal Tracker and start using it immediately to build the habit of filling it out, regardless of if it's the beginning of the month or not. You'll find instructions on how to use it on the second page, but these will differ slightly depending upon which format you choose to use.

Though I am partial to digital, I think it's important that you <u>use this tracker in whatever way you think will work best for you</u> because you'll need to *consistently* mark off all of the boxes that you accomplish so that you can have the most accurate snapshot of how you're progressing. You can choose from the following three options. You can print it, download it and use it as a clickable PDF, or you can use Google Keep like how I went over yesterday. If you choose this latter option, make sure you get a stylus so that you can write things down, because the PDF will be imported as an image and will no longer be clickable.

<u>I find the Google Keep option particularly helpful because it reminds you to fill out the Monthly Goal Tracker and it has the tracker conveniently accessible inside of the reminder notification.</u> I went over how to add an image and an alert to a note yesterday. But this is a little different because the link above is not an image. The simplest way to add the tracker to your Keep is to take a screenshot of it and then add that. Then click the bell icon up on the top right. Set it to repeat daily at the best time that works for you. I personally have mine go off every evening before bed.

Action Plan

Contemplate where your life is headed. If you continue living the life you are now, will you end up being a person with one of those regrets? How will you start changing this for yourself so you will not end up that way?

Resolve to take responsibility for your actions and where your life ends up from now on. <u>Take back any power you may have given away</u> by blaming other things or other people for setbacks or failures.

Consider what your Life Jar looks like right now. Is it situated how you want, or are you putting things in out of order? How could you begin prioritizing better?

Determine your goals using the Quick List method. Define them further by making them SMART. Break them down into smaller steps, list them in order of what needs to happen first, and then add them to your calendar. Make it a priority and set aside time to accomplish each step. Lastly, track your progress towards your goals using the Monthly Goal Tracker.

DAY 4:
DESIGN EFFECTIVE ROUTINES

A Little Side Note

I'm going to bypass everything else today and say that my goal for you is to just get through today's chapter. Of course, doing the suggested steps and the Action Plan would be optimal. But statistically speaking, the majority of you will not make it much further than here, let alone finish the thirty days (only 5-15% of people complete online courses, which this could be considered). So if you've made it this far, I'm proud of you.

I just want to take a quick second to talk to you if you're currently thinking "I'm not going to do this anymore", "This is harder than I thought it would be", or "This isn't fun." John C. Maxwell, says that "Successful and unsuccessful people do not vary greatly in their capabilities. They vary in their *desire* to reach their potential." How much do you desire this?

Right now, you have the opportunity to change your present and your future. Your future self *deserves* to know the things you will learn in the coming chapters. Are you really going to deny her by stopping at the beginning of your journey and becoming a part of the statistic that goes no further?

Let me make a deal with you. I promise that if you do nothing else but read each chapter, finishing out the thirty days without doing any more of the activities or assignments, this guide will still be here for you to come back to later. There is no reason why you can't just read through it and then return to it again to do a little more, try a new suggestion you didn't try before, and be reminded of things you forgot when you read through previously. You can come back any time to go through it once more.

With that in mind, I challenge you to keep going and not give up. Remember, persistence over progress.

Design Effective Systems

Yesterday, we talked in part about making and setting goals. Goals are important to have because being excited about and looking forward to something is one of the things in life that brings us joy. Hope (of reaching those goals) makes life worth living and prompts us to keep striving and improving. Unfortunately, not every day is a day when you achieve a goal though. Most of your days will be spent working *towards* your resolutions, which is why today we're going to focus on what you do the rest of the time.

The things that you have a habit of doing regularly build a routine. These routine habits can also be considered your system. James Clear differentiates between goals and systems in the following way: "Your goal is your desired outcome. Your system is the collection of daily habits that will get you there."

Your Current Routine/System

You may think that you don't have a routine right now but, as I just mentioned, whatever you're doing regularly *is* already a routine. Whatever you have a habit of doing creates the trajectory of your future, so you might as well put some thought and purpose behind the actions you take.

"We are what we repeatedly do. Excellence, then, is not an act, but a habit."
- Aristotle

On the other hand, you may have jumped on the trend that surged in popularity in recent years, and already have a morning and nighttime routine. If this is the case, it is still good to reassess and adjust things occasionally so that you can continue improving your processes.

You will not get where you want to by chance. So today you're going to design a daily routine, regardless of if you already have one or not, and you're also going to create a *weekly* routine as well. The reason being is that a week is, as Steven Covey puts it, "a complete patch of time in the fabric of life... [as] it is close enough to be highly relevant but distant enough to provide context and perspective."

Make a New Routine/System

What system could you create that would lead you to your desired outcome, to achieving your goals? What daily habits would that system consist of?

Spend some time brainstorming what you want your daily and weekly routines to look like. Are some of the things that you're already doing benefiting you? <u>What habits should you keep and what should you replace?</u>

Read the suggestions below on what makes a successful routine, and then feel free to do some research on your own either by gathering ideas or by asking a mentor what they do. Lastly, follow the instructions to lay out your new routines.

Keys for Success:

<u>Make It Realistic</u>

I'd love to say that if your ideal routine involves running five miles up a mist-covered mountain first thing in the morning only to break through the fog and breath in the fresh air while having the sunshine hit your face at the top is your thing, that you should do it. However, if you don't run let alone live anywhere near a mountain, that's not realistic.

Your routine needs to be physically possible, but it also needs to be made up of actions that you'll be *likely* to take. You could physically wake up at 5 am. However, if you're unlikely to get up at that time every day, then you shouldn't make it a part of your routine.

<u>Make It Uniquely Yours</u>

As I've said before and will continue to say, if you want to succeed, you need to take the ideas and suggestions in this guide and make them your own. Make your routines *yours*, not what your favorite influencer or best friend does.

Yes, I did say to get ideas from others but put your own spin on them. If you think someone else's routine or part of their routine would work for you then, by all means, add it. But <u>just because something works wonderfully for someone else, does not mean that it's the right fit for you</u>.

<u>One of the resources I recommend you check out to see if any of the suggestions would be the right fit is my own odd and scientifically-based morning routine.</u> My routine has changed quite a bit since writing this. However, there are still good ideas in it that are worth considering.

Block Your "Rocks"

Now that you've researched and brainstormed how you want your daily and weekly routines to be set up, we're going to use Google Calendar in combination with time blocking to lay out and structure them.

Time blocking is essentially just blocking off periods of time on your calendar when you will do a bunch of similar tasks or tasks that need to be done around the same time. It takes your priorities off of a to-do list and puts them into your schedule so that nothing gets forgotten. It ensures that every task gets the time that it needs by keeping you moving from block (or group of tasks) to block, instead of getting hung up on one thing while neglecting everything else.

<u>Seeing all of your time laid out on your calendar in blocks will help you visualize just how much of it is being taken up by certain activities</u>. You'll then be able to make a more informed decision about your routines, and decide if the ideas you came up with are realistic or if you need to adjust them.

When I first heard about time blocking through this video, it completely blew my mind. The way that the woman likens time blocking to the schedules that we used to keep in high school makes so much sense! I feel like she switched on a lightbulb for me, and I hope that you too will find it just as enlightening and helpful.

In the video, she talks about how when you were in science class, you focused on science. You worked on your science projects or homework and didn't work on other subjects. Then, when the bell rang, you stopped what you were doing, picked up your stuff, and went to your next class. You didn't stay in science class and keep working on that subject.

Despite having *so much* to do back in high school, this system helped you keep a somewhat balanced schedule. You're going to use time blocking to construct something similar so that you can once again enjoy a balanced schedule and tackle everything you have going on.

<u>How to Time Block:</u>

Whether or not you watched the video that I just mentioned, be sure to watch this video now to learn how to time block your routines using Google

Calendar.

You already have your goals, and time to work towards them, blocked off on your schedule from yesterday. We did this *first* so that you'd be sure to have time for your most important things. Now, you're going to follow the example in that video and block off time for all of the other things you do regularly, not just your goals.

If you have time, I recommend watching both videos as they offer a lot of good ideas and advice. One represents a more general way of time blocking, while the other video gives a more detailed approach. Likewise, you can make your schedule as vague or as specific as you want. I recommend that you experiment to see what you like best and do what works for you.

Tips to Make It Work:

Treat scheduled tasks like an appointment. If something is on your schedule or scheduled into a block, treat it as though it is an appointment or something *very* important that can not be skipped or left undone. This is especially important for later when we get to the sections where we go over putting yourself first and scheduling "Me Time."

I thought that in her book *Girl, Stop Apologizing*, Rachel Hollis makes a hilarious example about this that drives the idea home. She likens keeping your appointments with yourself to going on a date with Chris Hemsworth. Would you blow off a date with him to go do something else, or would you make sure that you showed up because "It's Chris-freaking-Hemsworth" and your date is really important? It's the same concept. Show up and keep your appointments with yourself.

Group similar tasks. You can use time blocking to help you be more time-efficient by grouping tasks that are alike. If for instance, you have a lot of errands to do, it wouldn't make sense to do one at a time. Instead, you could block off a period of time specifically for errands, and then do as many as you could within that time frame.

Set alarms. Just like how the bell went off in school letting you know that it was time to switch classes, set your Google Calendar to notify you when it's time to switch blocks. You can also just set alarms on your phone. I highly recommend that you set an additional alarm to go off a little bit beforehand as well. This way, you receive a heads up when the block is going to end soon and can wrap things up, clean up, and prepare to switch tasks.

Block realistically. You might be able to guesstimate how long you should make a block of time or how long a sequence of activities will take you. However, you won't know for sure. For now, if you usually have extra time leftover, reduce the size of the block. And if you tend to run over, increase it.

Once you complete the exercise in the time management section where you time how long it takes you to do each activity you do throughout your day, I recommend you revisit your schedule once again. Adjust the time that you allotted each block so that it will be more accurate, but be sure to also consider the next point when you're adjusting amounts.

Leave breathing room. You may choose to have everything be scheduled back to back. However, inevitably something will run late and spill over into the next time period. To avoid this, I recommend you leave gaps between each block.

Having this space will help you feel less stressed as you'll have a little bit of room to catch up whenever you fall behind. This will also serve as a transition time for your brain as it switches from one task to another (we'll talk about this in the time management section as well).

Don't overdo it. Not everyone will flourish from scheduling every single little thing. Even if you *enjoy* having a super detailed schedule, it might not be what ends up working best for you. This is one of the great things about time blocking. You can schedule more if they want, but you don't have to for it to work.

For example, instead of overwhelming yourself with a long list of tasks to do during your night routine like brushing your teeth, washing your face, putting on face lotion, etc, you could simply say that you will get ready for bed during that block.

Similarly, instead of setting one block for driving to the gym, a second block for working out, another block for driving back home, and a final block for showering, you could lump everything that has to do with or is a result of exercising into one large block.

Be flexible. Don't get stuck thinking that what you create today is never going to need to change. I'm going to be giving you more ideas and suggestions throughout this guide that you'll need to add into your routines. Working out a time to clean, pay bills, look at your finances, and work on yourself is all very important. So you'll need to remain flexible and add these things, as well as anything else that life throws at you, into your schedule.

Never stop improving. The routines that you set up today are just a general framework for what *might* work. As you begin putting them into practice, you'll see what does work and what doesn't. Keep revisiting and tweaking your routines often to make them as optimized and effortless as possible.

Support Your Future Self

The Time Management Matrix & ABC Method

Organizing the remnants of your brain dump from a couple of days ago might not seem like it has anything to do with routines. However, because doing things on your to-do list is something that you do daily, I've chosen to include it in this section.

We're going to be organizing and prioritizing your Google Keep note that you made on Day 2 with things you need to accomplish using the Time Management Matrix. This idea comes from the book *The Seven Habits of Highly Effective People* by Steven Covey and is also sometimes referred to as the Eisenhower Decision Matrix.

Watch this video to learn about the matrix before you continue.

When I first used this matrix to make sense of my to-do list, it certainly improved things. However, I still felt like it was missing something. That's when I discovered Brian Tracy's organization method in his book *Eat that Frog!*, and decided to combine the two methods together in a new way that I'd never seen utilized before.

To avoid confusion, I'm only going to borrow one part of Tracy's method so that the two tactics can be blended. You can see it displayed below.

Take special note of how each quadrant or box is labeled with a letter. Tracy labels each task according to the letter of the box that it falls into. He then further organizes his list by adding ascending numbers to items when multiple tasks fall into one box.

For example, if you have multiple items that fall into the first box, you'll label them as "A" tasks. You'll then prioritize them by determining which of those will be your top priority and dub it "A1". Your second priority in that same box will then be dubbed "A2", and so forth.

You might think that the tasks in Box C do not need to be organized as you won't necessarily be the one doing them. I would argue against this, as some things in this box might indeed get done by you, just through automation. However, if a task does get delegated, it's helpful to know the order in which things should be done for whoever ends up doing them.

To illustrate, if you hire someone to fix things around your house and you have a limited amount of funds, you'll need to know the things that are most important so that you can have them fix those things first e.g. fixing a leaky roof before fixing a squeaky door.

Lastly, it should go without saying that anything that falls into Box D can just be axed.

Now it's time for you to organize your to-do list by using these two methods together. First, use the Time Management Matrix to determine which box a task falls into. Then label it the letter that corresponds with that box. Finally, if you have multiple tasks that fall into the same box, prioritize them by marking them with ascending numbers with one being the top priority.

Once you've completed this, you'll be able to refer back to your list anytime you're working in a block and know what tasks to do (those that are in the category assigned to that block) and what order to do them in.

Plan Ahead

"People seldom achieve anything significant by stumbling around day to day." - Grant Cardone (*New York Times* best-selling author, founder and CEO of Grant Cardone Enterprises)

You now have a wonderfully organized to-do list with your priorities straightened out, as well as a beautiful new weekly and daily routine set up on your Google Calendar. You have these tools at your disposal, but how do you implement them into your life? What system could you use to then use these systems?

Plan For the Week

Steven Covey recommends that you look ahead and spend about 20-30 minutes planning your upcoming week every week. Go ahead and add this time into your schedule now so that it does not get forgotten, and make it a part of your weekly routine. Perhaps Sunday evenings would be the best time for you to do this.

When you're planning your week, pull up Google Calendar and see if anything needs to be moved around or adjusted. If you have a doctor's appointment when you'd usually go exercise, where could you move your exercise block to? Better yet, could you reschedule that doctor's appointment to a block when you're free or to a block when you're out running errands and close by to the doctor's office?

This is also a good time to assess how you're coming along with your big goals as well as your little ones, or any habits that you're trying to build. <u>Did you check off everything that you planned to do on your Monthly Goal Tracker last week?</u> If not, how could you change things so that you can get better at continuously pursuing your goals and building the habits you want to implement? Do any steps need to be broken down into smaller pieces?

Plan Every Day

Besides having a weekly check-in, it's also very helpful to have a daily check-in as well.

To set yourself up for success, I recommend you take a few quick minutes every evening to look at the next day and plan ahead. As the saying goes, <u>a good morning starts the night before</u>, so pause and reflect on what you need to do so that you can make the best use of your time tomorrow.

Do you have somewhere that you need to get to before work? Then you need to set your alarm to go off earlier. Is it going to rain tomorrow? Then you need to set out your umbrella so that you don't forget it in the morning. What are you going to eat for lunch? Get it all packed up and ready to go in the fridge waiting for you. Is your brother's birthday coming up in two weeks? Then make it a priority to purchase him a gift tomorrow.

If something is a priority and you need to make sure it happens, list it as one of three top priorities for the day. You can certainly do more than just three things, but *only* after you've achieved those top three (your A1 or B1 tasks).

Why only set three priorities or goals for your day? By focusing on just a few items, you're more likely to end the day feeling proud of yourself having accomplished all that you set out to do. This is opposed to ending your day feeling disappointed because you didn't complete all forty things on your to-do list.

RescueTime (a productivity and time tracker that I'll go over in a later chapter) surveyed hundreds of its users. They compiled the information and looked for trends of those who complete their goals consistently. Their findings show that the average person sets four goals. However, people who only set three goals per day are more likely to achieve them.

In that same survey, they found that those who set their goals the night before (like I recommended you do) are 11% more likely to be successful. Interestingly, 0% of the people who do the same thing, but set out their goals in the morning on the day they hope to complete them, achieve all of their goals.

Why write down your daily goals in the first place though? Psychology professor Dr. Gail Matthews, from the Dominican University in California, conducted a goal-setting study with roughly 270 participants. She found that you are 42% more likely to achieve your goals if you write them down. So that's what we're going to do.

I've created a downloadable/printable for you where you'll be able to write down your top three priorities every day. It is a supplemental tool to be used in addition to your daily schedule. Download the Daily Check-in now and add time to complete it into your schedule. Make it a part of your routine to go over it every evening for the following day.

When you go over it, follow the instructions in each section. Fill it out and look over your schedule, your to-do list, and your goals. Use it to remind yourself of anything you need to do. Some of the sections that it includes we have not covered yet, so ignore the parts that are not applicable until we go over those topics.

You'll see on the backside that I've added the Time Management Matrix for you, to serve as a helpful reminder and guide for prioritizing. Underneath it, you'll also see a section dedicated to your to-do list. You're welcome to use this as your new place for keeping track of everything you need to accomplish or continue using Google Keep, whichever is easier.

Lastly, be sure to set this printable to pop up in a reminder on Google Keep, or use it in whatever format you decided to use for the Monthly Goal Tracker.

Action Plan

Consider how you'd like to structure your day and week. What daily actions have you already been doing that will lead you to your desired outcome? What habits do you need to add to build a better system, and what habits do you need to remove?

Block out your new routines on Google Calendar, and add alarms to notify you when a block is about to end as well as when it has ended. If you have time, watch both videos about time blocking so that you can gather a better understanding and see if one way would work better for you.

Pull up the to-do list you made the other day and organize it using the Time Management Matrix along with the ABC Method.

Block off time on your schedule to review and plan for the upcoming week on a repeating basis. Block off time every evening to plan for the following day as well. Download the Daily Check-in printable, and begin implementing the parts that we've covered already, including using your prioritized to-do list to determine your top three priorities for the day.

DAY 5:
MAKE TIME PART 1

Understand Your Two Limitations

For the majority of your life, you've probably heard about and sought after ways to save time. You thought if you could just get more hours in the day, or work your schedule better, you could fit everything in. You thought lack of time was the problem. But what if I told you that you were missing a *crucial* piece of the puzzle?

Up until a little while ago, I too only focused on the clock and the calendar. I would end most of my days feeling frustrated, stressed, and disappointed in myself because I hadn't gotten everything done on my to-do list for the day. I thought, as you might have thought yourself at some point, that if I just worked *longer*, pushed myself *mor* e, took fewer breaks, or even skipped them altogether, I'd finally have the time to get everything done. I thought I could make the time by *forcing* things to get done, by forcing myself to continue working on them even when I was completely exhausted. Because if I didn't force myself to keep working until they were done, when would I ever find the time?

Inevitably, my brain would end up so fuzzy that I'd have to take a break. I'd then scroll through social media while my brain had its much-needed moment of rest, but later, I'd feel *guilty* about it! "I made my schedule to fit everything in. Why couldn't I stick to my plans and get those things done? Instead of spending my time on the things that are important to me, I was *lazy*, and spent my time scrolling on Facebook!" I thought.

Does this sound familiar? You might not have gone to the extreme that I did, but perhaps you can relate to thinking that working harder and longer is the answer. You might have burnt the candle at both ends, borrowing time from things that were important but not urgent (like your health) to give time to the urgent but less important things (work or homework due dates). Time and time again you found yourself burnt out and depleted.

Time management on its own may prove constricting and inflexible. It says to schedule every minute of your waking hours, because if time is not being put to good use, then it's being wasted. Right? Time management leaves no wiggle room for life to occur, and it expects you to work at your full potential constantly, but you're not a robot!

When performing a task or a goal, you are restricted by not one limitation, but two, time *and energy*. "It's not how many hours you put in that determines how productive you are, it's how much energy you are able to invest during the hours you work," says Tony Schwartz, energy expert, and author of *The Way We're Working Isn't Working*.

You're now scheduling everything in your calendar, but if you don't plan your schedule with your energy levels in mind, you'll be too exhausted to complete those plans. Both time and energy need to be managed, and they must be balanced in a way that works for you.

Manage Your Time

Find Out Where It's Being Spent

How long do you spend doing things? Where does the time go? The answers may surprise you! People measure the calories they consume or the money they spend. But few people track time, a limited resource, and arguably more valuable than the other two.

"What gets measured gets managed." -Peter Drucker

To improve your time management, we must first measure, or track, where you currently spend your hours. After you've chosen which of the two following methods you want to use, you'll then track your time for one week, or at least a few days. This will take some work, but the longer you track, the more data you'll get. The more data you get, the more accurate of an assessment you'll have of where your time is going. So I encourage you to do this for as long as possible.

You don't need to track the things you do during your work hours as you won't have a lot of say in changing them. However, you're certainly welcome to if you want. Regardless, track your lunchtime as that is your personal time.

You may find that timing how long it takes you to do activities will keep you focused on getting them done, and may even help you to do them faster. When I stopped tracking things, the amount of time it took me to get those same activities done increased. For these reasons, <u>it may be worth it to you to continue tracking your time even after one week has passed</u>. I've chosen to carry on tracking some tasks, to make sure I'm completing them within the shortest amount of time I know I'm capable of.

Track Your Time Manually

The first option is free and uses Google Keep. It is the simpler of the two methods and requires no time to set up.

To begin tracking, open a new Google Keep note and type in each activity you do. Write what time you *stop* doing it beside it. After, subtract the time difference of the activity you just did from the one you finished previously, and write that down as well.

Here is an example of how this will look:

Woke Up: 7:00

Made Bed: 7:05 5 Minutes

Got Dressed: 7:11 6 Minutes

In this example, you woke up at 7. You then started a new activity, making your bed. You *finished* that at 7:05, so you subtracted that time from the activity before it (waking up) to get the total time you spent making the bed, five minutes. You then started the third activity and wrote down when you finished that, 7:11. You subtracted that time from the time of the previous activity (7:11 minus 7:05) to get how long it took you to get dressed, six minutes.

I recommend you <u>do the math for the previous interval when you're writing down the next activity you're starting</u>. However, if you don't have the time to do it right then, you can always go back later to do it.

This method works well, and you can learn a lot about yourself by doing it. However, it can be a little difficult to analyze the numbers you're left with and get something of value out of them. <u>Apps, on the other hand, offer an easy way to interpret your data</u>, and once set up, will allow you to track your time much more quickly.

Track Your Time with Apps

There are multiple time tracking apps out there, but I've found ATracker to be the one best suited to our needs. It will serve the same purpose as the previous method, but with a built-in timer, colorful icons, and comprehensive pie charts. However, if you don't like this app, find one that you do so that you'll be more likely to use it.

There is a basic version of it, but you can't do anything worthwhile with it, so I recommend you get the Pro version of ATracker as it has everything that you'll need. Depending upon which device you have, this will cost you a one-time fee of $3-5.

Download the ATracker app, purchase the Pro version, and start setting it up. The interface may be a little confusing at first, so watch this tutorial if you need a walkthrough.

While setting it up, be sure to enable the note feature as you create each new task. You can do this by scrolling down the task's page and turning on the toggle that says, "Note: Enter note after finishing this task." This will make it easier for you to do another activity which we'll talk about later.

Listing all of the tasks you do and figuring out how you want them categorized will take some effort, but once it's all done, tracking your time with ATracker will be as easy as pressing a button.

This app offers a blend of manual and digital tracking, but whenever you can have things be fully automated, I recommend it. That's why I also suggest you download RescueTime. This will automatically track how long you spend on your devices so that you won't have to worry about entering screen time into ATracker.

There are lots of apps out there that will do this for you as well, but this one does offer a free version with everything on it that you'll need, and it is also available on all devices.

We'll talk more about this tomorrow, but RescueTime also has a premium version with the ability to block you from visiting certain sites if you tend to get easily distracted. So consider getting the premium version if you think you need it.

Because you don't have to do a lot with this particular time tracker, other than let it run in the background, we'll be using it for two weeks as opposed to only one week like the rest.

To begin collecting data, download the app on all devices that you use, and then use them like you normally would. After the first week, review your data and determine how you'll spend your time differently. Use the second week to implement those changes, and at the end of it, review to see how well you did.

What to Do Once You've Tracked It

You put in the hard work and diligently tracked your time for one week. Now you're left with a bunch of numbers and data, but how do you use this information to free up your time?

Similar to using RescueTime, you'll want to review your findings and then use what you've learned to adjust your habits.

Go back and compare how long it took you to do the same activity across multiple days. Your time probably fluctuated a little, but look for common patterns.

Consider if the amount of time you typically spend on that activity is acceptable to you. If you regularly spend thirty minutes getting ready for work, do you want to increase that so that you can put more effort into your appearance? Or do you not care as much as someone else might, so you want to decrease that amount of time? What you decide to do with your data is *personal*. No one else can tell you you're spending too much or too little time on something.

Take a while to look through your information, and based upon what your results show you, make a list of ideas of how you could save time and what changes you want to make to your habits.

I had quite a few realizations when I did this activity, as I imagine you'll have as well. One thing I learned was how much time multitasking was costing me. When I timed myself getting ready for bed without my phone, brushing my teeth and putting on my face lotion only took me twelve minutes. But when I did the same activities while watching YouTube, it took me eight minutes longer. I used this information to tailor my habits, and now I try to get ready for bed without my phone most nights.

Another thing I learned through this activity is that <u>transitions take a lot of time</u>. When you're changing from one activity to another, you're not necessarily getting anything done. However, it still takes time and requires your brain to undergo a mental switch. We'll talk more about mental switching tomorrow. But I was shocked to learn that my transition time from getting out the door to driving away was vastly longer than I had thought it was. Something that I thought took about three minutes, grabbing my stuff, walking out the door, starting the engine, and driving away, actually took me upwards of fifteen minutes. No wonder I was always late! I'd never timed myself, so I'd never known that the buffer time I had set, a mere five minutes, was inadequate.

Spending this much time in the transitioning phase was unacceptable to me. So I adjusted my behavior by one, figuring out how to get out of the door faster. And two, by setting aside the appropriate amount of buffer time that I needed, so that I would get places on time.

The last step in this exercise is to implement your list of ideas and changes so that you can manage your time better in the future.

A good way to see if your ideas are working and if you're sticking to them is to… you guessed it, track your time for another week! I know most people will not want to do this, and that's perfectly alright. You'll already have gained valuable insight into your habits from having tracked a single week. <u>But if you want to take this activity to the next level, track your time for an additional week while putting your ideas into practice. Then review your results once more and compare them to the first week.</u>

Manage Your Energy

Time, as we went over, is limited. However, energy is not. It is a renewable resource that can be increased and extended.

When you think of energy, you may picture it as being linear, something that peaks when you wake up and then gradually diminishes. Yet energy actually ebbs and flows over the course of the day, and these fluctuations are perfectly normal.

Your energy levels naturally rise and fall in a twenty-four-hour cycle of sleeping and waking, called the Circadian Rhythm. But as a female, you also have a secondary "clock" to think about, one that you've probably never heard of. You also have an Infradian Rhythm, a twenty-eight-day cycle of energy and hormones that is caused by your menstruation.

"Most research in health and fitness is done on *men* and not appropriate for you." That is according to the book *In the FLO*, which introduced a revolutionary new concept for women, that our hormones affect us in four different phases. Depending upon which phase of your cycle you're in, Menstrual, Follicular, Ovulatory, or Luteal, your body has different needs and will react differently. We can use this knowledge to our advantage to work with our biological rhythm rather than against it.

This is really good information to know because at certain times of the month you won't have a lot of energy and at certain times you will. Instead of scheduling a lot to do during your Luteal phase, when you will typically feel less energized and are prone to overwhelm, you could understand that those feelings are normal and accommodate them. You could plan ahead for this time of the month because your energy patterns are *predictable!*

If you're interested in learning more about your hormonal patterns so that you can better understand your energy levels, grab the book or check out the author's YouTube channel. Alisa Vitti, the author, also made an app called MyFlo, which will not only help you track your cycle, but will show you which phase you're in, suggest activities and nutrition based upon that phase, and educate you.

Your energy levels additionally change weekly, monthly, seasonally, and over the years. You probably feel more energetic on the weekends, compared to the weekdays when you have to go to work. If Christmas is your favorite holiday, you probably feel more energetic during the holiday season, compared to the lull after the holidays are done. Lots of things change depending upon the seasonalities of life, and your energy levels are no different.

In order to manage your energy, it's important to take note of how you're feeling, when you're feeling it, and what makes you feel that way. You'll figure these things out by conducting an energy audit.

Conduct an Energy Audit

You may already be aware that you're a morning person or a night owl, but conducting an audit allows you to know *exactly* when it is that you'll feel energetic.

It's helpful to know when you'll be performing at your best so that you can schedule your most important tasks for that time. This way, you can plan to work on your goals when you know you'll have energy for them, as opposed to working on them whenever they fit into your schedule when you might no longer have any energy left.

If you're married, it's also really good to know your spouse's typical energy fluctuations. Do you know when your significant other's peaks and dips usually are? My husband is not a morning person, but I am. I had to learn over the years to not have any deep conversations with him when he first wakes up. This may be an interesting thing that you could do together so that you learn how to interact with each other better, like when it's a good time to talk to them about something important, or when they need to be left alone.

With this audit, you'll also discover exactly *what* excites you. This information is good to know because when you have the need, you'll have an arsenal of energy-giving activities you can draw on to wake back up. You'll also learn what activities drain you, so you'll know what things to avoid doing. To get a full understanding of your energy levels and how to better manage them, you'll need to perform two different activities for the audit. With both the activities, you'll again be excluding anything you do or any time you spend during work hours. However, you'll still be including your lunch break or any time that is considered your own.

Find Out What Gives You Energy

The following idea is inspired by James Clear's Habits Scorecard. While you're writing down what activities you do throughout your day, you're also going to jot down how each one makes you feel.

As soon as you finish doing something, at the time that you're writing down how long it took you to do it, you're going to rate the activity. Use the following symbols to do so: Give a "+" symbol if doing something *excited* you. Give items a "=" symbol if an activity elicited a *neutral* response, and put a "-" mark next to tasks that *drained* you.

This is simple if you're using Google Keep, as you can mark how an activity made you feel right beside it.

It's not quite as simple if you're using apps. However, it's still pretty easy. This will be when you make use of the note feature you enabled earlier. After you finish an activity, type your rating into the note section of that activity. If you forgot to turn that feature on when you made a task, swipe left on that task while on the "Today" tab, and then hit the pencil icon to edit and add a note. When it comes time to review your ratings, you'll need to open up the "History" tab located at the bottom of the screen, and then click each task to reveal the note and rating.

Find Out When You're Most Energetic

To begin the second part of the energy audit, set a timer to go off hourly. When the timer goes off, score where your energy is at based upon these five ratings: "-2,-1,0,1, and 2." A "-2" means your energy level is extremely low. A "-1" means that your energy is somewhat low. A "0" means you are not drained or energized. A "1" means you are somewhat energized, and "2" means you are extremely energized. Do this for all of your waking hours.

Keep a running list of this in Google Keep and track it for one week. Afterward, you may choose to construct a chart to serve as a visual representation of the flow of your energy levels, or you may choose to simply take note of what hours you usually feel good and when you feel sluggish.

What to Do Once You've Tracked It

Once again, use the information you gathered to find *patterns*. Use the patterns of the different halves of the audit to work *together* to determine ways to improve your energy.

For example, you can use the activities that had a pattern of giving you energy in the first part of the audit to address the hours of the day when you had a pattern of feeling tired in the second part of the audit. If you found that you're usually tired after getting off of work, and separately that talking to a girlfriend energizes you, you could make a new habit of calling one of your girlfriends for a chat around that time.

Make a list of all of the things that usually increased your energy. The next time you feel a lull coming on, pull one of these "tools" out of your energy "toolbox." You may even consider rating these activities based upon how much energy they gave you, or which ones *sometimes* had high ratings compared to other activities which *always* had high ratings.

Consider also making a list of the activities that typically left you feeling tired. <u>If you must do those things again, plan to accommodate them by leaving yourself a rest period afterward or by scheduling energizing activities after them.</u>

Make the Most of Your Energy Peaks

You've probably heard the saying, "The early bird gets the worm." While there is some truth to that, it's not completely true. Sleeping in has become synonymous with laziness, but that's not the case for everyone.

If you're a night owl, it's not a bad thing. You still have just as many hours in the day as a morning person. Sure, you get up later, but you're also able to work later as well. <u>Don't let other people tell you when you should or shouldn't have energy</u>. Make the most of whatever time of day your energy is at its peak, regardless of how others might feel about it.

You can make the most of those peak hours by scheduling to work on your priorities then. If this time just so happens to be when you're at work, I know you probably won't have much of a say in how that time is scheduled. Regardless, <u>you can still schedule the rest of your day with your energy levels in mind</u>. You and your goals deserve the best you have to offer, so plan on working towards them when you know you'll be on your game.

If for instance you're a morning person, you might feel too drained to study for a class after work. By considering your peak energetic hours, you might move your schedule around so that you can work on your priority (your school work) *before* work when you know you'll be fresh and energized.

Raise Your Energy

While we shouldn't fight against our body's natural rhythms, there are still things that we can do to perk up our energy levels a little and minimize the dips.

Of course, there's the list of energy-giving activities that you just learned about and wrote down.

There's also the energy that you get when you do things that mentally excite you or that give you a sense of purpose. Speaking in front of crowds excites me, and teaching people how they can improve their lives gives me purpose. But to many people, public speaking is draining. You need to find and do things that energize *you*.

You might not know what those things are, especially if you didn't do them during the week you were tracking. And I can't tell you what they are, because they'll be different for every person. But you will learn if you keep your eyes open and continue to weigh how different activities make you feel.

Other things you could do to increase your energy levels include getting more sunlight or getting a light therapy lamp. One of the first things I do in the morning is open up my curtains and let the sunlight flood my room. Sunshine works with your Circadian Rhythm to let your body know when it's time to wake up.

In the darker, colder months, it can be hard to get enough sunlight to feel alert. And even in the summer when it's raining or cloudy, you may feel sluggish. To circumvent this problem, you can get a light therapy lamp which has the added benefit of treating seasonal depression that often comes in the winter months, also known as SAD (seasonal affective disorder).

You could meditate and do yoga. According to a study by the University of Waterloo, meditating for as little as twenty-five minutes a day while doing Hatha yoga can not only give you more energy but also "significantly improve brain function ." Don't be intimidated by this idea if you've never done yoga before. Hatha yoga is one of the more commonly practiced styles. It's beginner-friendly, slow-paced, and consists of simple stretches. Having a period of mindfulness where you lay on the ground first thing in the morning (as some Hatha sessions have you do) may energize some, but may cause others to fall asleep. Again, you need to find the things that energize you. But why not give this a try and start your mornings feeling energized *and* relaxed? If interested, here is a twenty-five-minute guided Hatha yoga session to get you started.

You could intermittent fast. While not a commonly accepted practice, the fasting movement has been gaining popularity in recent years. I started my fasting journey two years ago. Surprisingly, <u>one of the biggest benefits I've received from it is having a more constant state of energy</u>. This one benefit has been so profound that I'm not sure if I'll ever go back to eating three square meals again! I'll go into more detail about intermittent fasting later in this guide.

Other things you could do include getting more sleep and getting sleep that is better quality, eating healthier, and exercising. We'll talk about these in another chapter.

Embrace the Dips

Sometimes, you need to raise your energy levels. But your body can't sustain a constant state of "on." It's important to give it breaks. When it's work time, work. And when it's relaxation time or break time, take a break!

I know this is going to be hard for some of you, but in order to come back rejuvenated later, you need to embrace the lows for a little while. Instead of asking, "How can I get back up sooner?" or "How can I get back to work faster?" a better question would be, "<u>How can I take better care of myself during this dip?</u>"

Listen to your body. Dips are its way of saying it needs something. Do you need a snack? Do you need to drink some water, take a nap, or mentally check out for a few minutes?

Fully disengage from whatever you are doing. Then decompress in a way that rejuvenates *you*, however that may look.

Tomorrow, we'll be going over ways to save time, and reducing distractions, such as social media, is listed. However, <u>things like that *can* have their time and place</u>, and if that's something that recharges your battery, do that for your break.

That's what I appreciate about incorporating energy management into our lives. It offers a healthy balance to time management's rigidness. It acknowledges that we are, in fact, human. We need breaks, and that isn't something to be ashamed of. It *isn't* a sign of weakness. Remember, you're not a robot. So take that break girlfriend!

Action Plan

My goal is not to overwhelm you, but to give you the tools you need. So if life already has you feeling overwhelmed, do not feel that you have to do the activities in this chapter at this exact moment, especially as they require a lot of effort. Instead, <u>plan to do these exercises at some point when you're ready and able to</u>.

When you're ready, determine how you'll track your time, and do so for one week. Afterward, review the data and make changes to your habits. <u>Consider if it would be beneficial to you to track your time for a second week</u>, to see how well those changes work for you, or to see if you need to take a different approach to managing and saving your time.

Conduct your energy audit, and if you're married, consider having your spouse join you so that you can learn about each other. After one week, review your data, look for patterns, and use this information to change your habits. Begin scheduling your priorities around your best hours, and utilize the energy-giving activities you learn about to increase your energy when and where you need it.

DAY 6:
MAKE TIME PART 2

How to Find More Time in Your Day

Stop Procrastinating

We *all* struggle with putting off tasks occasionally. <u>A common misconception is that procrastination is laziness, but that's not always the case</u>. Sometimes it's perfectionism, fear of failure or criticism, low self-esteem, trouble focusing, or it could be depression or anxiety. There are a number of reasons why you could self-defeat before you even start, and sometimes it might be more than one. A good first step in conquering procrastination is figuring out why you do it, and also getting rid of any shame you might feel because of it. Like I said before, we all do it at one point or another.

After you've figured out your possible underlying reason for practicing avoidance, consider how you could change it. For example, if you have trouble focusing, could it be because there are a lot of distractions? How could you reduce them? Is it because you have a lot going on right now in your life? Give yourself a pass. Is your mind wandering because you're exhausted? Get more sleep. Could there even be an undiagnosed disorder such as ADHD? Make an appointment to express your concerns with your doctor.

Next, read through these procrastination busters and pick out the ones that you think will help you overcome that underlying reason. Keep a lookout for additional ideas throughout the rest of this chapter, as a lot of the other points will apply to procrastination as well.

Eat Your "Frog" First

Mark Twain once said, "Eat a live frog first thing in the morning and nothing worse will happen to you the rest of the day." One man ran with this notion. According to Brian Tracy, <u>the task you put off is often the thing that'll have "the greatest positive impact" on your immediate life</u>. Therefore, he encourages you to start your day by doing your biggest, most daunting task first.

He wrote a short, easy-to-read book detailing this notion, which is filled with practical applications. You may recall that I've already mentioned this book a few times so far. It has been so revolutionary that it has become an international bestseller. So if procrastination is a big issue for you, consider checking it out: *Eat That Frog!: 21 Great Ways to Stop Procrastinating and Get More Done in Less Time.*

Be Wary of Productive Procrastination

Sometimes we fall into the trap of thinking that procrastination *only* means playing on our phones or watching TV. But if you find yourself organizing a drawer, when you're supposed to be cleaning your whole house, that's getting sidetracked.

<u>You can be procrastinating *even* if you're checking things off your to-do list</u>. This kind of procrastination is easy to miss because you're still technically being productive. But if you're putting off the important things that you're supposed to be working on (like your "frogs"), in favor of lesser things, you're procrastinating. <u>Try to notice when you're doing this so that you can redirect your focus back to the thing that you're supposed to be working on.</u>

Set a Timer...

If you're struggling to get started on a task, begin by setting a timer for just five minutes. <u>This period of time may be considerably shorter than what you'll need to finish the project, but it'll also be short enough that you'll be able to complete it somewhat easily</u>. After all, you can do almost anything for just five minutes.

This works for a few reasons. It gets you to start right now, and not keep putting off a task because *the clock is ticking*. It gives you some relief knowing that you can stop in a few short minutes. It makes an otherwise boring task slightly more fun, as you challenge yourself to complete it within the time you've given. And it encourages you to work on one thing and not get sidetracked, because then other things would take up that task's time. Occasionally, you might even keep working after the timer goes off because you'll have gotten over the hump of getting started and into a groove.

...Or Set a Pomodoro

This leads us to the Pomodoro Technique, which Francesco Cirillo came up with in the 1980s. He named it the Italian word for "tomato" after those cute little tomato-shaped kitchen timers, but you don't need one of those to make this technique work for you.

To do it, set a timer and work hard for twenty-five minutes. Then take a break and reward yourself for five. This is a completed Pomodoro. If however, you need more time to finish your project, repeat the cycle until you're done. If you're working on a particularly large project, take a longer 15-30 minute break every four cycles.

This technique helps you conquer procrastination by lowering the barrier to getting started, and by giving you the ability to break big tasks into manageable chunks. You might even have more productive and efficient work sessions by feeling refreshed from frequent breaks, and by giving your full focus to the project at hand.

If you haven't already noticed, you'll begin to see a pattern with a lot of these time-saving tips. We'll go into more detail about this later, but a key reason why they work is that many have you focus on one thing at a time. Likewise, the Pomodoro Technique won't be very effective if you multitask. So give your work your full attention during those short twenty-five minutes. Read more about this technique and other similar time cycles if you're interested.

Use the Five Second Rule

This simple rule by Mel Robbins was first mentioned in a Ted Talk that has since affected millions of people's lives. It's based on the idea that while you're not always going to *feel* like doing something important to you, you need to push yourself to do it anyway. Her hack to overcome this lack of motivation is to count backward from five. And when you reach one, to power through that thing, regardless of how you feel.

Robbins claims this rule will help you "end procrastination forever," but it's also helpful for improving your productivity and many other things as well. Check out her book *The 5 Second Rule : Transform your Life, Work, and Confidence with Everyday Courage* or watch her Ted Talk to learn more.

Do It Now if It's Two Minutes or Less

"The dread of doing a task uses up more time and energy than doing the task itself." - Rita Emmett

The Two Minute Rule was invented by David Allen, a productivity consultant who wrote the famous book *Getting Things Done: The Art of Stress-Free Productivity*. He says, " If an action will take less than two minutes, it should be done at the moment it's defined. " So instead of considering whether you should rinse your dish and put it in the dishwasher, you do it *now* because it'll take less than two minutes.

This kind of immediate action won't just help with procrastination but has the potential to transform all aspects of your life. Instead of pausing to let dread of doing a task, the ever-popular planning for a task, or procrastination creep in, you just do it. You stop wasting time *thinking* about it or hating on yourself for not having done such a small thing already. And you prevent tons of tiny tasks from building up and stressing you out.

The next time you're faced with the conundrum to do or not do a two-minute task, say to yourself Nike's slogan, "Just do it."

Stop Waiting for an Arbitrary Number

Most things are scheduled to begin at intervals like 1:00 or 1:30. So it's understandable that we'd be inclined to do the same with our own activities. However, when you put off a task until it's a certain time, regardless of how you might rationalize it, it is still procrastinating.

For instance, if it was 12:57 you might think to yourself, "I'll just wait until 1:00 to start." This initially wastes three minutes. But what often happens is that we get so engrossed in other things while waiting that we miss that "ideal" time. This then leads to a cycle where even more time is lost, because beginning at 1:04 just doesn't sound "right" compared to beginning at 1:05.

Do you see how ridiculous this is? How much of a time-waster it is? It's the same kind of silly concept as waiting until the New Year to make resolutions. You can improve yourself any day, any time. You don't have to wait until January 1st to take action.

Clocks are man's attempt to measure something we have no control over.

You could turn the hands on a clock and change it to 1:00. Then you'd have achieved the same "point in time" that you were waiting for while not having changed time itself. Therefore, waiting for a special or specific time is pointless. So begin when it's time, not whenever it's a *certain* time.

Increase Your Motivation

Your tendency to procrastinate may simply be an issue of not being motivated enough. So how do you increase your motivation so you stop wasting time dilly-dallying? Essentially, you increase the reward that you'll receive from doing the task that you're procrastinating on, and you decrease the time until it's due.

This is better explained by the formula for Temporal Motivation Theory (TMT):

MOTIVATION = ↑ Expectancy x Value ↑

↓ Impulsiveness x Delay ↓

In this formula, Expectancy is the likelihood, or your expectation, that you will reap a reward for your efforts. Value is how much that reward appeals to you. Impulsiveness comes down to your ability to resist urges to do things that are not task-related. And Delay is how long you have to complete the task.

This theory claims that <u>to be more motivated you need to *increase* the things on the top of the formula, and *decrease* the things on the bottom</u>.

Also according to this theory, motivation increases the closer a deadline gets because you view the benefit or usefulness of getting that task done as progressively more valuable. So <u>take advantage of this increasing motivation by setting deadlines for tasks</u> (we'll talk more about this later).

So how do you use this in real life? You could use it to get motivated to clean your car. Plan an activity with a friend for this evening, and offer to pick them up and drive together. According to the formula, you'll have to believe that your efforts will result in a clean car (Expectancy). Can it be cleaned? Of course it can! Having a clean car will suddenly become more important to you (Value) because having a filthy car would be embarrassing! If you'll be tempted to scroll on your phone while trying to clean, you'll have to limit your activity on it (Impulsiveness). And because of the limited time that you'll have (Delay), you'll need to clean faster and procrastinate less.

Complete Tasks Faster

How could you do the things you need to do just a *little* bit quicker?

Speed Them Up

This seems rather obvious. Doesn't it? How do you get something done faster? You speed it up. But a practical application of this is to quite literally increase the playback speed of YouTube videos and audiobooks. You don't need to increase them to the point where you can't understand them though as an incremental change will *still* save you drastically. Listening to a six-hour audiobook sped up by *only* 0.25x will save a whole hour and twelve minutes!

To change the playback speed for YouTube on your phone, open a video and click the three dots. Then click "Playback speed," and adjust it to your liking. Different audiobook apps have different setups, so I can't tell you how to do this for all of them. But if you use Libby, a digitized library app that I'll talk about in a later chapter, open a book and hit the dial symbol at the top middle of the screen to access the speed adjustments.

Another way you could speed things up would be to set a timer, like was mentioned earlier, and to race yourself. Make it a game and see if you can beat your previous time for the same activity.

Lower Expectations

I once heard a tale of three women. All had children, who for some reason or another, forgot to tell them that their school was having a bake sale until the day prior.

The first woman drove around to different stores hunting for the best ingredients, flour hand-ground by monks in Malaysia, and sugar stripped from the canes by the weathered hands of workers in Brazil. Then she went home and proceeded to spend *hours* baking cookies from scratch, her plans for that evening long forgotten.

The second woman hurried out to the store as well, but she bought cookie dough. Regardless, she still spent most of her evening frantically baking, spooning out the proper amount of dough, changing out the baking sheets for another dozen, and delicately setting out the cookies on cooling racks. This took some time, but it took way less than it took the first woman because the dough was already made.

But the third woman... Can you guess what she did? She went out and bought cookies.

<u>All three women ended up with the same result, but how much time they took to get there was vastly different</u>. In what ways are you currently "baking cookies from scratch" when you could just "buy" them?

<u>Not everything in life needs to be done well</u>. Sure, there are some things that you should spend more time on. But there are also a lot of things that as long as you're getting the basic requirements met and the job done, you're golden!

A thrown-together meal that is bland, slightly burnt, or maybe not the healthiest, is still a meal. A hurriedly swept floor with a few crumbs missed is still a swept floor. And a rushed workout with a few fewer repetitions than you wanted to do is still a workout. <u>Learn to recognize when good enough is good enough.</u>

Get Rid of Perfectionism

Getting rid of perfectionism would certainly help you complete tasks faster. But I've chosen to separate this section from the previous one about lowering expectations, despite being virtually the same thing, because there is a difference between *wanting* things to be done well, and *needing* for them to be done well.

Perfectionism, while idolized or even joked about by society, should not be worn as a badge of honor. Instead, Brené Brown, a researcher and *New York Times* bestselling author, describes it like this:

<u>Perfectionism is not the same thing as striving to do your best</u>. Perfectionism is the belief that if we live perfect, look perfect, and act perfect, we can minimize or avoid the pain of blame, judgment, and shame. It's a shield. <u>It's a twenty-ton shield that we lug around thinking it will</u>

protect us when, in fact, it's the thing that's really preventing us from taking flight.

I challenge you to use these next points to help you put down your shield, not only so that you can save time, but so that you can take flight in *all* areas of your life and no longer be burdened by the weight of perfection.

Perfection Isn't Real

It's sad that some of us, myself included, obsess over this considering that perfection doesn't even exist. Perfection is subjective, thereby contracting the very definition of what it means to be perfect, "being entirely without fault or defect" (Definition by Merriam-Webster Dictionary). It's subjective because what you think is perfect, someone else may find fault with. And even something that you used to think was perfect, may be something that you now think could use a few tweaks.

Holding yourself to a standard that *doesn't exist* is setting yourself up for *failure* because it is *impossible* to achieve.

Know Your Worth

While I was researching for this section on perfectionism, a common theme emerged, that perfectionism stems from the belief that your self-worth is wrapped up in your achievements. But based on my own experience, I believe that perfectionism, like procrastination, can be caused by a multitude of different reasons. However, let's talk about self-worth for a little bit, in case you feel that it may very well be the reason why you act this way, and also because every one of us could use a bump up in that area.

According to Brian Tracy, you can improve your self-esteem by saying positive affirmations to yourself, and by telling yourself how awesome you are. If you need some ideas to get started, I have a thoughtfully created list of 51 Positive Affirmations to Start Your Day Right that I think you'll love.

If however, you have a hard time saying, let alone believing, positive affirmations like how awesome you are, I have some news for you. You *are* awesome! You are a woman who cares about her future. You are taking strides to improve yourself, and you are a hard worker. How do I know this? Because you're here, going through this guide, reading and learning all this material, and doing the daily actionable steps. It's a *lot* of work, and you're killing it!

I want to remind you that even the big guy upstairs thinks you're pretty sweet. God made you with his own two hands and afterward said, "[she] is very good" (Genesis 1:31), you are "wonderfully made" (Psalm 139:14). Notice how he didn't just say, "Eh, you aight." In other words, you were *created* worthy. Nothing you could do, make, or be could *make* you worthy, because *you already are*. And nothing you could do, make, or be that *isn't* perfect could make you *un* worthy.

Tracy also believes that completing projects improves your confidence and the bigger the goal you complete, the higher your confidence will spike. This gives you all the more reason to keep on plugging away at those big goals you set in that earlier chapter. Additionally, you can boost your self-esteem by writing down and reviewing past accomplishments that you're proud of.

Lastly, begin thinking of yourself as a friend and speaking to yourself as such. Would you talk down to a girlfriend, and tell her that she is *horrible* at doing something? Would you tell her that she is a hot mess and *always* gets everything wrong? Of course not! If someone did that to you in real life, you wouldn't hang out with them (or at least I hope you wouldn't). So don't do that to yourself. Instead, speak words that are loving and encouraging. Build your self-esteem.

Practice the 70% Rule

This rule helps you overcome perfectionism by relaxing your standards, by resetting your level of acceptability.

The idea, in theory, is simple. If 100% equals a perfectly completed project, then you should stop working once you reach 70%. Now your number may be different than 70, and you may occasionally put more effort than that into things that are important to you, but the idea remains the same.

You may have issues with the idea of willingly putting out less than your best. But to be clear, I'm not saying to put out subpar work, but to find a healthy balance somewhere along the line that isn't extreme.

So instead of procrastinating on doing a project for fear that it won't turn out exemplary, you can start right away, confident in your ability to reach only slightly above average. And instead of painstakingly working to make something flawless, you can stop much sooner, saving yourself a lot of stress and time.

Lowering your level of acceptability will help you get things done *faster* which will, in turn, help you do *more*. And the more you do something, the better you become at it. This is because of the experience you gain, the feedback you receive from others, and the feedback you give yourself. So while we've often heard the phrase, "Quality over quantity," perhaps it should be the opposite, as quantity *leads* to quality.

This is illustrated in the interesting read *Art & Fear* by David Bayles and Ted Orland. The book tells the story of a professor who split his photography class in two. One half was given the assignment to take the single best photo (quality), while the other half was tasked with taking as many photos as possible (quantity). At the end of the semester, the photos were judged, and the winner of the best image came from the quantity group.

Their success was believed to be due to them learning from their experiences. By taking many photographs, they figured out what worked and what didn't, improving their skills. I also believe that the quantity group excelled because they did not hold themselves back for fear of something not being good enough.

So the next time you're tempted to waste time making something perfect, try to stop once you reach 70%. In doing so, you'll be able to achieve more, which will inevitably help you turn out better work.

Understand the Law of Diminishing Returns

You can use the previous rule as a guiding benchmark for this law which says that essentially the further along in a process you become, the fewer results you will achieve. Eventually, your efforts will no longer give you a better result but a *negative* one!

I think the best way to visualize this is through a graph:

Imagine that you begin working on a project. On the first day, you get a lot done. You pick out a name, make a plan of action, and you get some of the main balls rolling. On the second day, you spend equally as long working, but not as much progress is made because you spend your time working on the finer details. But on the third day, despite working just as long as the other days, *no* progress is made. In fact, considering that time is a valuable resource, you begin to *lose* returns the more time and effort you invest into that same project.

The third day of this example is usually when perfectionists stop working. Ideally, if you want to optimize your efforts and save time, you should aim to stop *before* things start to dwindle, somewhere before surpassing that 70% (or whatever number it is that you decided you will stop at).

This law also serves as a good reminder that sometimes sinking more time, money, or effort into something isn't the answer. <u>Sometimes, it's best to just cut your losses and walk away.</u>

If you'd like to learn more about overcoming perfectionism, I recommend the book *How to Be an Imperfectionist: The New Way to Self-Acceptance, Fearless Living, and Freedom from Perfectionism.* It focuses on helping you make small changes towards embracing imperfection, so you can eventually live a life that's happier and l ess stressful. T he book is easy to understand, and its practical suggestions can be applied immediately.

Before we wrap up this section, I'd like to add that if perfectionism, or procrastination for that matter, are hindering your daily activities, it's okay to see someone about them. There is no shame in working to understand and improve yourself.

Eliminate Unnecessary Tasks

When looking at your big list of to-dos ask yourself, "Does this *need* to be done?" We already went over eliminating unnecessary tasks back in the section about prioritization. But as this is such a problem for so many people, it's worth mentioning again. Refer back to that section, and reread it if you need to.

Automate

I can't recall where I heard this quote, but it goes something like, "If you do something more than once that can be automated, you're *choosing* to waste your time." That stuck out to me because I wouldn't ever intentionally waste my time. Yet, there were many things I was doing manually that could have been automated.

I know that time is valuable to you, and you certainly wouldn't ever purposely waste what little time you have either. That's why a lot of this guide is dedicated to helping you automate things, because anything you can create a process for today, will save you time tomorrow. So let's take advantage of the advances in technology, and <u>make the little "robots" in your pocket work for you</u>!

Delegate

Ask yourself, "Does this need to be done *by me*?" If the answer is "No," delegate it. We'll go over different ways you can pass off responsibilities later in this guide, but a couple of examples would include sharing chores with those who live with you and hiring someone to mow the lawn so that you don't have to.

Maximize Time & Efficiency

People often say, "Work smarter, not harder." The hope is that by working smarter, you'll work less, which consequently saves time. But *how* exactly do you do that?

Work on One Thing at a Time

We've convinced ourselves that we're good at multitasking as it keeps us feeling busy and productive. After all, why not get two tasks done instead of only one? Yet, research shows that despite us thinking we're accomplishing *more* by doing this, we are in fact *lowering* our efficiency as well as our performance.

This is because our brains can only focus on one thing at a time. "You really can't focus on multiple tasks at once, with the exception of automatic tasks such as digesting or breathing," claims Susan Weinschenk, Ph.D. <u>When we're "multitasking," our brains are actually switching back and forth rapidly between tasks.</u>

Researchers at the University of Michigan conducted a study to measure this switching or mental "gear shifting." <u>They found that when participants changed from one task</u>, such as solving math problems, <u>to another task,</u>

like classifying geometric objects, they *lost* time *every* time. And as the tasks got more complex, or were something that the participants were unfamiliar with, it took even longer for their brains to make the switch. While some switching only resulted in the loss of a tenth of a second, those losses added up. David E. Meyer, Ph.D., who was one of the researchers, concluded that the mental process of switching between tasks could reduce productivity by as much as 40% in some cases!

This study found that we are most productive when focusing on a single task at a time. So set aside time to work on one thing, and discipline yourself to *only* work on that thing during that time.

Eliminate Distractions

To stay focused on that singular task, you'll need to eliminate, or at least reduce distractions.

If people are distracting you, you may need to ask them for some quiet time, ask them if you could have the space to yourself, or you may need to move yourself to another, less distracting area.

If technology is distracting you, you could put it into airplane mode. Alternatively, you could turn off all notifications on your phone and computer for things like emails, messages, and any other popups that might interrupt you (besides calendar events). This will not only help you be more productive by eliminating distractions, but it will have a *profound* impact on lowering your stress.

Take back control over your time by implementing this no-notifications boundary. With today's technology, it's become regularly accepted, if not expected, for people to immediately reply to messages. There is no excuse not to immediately reply, as everyone always has their phone with them. Right? Wrong. There is no rule that says you have to reply *right now*. So turn off your notifications, and don't allow other people to hijack your time by interrupting your focus and harming your productivity.

If you choose to eliminate distractions in this way, make sure you set a regular schedule for getting back to people and replying to emails.

There are also apps and browser extensions that will limit your usage on social media and other websites. This is a great option if you want to keep your notifications on but still limit distractions. Some of the apps will limit when and how long you can access a site. And if you need to stop all access, some will even fully block sites as well. Look through this list of website blockers and download one if you think you need it.

Multi-Task the Right Way

Now that we've gone over how multitasking can mean the death of your productivity, I'd like to let you know about an exception to that no-multitasking rule.

A second study performed by the University of California, Berkeley concluded that the findings from the first one weren't absolute. Three different experiments proved that people *can* multitask, without too much interference, if the two tasks are cognitively different and are both mastered.

Said differently, if you combine one task that you are proficient with, or one that is mindless, with another mindless task, you can accomplish them simultaneously. Just be wary. If you notice that your *quality* of work goes down, or if pairing them up causes you to work *longer*, then you've defeated the purpose of multitasking. And both actions should be done separately once more.

An example of a good pairing would be using your commute time to listen to audiobooks and learn something of value. Please use this suggestion wisely. This would only work if you knew how to drive, knew where you were going, and if the books didn't take too much of your concentration. This *wouldn't* work if you were new to driving, as most of your focus would be preoccupied. Of course, you should only use a hands-free listening device when allowed by law and if conditions permit.

A similar example to this would be listening to audiobooks or podcasts while exercising. I enjoy listening to books while walking my dog, but some people even do this while lifting weights or running.

As you can see, listening to information is a great way to multitask, and it can save you a lot of time. But what if you have something *physical* that needs to be read? Check out this list of free text-to-speech apps if you'd like to convert any text into audio.

A third example would be <u>using the time that you're waiting in the shower to clean a portion of it</u>. Instead of twiddling your thumbs while waiting for a hair mask to soak in or a face mask to dry, you could scrub down a wall.

The last example would be <u>painting your nails while watching a movie</u>. Movies are typically two hours long, which I've found to be the perfect amount of time needed for polish to dry. Plus, if mindlessly munching on food while watching films is a problem for you, having wet nails would prevent you from doing this.

Pareto's Principle (The 80/20 Rule)

Pareto's Principle, unlike other principles, is not a law but more of an observation, that <u>things in life are not always evenly distributed</u>.

While you might think that you should receive an equal amount of output for an equal amount of input (like a transaction), the reality of distribution is *unbalanced*. However, it's unbalanced in a predictable ratio, that approximately 20% of your efforts will lead to 80% of your results.

So if you want to save time and reap the greatest reward for your work, use your time efficiently by working on the big-ticket items that'll have the greatest impact. These "vital few" as they're called, typically only make up 20% of your workload. So <u>by doing *less*, you'll actually achieve *more*</u>!

Likewise, you must work as little as possible on the 80%, on the tasks that have little to no value. Otherwise, you'll be like a donkey at a mill who walks around in circles. <u>You'll stay busy, doing little tasks over and over, while going nowhere</u>.

Parkinson's Law

Did you ever have a big project that you procrastinated on for weeks until it was due the next day? Then you buckled down and *somehow* finished it in time. Or did you ever whip your messy house into shape faster than you knew was possible when your relatives said they were coming to town? These are both examples of Parkinson's Law.

It states that "work expands so as to fill the time available for its completion." Basically, without a deadline, a task will suck up as much time as you give it.

Think of work as being a hungry little gnome who will eat all of the time you feed it. How do you keep it in check? You set deadlines. Don't just think, "I'll work on this project until it's done," because the project will take longer than necessary.

Instead, use the time tracking techniques you learned about yesterday to determine a *realistic* amount of time you need to finish a job. Then, for all similar jobs in the future, use that same amount of time, or slightly less if you want to push yourself. This works for small, short-term projects that only need a few minutes, as well as large projects that need multiple months.

The Reality

Now that you have all of these time-saving tricks up your sleeve, it's time for a reality check. At the end of the day, it doesn't matter how efficient you are, how fast you work, or how good you are at time management. Time is going to pass by either way. But as Lao Tzu, an ancient Chinese philosopher put it, "Nature does not hurry, yet everything [gets] accomplished." In other words, everything that needs to be done will eventually be done.

So don't stress trying to fit it all in and get it all done. Don't use these techniques to try to stuff even more into your busy schedule. Instead, stop and smell the roses once in a while. What does all of this time saving do for you if you don't spend some of it on things that matter?

If you're still feeling like you don't have enough time though, keep an eye out for the additional time-saving tips that are sprinkled throughout the rest of this guide.

Action Plan

How will you apply the things that you learned today to your life?

If you're a procrastinator, reflect on why you tend to put things off. Then pick out one or several points that might help you address this and determine how you'll make them work for your situation.

If you're a perfectionist, follow the same steps. You might consider how you could improve your self-esteem. Or you might determine if 70% perfect is good enough for you, or if you need a higher level of acceptability.

<u>If you don't identify as either</u>, which of the points still speak to you? Are you going to set timers from now on? Are there any things in life that you've been "baking" that you are now going to "buy?" Are you going to download one of those website blocking apps so you can limit your time on distracting sites? What are two mindless tasks that you could still perform effectively if you did them at the same time?

DAY 7:
STOP PUTTING YOURSELF LAST

Why You Need to Put Yourself First

Have you heard of the quokka? It's this adorable little animal that exemplifies putting yourself first more than any other example I can think of.

When it's chased by a predator it does its best to get away. But as a last resort, it relaxes the muscles in its pouch which causes its baby to tumble out. The mom knows that the baby will make enough noise that the predator will be drawn away from her so she can escape. What a great mom, right? But why does she do this? She knows she must put herself first because she can't make more babies if she's dead!

While you might not have heard of that before, you probably have heard of the airplane and mask analogy. For those who haven't flown, or haven't in a while, it goes something like this: When you're riding a plane the stewardess will say, "In case of an emergency the compartment above you will open and a mask connected to an air tank will drop. Put your mask on yourself *first* before you help the person next to you and put their mask on them."

Despite having heard these words many times before, it never occurred to me to apply them to everyday life. By the time I heard of putting your mask on yourself first, outside of the context of an airplane, self-sacrificing ideologies had long been planted in my mind.

I mentioned before that a big reason why I was let go from my previous job was because I was a hot mess. I won't regale you with the tales of my misfortune now, though I have sprinkled a fair bunch throughout this guide, so you can learn from my mistakes and so we can laugh at how much of a mess I was together. But quite simply, I was a hot mess in my personal life and I was a hot mess in my professional life. I was a hot mess physically and I was a hot mess mentally. Some of it was just naturally who I am. But the things that could have been helped, such as getting my priorities straight and taking care of myself, were completely ignored.

I thought that postponing my own needs for the needs of others was the *right* thing to do. I thought it would be *selfish* of me to think of myself before thinking of anyone else. I kept saying I'd eventually get around to taking care of my own needs and wants, but something else always seemed to come up. I put my own needs in the backseat for years, until everything in my life was falling apart. And it all came about as a ripple effect from me putting myself last.

Admittingly, I had begun turning outward for approval, when I should have turned to my religion or myself and loved ones. Instead, I hoped that the people around me would acknowledge and appreciate how dedicated I was if I put their needs above my own. The reality was that they didn't.

One hard lesson my naive self had to learn was that the people around you will never care about you as much as you care about yourself. Most people have their own interests at heart, even those in places of authority whose responsibility it is to watch over and care for you.

If you put your needs last in an effort to bend over backward and serve others, a lot of people will take advantage. They will expect more and more from you until you have nothing left over for yourself. That sounds extremely pessimistic, but <u>even those who mean well, who don't intentionally ask for more than you can give, may do so without realizing it</u>.

That is why you must be your own advocate. You must put yourself first and make sure your needs are being met because no one else will. And <u>you must be the one who lets others know your limits because no one else will know what they are or when they have been reached.</u>

"Putting yourself first is a nice idea, but it's not reality," you may be thinking. "Women are the caregivers. We sacrifice for others. That's who we are." Yes, that is in our nature, and we still need to find a *healthy* balance.

I'm not saying that to put yourself first you must put everyone else *last*. Nor am I saying that you should be first *all* the time. Putting yourself first doesn't mean that you don't care about others. <u>Certain seasons of your life will call for priorities to be moved around</u> and require you to put other things and other people above your own needs. <u>But these seasons should never be long-term, and your needs should never be last place. Because if</u>

<u>you ignore your own needs long enough</u>, eventually something is going to give, <u>something is going to suffer because of it</u>.

What I didn't understand before was that for us to be better wives, friends, employees, volunteers, you name it, we need to be able to be present in the moment and well enough that we can do the things that we need to do. You can't love, serve, and care for others as well as you *could* if you're barely hanging in there yourself.

"You can't pour from an empty cup." - Norm Kelly

By putting your own needs and wants in front of others, you'll be able to show up as your *best* self and consequently show up better for others as well.

How to Start Putting Yourself First

Now that you know how important it is to put yourself first, how do you begin doing that?

Consider what your current priorities are and rearrange them if needed. We just went over your priorities yesterday, but it doesn't hurt to have a second look at them. <u>What things have you been allowing into your life that use up your time and energy when you've been lacking these very same things for yourself?</u>

<u>How could you reduce, or if necessary eliminate, these things that are no longer top priorities?</u> Downgrade these from rock status to pebbles in your time jar.

Also, be conscious of any priorities that others may have set for you. You'll need to decide if these things really should be at the top of your list, or if you're going to have to do some rock rearranging.

Next, set aside the time and means to accomplish your new priorities. Determine how you could make these things happen, and make the necessary arrangements to ensure that you get your "Me Time." That means that if your tiny dog can't hold their bladder long enough for you to go exercise after work, you need to ask your neighbor to let them out for you. That means that if you want to start getting a pedicure monthly, you need to spend less money by not going out to eat with friends as often.

Let others know about your new top priorities and set expectations, like informing your boss that you'll no longer be taking projects home to work on in your free time. <u>Let them know how they can support you in this venture of putting yourself first.</u> But if they're not used to the idea, let them know that you'll be able to show up better for them if they help or at least do not hinder you in caring for yourself.

<u>Some may accept these changes, but even those who love you may intentionally or not push back against your new way of living</u>. Some people will make a fuss when you suddenly start putting your own needs above theirs when they're used to you bending over backward for them. This is where boundaries come in.

You may need to set down some hard and fast rules regarding these things if others do not respect your needs and wishes. People may ask you to do something multiple times or word their request differently. Don't let the raised eyebrows of people convince you to make exceptions or compromise to some degree. Don't let pressure or guilt trips deter you. Let your "No" mean "No."

I know that the idea of declining something or setting boundaries can be intimidating, but we'll be covering all of that tomorrow so that you can learn to boldly and confidently put your own needs first.

Action Plan

Go back to your time jar once more and review what your current priorities are. What things have you allowed into your life, or have you allowed others to put into your life, that should not be a top priority anymore?

How will you adjust your priorities so that you can begin taking care of your own needs and wants, or taking care of them *better*? What arrangements do you need to make so you can support your future self in this endeavor? Do you need to adjust your schedule, your budget, or speak to anyone about your new priorities?

DAY 8:
THE ART OF SAYING "NO"

Setting Boundaries Isn't a Bad Thing

Most people struggle with saying "No" to some degree, especially us women because we tend to be more agreeable. We want everyone to be happy, and we want to seem nice and not appear uncaring, rude, or selfish. So we say "Yes" to things that we want to do and even say it to things that we *don't* want to do. We say "Yes" so often that saying (or hearing) the opposite response can be quite alarming.

I remember asking a friend's husband in passing if they wanted some more of the fish my husband and I had caught. I had dropped some off at their house a month prior and still had a freezer full that I didn't want to toss out. Without blinking he said, "No." I was taken aback. "No? How rude!" I thought. I was offering him something and he couldn't at least soften the blow of "No" by saying "Thank you" with it?

After a bit of reflection on this interaction, I realized that his saying "No" didn't make me dislike him at all. In fact, it made me *respect* him more. He was assertive and clear about his limits. He didn't beat around the bush or come up with a lame excuse.

Sure, I was offended and slightly hurt at first. But I still considered him a friend. This made me realize that I could act in the same way that he did, and people wouldn't hate me! Maybe, like how I came to appreciate his straightforwardness, others could also come to appreciate it if you and I didn't lead them on or fake enthusiasm. Maybe, we could invoke that same kind of respect if we were *honest* and actually said what we meant.

Many people are too afraid to do what this man did. We are too afraid to say "No," and consequently allow others to walk all over us, intentionally or not, determining what we do with *our* time and *our* days. We let others get into the driver's seat of our own lives! One of the best ways you can take back your life, take back your control, and stop being a hot mess, is to learn to say "No," especially to things that don't align with your goals and priorities.

You have every right to decline things and protect your time jar. The extra things people ask you to do, those things are just sand, which can fill in the gaps *after* you've already put in your rocks and pebbles. I used to struggle a lot with wanting to do and say "Yes" to everything. I would feel *guilty* if I didn't! I'd volunteer to clean up highways when my own house needed to be cleaned up. I'd say "Yes" to feeding the homeless when I didn't even have the energy to cook food for myself and my husband. Learning about the time jar helped me, as did determining if I *wanted* to do things or if I was just feeling *obligated* to. I've gotten so much better with this, but even now, I still occasionally feel a twinge of guilt when I say the word. However, I'm almost always glad that I said "No," and I think you will be too.

How to Set Boundaries

Telling other people "No" and setting limits to what you will or won't do can be difficult for people pleasers and those intimidated by confrontation. It's especially difficult when we don't know what to say, how to say it, or get all tongue-tied when trying to express how we feel. We can't expect others to know our boundaries unless we tell them though. Thankfully, it doesn't have to be a difficult conversation.

Examples of how to politely decline:

I'd love to, but my schedule is full.

Sadly, I have other plans.

Unfortunately, now is not a good time.

I'm honored you thought of me, but I can't.

Thank you for thinking of me, but I'll have to decline.

I'm not sure I can do that. I'll have to think about it and get back to you.

No thank you, but it sounds like fun!

I'm sorry, I can't fit anything else into my schedule right now.

Unfortunately, I won't be able to make it.

I'm sorry, I have other commitments at that time.

It is very important with some of these examples, or when you say "No" in any other way, that you do not tell someone to ask you again later or say that you would like to do something if you do not want to do it. <u>Saying that you want to do something will leave you open to being asked again</u>, which will mean you'll find yourself in the uncomfortable position of having to decline once more.

Out of *respect* to the other person, their time, and to make things easier on yourself, don't say what you don't mean! This will help ensure that valuable spots or things are not reserved for you when you don't intend to be there. This will also save you a lot of anxiety and save others from hurt feelings, confusion, and frustration when they wonder why you don't do something when you keep saying, "I'd love to."

Instead, be clear with your intentions. Do not say "I'll think about it," or "I'll get back to you," unless you *really* will get back to them and are just checking your schedule or are trying to coordinate things. <u>If you already know that your answer will be "No" later on, then you've already made up your mind. Don't string them along by saying "Maybe"</u> and stress yourself out in the meantime.

"Let your yes mean yes and your no mean no." - Matthew 5:37

Keeping those things in mind, look back at that list and pick a phrase, make a combination of phrases, or create your own that you'd be most likely to use. Make that your go-to phrase for declining, and practice saying it in situations where there is less pressure. You might practice saying it to a clerk who asks if you want to apply for a store credit card or to a door-to-door salesman.

Saying "No" to a stranger is much easier than saying the same thing to people who you love and care about. So get comfortable with declining in these interactions, so that you'll have built up your confidence when you have to decline something with family and friends.

If you're worried about hurting peoples' feelings when setting boundaries with those closest to you, try to remember that the words "Yes" and "No" are just that, words. They do not carry emotion. Sarri Gilman, a marriage and family therapist, reminds us in her popular TedTalk on boundaries that "Yes and no are not feelings." <u>We must do our best to remove ourselves and our emotions from situations when defining our limits.</u>

<u>From now on, be *very* selective about what you say "Yes" to</u>, because when you say "Yes" to one thing you are giving an unspoken "No" to something else.

How to Get Out of Previous Obligations

I would be remiss if I told you to not do things in the future that you don't want to do without also addressing the things that you have *already* signed up for. Earlier, you took a second look at your priorities and may have moved some things around to put your own needs first. We talked about letting others know about these new priorities, but that now means that you'll have to have the awkward conversation of telling people you won't be doing what you said you would.

Saying "No" is difficult enough, but getting out of doing something that you already said "Yes" to is that much more intimidating. Communicating your intentions in a *timely* manner so that others can find a replacement for you is essential. Just because you will now be putting yourself first does not mean that you should *disrespect* others by not letting them know you won't be holding up your half of the bargain.

If it's within a short enough period of time that your backing out will leave others scrambling or worse for wear, you should go through with what you said you would do. We still want to be the type of person who maintains trust and respect in our relationships. Just make sure to say "No" next time.

So how do you gracefully bow out of previous obligations? Here are a few examples:

I made a mistake and overextended myself by signing up to do XYZ. I'm sorry for the inconvenience I'm causing you, but I simply can not take on anything more right now.

This XYZ is important. Unfortunately, I will not be able to give it the kind of time and attention it deserves.

I'm feeling a bit overwhelmed with everything else I have going on right now and I realize I should not have agreed to help with this.

I'm sorry, but I'll no longer be able to do XYZ. However, I do know someone who could do as good of a job or better than I could have. Would you like me to get in contact with them for you?

I'm not going to be able to complete XYZ due to personal reasons. However, I have already completed this much of it. Where would you like for me to drop it off?

I can no longer do XYZ due to unforeseen circumstances. I'm sorry for the inconvenience, but I'm honored that you asked me to be a part of it in the first place.

Unfortunately, something has come up that I have no control over. I could still complete this half of XYZ, but do you know someone else who could do the rest?

My plate is overflowing right now. Would there be a different way that I could still help you that requires less XYZ on my part?

As some of these examples suggest, it may help to ease the tension if you offer options, such as an alternative or compromise, when you are backing out of doing something. After all, the other person was counting on you. But if you can offer them a solution to their new problem, finding someone to fill your role or do the work you said you would do, then you won't be leaving them in a pinch. They may even be *excited* about you stepping down if you can provide them with a better alternative. But, <u>if you offer a compromise, only do so if you want to and can fulfill this new commitment.</u> Otherwise, you'll have to back out of yet another uncomfortable situation.

Stand Your Ground

It is *crucial* that you stick to your boundaries after you have set them. This may be the hardest part of putting yourself first, second behind letting others know your new priorities, because either you or others may waiver.

You may have mixed feelings about the situation, like wondering if you did the right thing. Or you may feel guilty about the limitations you set. You'll have to do some self-reflecting to determine if you made the right choice for yourself and if it's just your people-pleasing tendencies nagging you, or if you need to rethink things.

The people on the other side of the equation may be angry, or worse, disappointed. They'll be used to interacting with you in ways that you previously taught them were acceptable, with behaviors that you allowed. But now, they'll have to figure out their place in your new "normal." They may struggle with the change and do whatever they can to get things back to what they're used to.

As tough as it may be, <u>try to not take the other person's reactions to heart. You can only control and are responsible for how *you* behave</u>. If the other person wants to throw a "tantrum," give you the silent treatment, or call you names, that is on them.

If you give in to their behavior and revert to your old ways, you'll teach the other person that it is okay for them to push your boundaries. You'll essentially reward them by giving them what they want. You'll encourage them to push your limits next time, and teach them to disrespect you and your word. Do not do this! It'll be that much harder for you next time. Instead, stick to your guns and hang in there, regardless of how they act.

As much as you may feel mean or uncaring, and as much as the other person may feel abandoned at first, recognize that <u>you are setting these limitations out of love</u>. If you didn't care about the other person in some way, you wouldn't allow them into your life anymore. You setting these limits means that you love or respect that person enough that you are trying to work through a problem, build a healthier relationship, and *keep* them in your life.

Learn More

Today, we mainly explored boundaries in the context of declining requests and invitations so that you can free up your time and resources to care for yourself. But there is so much more to discuss and learn about the topic, such as setting boundaries for how people treat you.

If you'd like to learn more, I highly recommend the book *Boundaries* by Dr. Henry Cloud and Dr. John Townsend. If you've been a part of the Living a Sweeter Life family for a while, you know that it is one of my favorite books I always recommend. I especially recommend it to Christain women, as I feel we are often raised to serve others at the expense of taking care of our own needs. I've read through it multiple times and it has *really* helped me. In fact, this is the book I've given away most often, even to strangers who have taken the time to ask what it was about when I was reading it in public. There is also a new version of the book for those who are married which is fittingly titled *Boundaries in Marriage.* If saying "No" or setting any kind of boundary is a problem for you, I highly recommend you get one of these.

Action Plan

Determine what your default "No" response will be and practice saying it. <u>Work towards declining all events, activities, or requests from now on</u>, unless they are things you want to do or that support the kind of life you want to live.

Which prior engagements do you need to remove from your schedule? Create an actionable plan for doing so as long as there is sufficient time for you to be replaced. Do you need to call anyone this evening to let them know you will no longer be doing XYZ? Where do you anticipate people not respecting your new priorities and <u>what kind of boundaries could you be prepared to put in place</u> to protect them? If anyone is already overstepping boundaries that you have, how could you approach and correct the situation?

**DAY 9:
SOUL-CARE**

Yesterday we went over how important it is for you to put yourself first. You probably did some priority shuffling, and then had to have a few uncomfortable conversations where you let others know about your new priorities, dropped some prior obligations, and maybe even set up a few tough-love boundaries. Now that you've carved out this special time for yourself and set things in place to support you with this, what exactly should you do?

Do Things You Want to Do

You may already have an idea of the kinds of things you could do during your "Me Time." But for those of you who shrug your shoulders when someone asks what your hobbies are, or for those of you who have put off doing things for yourself so long that you've all but forgotten what you used to enjoy, here are a few ideas.

You could do more of what you already do that excites you. Look back at the energy-inducing list you created a few days ago. Since those are the activities that excite you and do not drain you, they are most likely also things that make you happy. Do these things more often or extend the time that you're already doing them.

You could pursue previous passions. Chances are that things that used to bring you joy, probably in some shape or form still could. What are some things that you used to love doing as a kid? What things did you enjoy doing even just a few years ago but stopped doing for one reason or another? Now you have the time and means, so pick these activities back up and see if they still bring you the same level of happiness they did before.

As you seek to breathe new life into old hobbies, <u>don't get stuck in the rut of thinking that you must do them in the same way you used to</u>. As you have grown and changed, how you interact with those previous hobbies may have changed as well. Maybe you used to love playing softball as a teenager. Now, you might not enjoy playing it, but you probably would love watching a game. You might have enjoyed finger painting as a kid, but now you might prefer to paint by number as it's a lot less messy. Personally, I could no longer get into reading. But when I approached things differently and began listening to audiobooks, instead of forcing myself to sit and stare at a page, I found pleasure in my old hobby again.

You could do something that you've always wanted to do. I imagine that there are a few more things you'd like to do that for whatever reason you did not put into your calendar. Maybe these things are on your bucket list, are not a priority right now, are so small they "aren't" worth mentioning, or are part of your "wild" imagination, so you don't think they'll ever really happen. <u>Use your "Me Time" one of these days to go do something you've always wanted to do</u>! If it's a larger goal, you may need to dedicate a few "Me Times" to accomplish the steps working up to that unspoken dream of yours.

You could try something that you've never thought about doing before. Next time your adventurous friend asks you to go do something with her, tell her "Yes" (keeping in mind what we talked about yesterday) *even* if you're not sure you'll like it. If you don't enjoy yourself, you don't have to do it a second time. But then again, you might end up *loving* the thing you're trying out, and unearth a whole new hobby for yourself.

Actually Care for Yourself

Another thing you could (and should) do when prioritizing yourself is self-care. However, I have a different name for it as I'll explain shortly.

Thanks to the invention of social media, any person can have their opinion heard, even on topics about which they have no knowledge. Because of this, self-proclaimed "experts" have been able to share advice that perhaps isn't the best or most accurate. While they might mean well, a lot of the self-care suggestions nowadays promote cliche practices with one-size-fits-all solutions and quick fixes that provide no lasting results.

Some of the more unhealthful ideas have pushed the notion that you can do whatever feels right as long as it's under the guise of self-care. This, I believe, has given rise to toxic self-care where poor practices such as cutting people out of your life because they upset you, instead of having a mature conversation about things, have become acceptable and even encouraged. It has transformed things that were meant to be good into things that you may no longer derive pleasure from, into a list of to-dos.

Understandably, doing whatever feels good in the moment is not caring for yourself at all. You can't avoid doing unpleasant or uncomfortable things for the rest of your life just because you don't feel like doing them. And you can't just solve real problems you have by drinking a glass of water or by saying three things you're grateful for.

Now some of the things that people suggest you do as self-care *can* be good for you. If you really do feel relaxed or refreshed afterward then, by all means, keep doing them. But I don't believe that caring for yourself should feel like a laundry list of tasks that only add more things to your plate and increase your anxiety. Instead, I believe that caring for one's self should be tailored to one's self. Moreover, and contrary to what the ten billion dollar self-care industry would have you believe, self-care doesn't have to require expensive trips to a salon or costly face products either.

Because of these misleading ideas and the negative connotations that the word "self-care" now carries for some, I suggest we practice *soul* -care instead.

When I refer to soul-care instead of self-care, I'm still essentially talking about the same thing. However, I hope that by referring to it like this, it'll remind you to care for yourself on a deeper level, in a nonsuperficial way. Soul-care is meant to be caring for yourself in the healthful ways that self-care was perhaps once intended to be. It is meant to be something that leaves you feeling refreshed and rejuvenated *long-term* in your mind, body, and spirit, not just caring for your external self temporarily.

Soul-care is about doing the things that help you, not forcing yourself to do the same old self-care activities that everyone else says you have to do. It is about still doing or having things that you enjoy, but doing so in moderation and without overindulging or oppositely, completely depriving yourself. It is about acknowledging when things are bad and seeking help or professional assistance when necessary, not just trying to positive self-talk your way out. <u>Soul-care is about doing something unpleasant when you know it is the best thing for you</u>, not running away from situations or cutting off people when things become difficult, inconvenient, or no longer fun.

What would practicing soul-care look like to you? <u>A good way to determine if something is soul-care or not is to consider if you'll be better off for doing it or if it will just provide temporary gratification.</u>

Let's go over some ideas and suggestions for how you might begin practicing soul-care. A lot of these are also the things that I hinted at in a previous chapter as being activities that will increase your energy levels.

Physical Well-Being

Get the Rest You Need

Why is it that in today's society sleeping for as few hours as possible has become something to brag about or even a challenge people can compete over? "You slept six hours last night? Well, I only slept five!" How can you expect yourself to *not* be a hot mess if you won't even allow your body to get one of its most basic needs?

According to the National Sleep Foundation Guidelines, you need 7-9 hours of sleep if you're age 18 - 64. So ignore those gurus or influencers who say they get up at 4 am and only sleep for five hours. They may indeed do that, but it's not *healthy*.

If you're sleeping less than is recommended, how could you change that? If you're burning the candle at both ends because you have so much to do and a lack of time to do it, I urge you to rethink your priorities once more. Sleep is so *fundamental*. It really should not be one of the things that you try to cut corners on.

Setting aside a proper amount of time to sleep is only half of the battle though. You also need to set yourself up to get *quality* sleep by practicing good sleep hygiene habits. This includes things like going to bed at the same time every night, only using your bed for sleep and sex (not watching TV), and reducing the light in your bedroom. My bedroom is pretty bright at night as our porch light shines inside it. After trying multiple different sleep masks, I finally found this one that I love and have been using for about three years now. Pro tip: add a drop of lavender essential oil to the outside of it to help you sleep even better. Check out this list of suggestions for other ways you can improve your sleep hygiene if you think that this is an area you need to work on.

Eat Right

You probably already know that you should eat vegetables and avoid junk food. But actually getting to the point where you eat better can be a bit of a challenge. There's a lot of information out there that you can dive into if you need help in this area, but I'll share a few quick tips with you while you're here. Find little tricks that will entice you to eat better. For example, I don't like carrots. But if I pair them with hummus, I'll eat them like candy! I also don't like corn, but I don't *pressure* myself to eat it. Instead, I try to make up for it by eating more of the vegetables I do like.

Another trick, one that I picked up from my mother-in-law, is to sneak veggies into dishes wherever you can. I add colorful peppers to my sauces. And anytime I make a stir fry, I consider tossing in some spinach as well. I try to add veggies into any dish where they will blend in and not be a distracting flavor.

Exercise

Exercising is probably another thing that you already know you should be doing. Perhaps again, the real problem is actually doing it. The CDC recommends adults participate in 150 minutes of moderate-intensity activity per week in addition to two days of muscle-strengthening. <u>This equates to *just* thirty minutes, five days a week</u>.

If you weren't already exercising, or if that seems like a lot at first, you can build up to that by <u>looking at where you're already spending a lot of your time and then incorporating a little bit of movement into it</u>. As they say in that CDC article, "*some* activity is better than *none* ."

One idea is to optimize the time you spend watching TV. Different sources claim different amounts, but according to Statista, Americans watch an average of 3 hours and 17 minutes of TV a day. This is a whole other topic we could delve into, but if that sounds like your typical evening, how could you still enjoy your relaxation time while also getting in the exercise you need?

You could <u>do a few quick exercises every commercial break</u>. You don't have to buy any special equipment. Just get up off the couch and use your body weight. Do some jumping jacks, squats, lunges, planks, or pushups. You could even use the couch to do modified push-ups, or do tricep dips off of your coffee table. If you're not sure what some of these exercises are, you can find demonstration videos for them on YouTube.

You could also <u>make things more fun by challenging yourself to do one</u>

<u>repetition</u> of a lightweight bicep curl, military dumbbell press, or tricep extension <u>every time a certain common word is spoken during your show or movie</u>. Again, you don't need any special equipment. If you don't already have a dumbbell, just grab an old textbook or a 5lb bag of flour. Get creative!

Another idea is to incorporate more physical activity into your social engagements. <u>Whenever you're planning to hang out with a girlfriend or go out on a date, add in some kind of physical activity</u>. Not all social gatherings have to revolve around food! You could do a city scavenger hunt that involves a lot of walking (you can find these on Groupon), do a bike tour, go to a group dance class, visit a rock climbing gym, or look up outdoor activities to do near you, such as hiking or canoeing.

We'll talk about exercising even more later on in this guide but start with these suggestions for now if you think any would work for your lifestyle. If they wouldn't, <u>how else might you be able to work more movement into your day</u> in your effort to practice soul-care? Previously, when I was putting my own needs and wants last, my excuses for not working out were always something along the lines of "I don't have time; I'm too tired," or "I'll be too tired afterward to do the other things I need to take care of." If any of these are your current excuses or fears, let me put them to rest.

Working out causes your body to produce more mitochondria. Mitochondria use oxygen and glucose (from that healthy food you're eating) to make fuel, essentially <u>increasing your body's energy on a cellular level</u>. Additionally, exercising boosts your oxygen circulation and strengthens your heart. Both of these will help you power through your day by giving you more stamina. So you don't need to be concerned about being too tired. In fact, you'll gain more energy and strength to do the things you need to do.

Lastly, don't allow lack of time to deter you. You now have this special time set aside for yourself. Use it to care for your well-being, and don't use excuses any longer to deprive your body of what it needs.

Mental Well-Being

Rest Your Mind

Besides resting your body, you also need to rest your mind.

I came across a very interesting interview with Dr. Caroline Leaf, a Chrisitan neuroscientist, who explained how the world has gotten more stressed in the last fifty years than it ever was previously. This sharp incline in anxiety has to do with technology and the way we use it.

Dr. Leaf goes on to explain how our brains are made to have a constant stream of thoughts, and how when we interrupt this process by not giving ourselves time to let our minds wander, we are worse off because of it. She recommends you take at least seven to sixteen minutes a day to do nothing but sit and daydream. Our minds need this time to process and do "housekeeping."

In a separate podcast, she explains that having this quiet time "reboots our brain and our body and [helps us] feel re-energized." By doing this we can enjoy an immediate sense of calmness, peace, cognitive clarity, improved creativity, and even improved intelligence from deeper insights. We can enjoy all of these benefits if we just allow our brains this time of rest. Let's work on taking time every day to practice soul-care by being quiet with our thoughts. How could you get better at disengaging?

You could start by eliminating any white noise or things that would distract you and pull away your attention. You could turn off the TV, hide your phone in a drawer out of sight, or turn it off as well. You could also check out that list of apps that I mentioned in a previous chapter that limit your time on certain websites. If you already looked through that list and didn't find any of them to be helpful, there are also cell phone lockboxes that you can find on Amazon for those especially addicted to their mobile device. If you need to, get a larger box so that you can additionally fit in your tablet, TV remote, gaming remote, and whatever other distracting technology you have.

Exercise Your Mind

When people think of exercise they generally think of moving their body. Most do not even consider the whole other very important "muscle" that also needs to be worked out as part of your caring for yourself.

Jim Kwik overcame multiple severe concussions as a child and was dubbed by a teacher as "the child with a broken brain." He resolved to learn everything he could about how we think and remember things so that he could improve his situation and also help others. Now, Kwik is a world-renowned speaker and brain performance coach who has worked with the likes of Will Smith and Elon Musk.

According to his blog post, our brains start to cognitively decline after just age twenty-five! So stimulating and training our brains should be something that we *actively* work towards. Kwik likens exercising our brain to exercising our body and cautions that " If you don't use your mind it atrophies. It's use it or lose it." If you're interested in improving your mental muscle, consider listening to Kwik's twenty-minute podcast: Tips for Brain Exercise. In it, he and his guest speakers have some interesting ideas for cognitive improvement. Two of the suggestions that stuck out to me were to simply improve your balance and to learn how to juggle.

Spiritual Well-Being

Spirituality means different things to different people. This_article articulates the difference in an easy-to-understand way. It says that "Religion is a specific set of organized beliefs and practices, usually shared by a community or group. Spirituality is more of an individual practice and has to do with having a sense of peace and purpose."

To some, this word may have more of a religious connotation and involve beliefs and behaviors centered around the Creator. To others, it may mean feeling connected to the earth, the world around you, and believing that your life has meaning. When you are facing difficult times, spirituality is the thing that gives you the strength to carry on and hope for better things to come.

Improve Your Religious Walk If you're a religious individual, how are you feeling right now about your walk with God? What is one thing that you think you could improve upon?

Perhaps, working on your spiritual well-being means that you need to get better about doing your daily devotions, or maybe, you just need to start them in general. It may mean praying more often, going to church regularly, or surrounding yourself with Christian friends who can encourage you in ways that align with your religious views. Working on your spirituality might mean that you practice letting go of any anxiety and fear that you have about your future and learn to trust God with your circumstances, whatever the Holy Spirit may be leading you to do.

If you're not currently in fellowship, I encourage you to seek out a church that's to your liking. "For where two or three are gathered in my name, I'm there with them." (Matthew 18:20) Going to church and <u>being surrounded by a like-minded community of individuals can offer you needed structure, encouragement, and comfort in difficult times</u>. These are people who want to leave the world a better place and who, like you, are working to become the best version of themselves.

In the meantime, get into the Word some other way. You could join a small bible study group *even* if you don't go to their church. You could also download the Bible app. This app has tons of different devotions covering all sorts of topics, all of which are free. A lot of the devotionals and even some of the versions of scripture can be read aloud to you for your convenience.

Spirituality Outside of Religion

As I mentioned before, different people view spirituality in different ways. Some view it as being connected to the earth and your surroundings.

The Japanese call the act of being in nature surrounded by trees shinrin-yoku, or "Forest Bathing." You can enjoy the health benefits of this activity by slowly walking through the woods with no particular destination in mind, using your senses to take in your earthy surroundings. What things can you see, hear, touch, and smell? Leave your phone behind and enjoy being present and alive surrounded by all the beauty that Earth provides.

<u>If being in nature is something that would help you feel more spiritual, how could you get better about reconnecting with the great outdoors?</u> You don't have to "go big" and plan a getaway to a national park or to one of those destinations in the article I just mentioned. You could just visit your local park this evening or take a day trip this weekend to see a nearby forest. And while bringing nature indoors won't be quite the same as being outside surrounded by it, you might still feel more connected if you were to bring a few live plants inside.

Another way that some people work on their spirituality is through meditation. One way you could do this would be to take a few moments to sit still, close your eyes, and shut out all other thoughts but that of your slow, steady breathing. Many practice meditation in combination with yoga, which is touted as being the trifecta of spiritual, mental, and physical well-being. To intensify the rejuvenating effects of these two practices, you could even do them together while in nature.

Yoga retreats, sometimes taking place in natural outdoor settings, offer guided sessions and provide an opportunity to get away and recharge. If this sounds like something you would like to do, consider attending a yoga retreat near you. There are now even online yoga retreats for those who do not want to travel or who would rather save their money. Check out this free online yoga retreat if you're interested in improving this part of your spiritual well-being. If you don't want to go through a whole retreat or if you're new to the idea of meditation and yoga, you can try it out and see if it's right for you by following along with a free YouTube video. Consider finding one set in nature, such as one where the instructor is on a beach where you can see the waves crashing and hear the seagulls cawing. It won't be the same as being in nature in person, but you may still find it relaxing and perhaps even spiritual.

Others may find their spirituality through being a part of something bigger than themselves, by working towards something they are passionate about. What is a cause that you are passionate about? <u>What gifts or abilities do you have that you could use to positively impact this cause and the people around you</u>? If you have the gift of conversation, maybe you would feel fulfilled by visiting folks in nursing homes and spending time talking to them and listening to their stories. If you've been touched by the plight of homeless people in your city, volunteer at your local food bank or soup kitchen. Help build a house for those less fortunate than yourself with Habitat for Humanity. If you love spending time with children and would enjoy being a big sister, you could volunteer to be a mentor through BBBS. And if you're a trauma survivor, turn your experience into a blessing for others who are currently going through something similar by volunteering to offer support and love in the special ways that only you know they need.

Making an impact on someone's life can give purpose and meaning to your own. So while in the majority of this guide I will caution you against volunteering *too much*, it can be a wonderful thing. However, serving others and volunteering is not for everyone. That is why you must determine what way is the best way for you to work on your spiritual well-being.

Being a part of a group of people who are passionate about something that you are passionate about will give you a sense of community and belonging, two things considered to be spiritual attributes. But you do not have to be a part of a group working for a cause to enjoy community. Some find spirituality and support through their connection with family, friends, and even coworkers.

One final suggestion for how you can practice soul-care, besides those ideas we just went over, is to take care of your hygiene and appearance. We'll go over both of these in the chapters on personal appearance later on.

Do It Regardless

Something that may hinder you from doing what you want or need to do is a lack of people to do it with. If no one wants to do something with you, then you need to do it by yourself. This won't be as difficult for independent women. But it may be a struggle for social butterflies or those intimidated by doing something new without someone there to support them.

Girlfriend, life is short! Don't let a lack of comradery keep you from doing things that would make you happy or keep you from living a better life. Doing something on your own without anyone there is *not* embarrassing, pathetic, or sad, nor does it necessarily mean that you'll be lonely. Doing something by yourself can be *empowering*. You could learn so much about who you are and grow as a person. You'll probably also meet new people, people who share a common interest with you which makes them potential friends.

So the next time you want to go to a movie that no one else wants to see, I challenge you to go by yourself. When your roommate doesn't want to go work out with you, go exercise for your own health. When your friends don't show up to run with you, I challenge you to *still* work towards your dream and practice for that half marathon anyway. <u>Be the girl who shows up for *herself!*</u>

Action Plan

Come up with a few ideas for things you could do during your "Me Time." What things did you use to enjoy doing? Are there any that you want to pursue again or any new things that you'd like to try?

How will you practice soul-care? If you were already taking time for self-care previously, are there any activities that you've been doing that have not been serving you but stressing you? What soul-care practices could you swap them out with, or could you find a new more healthful way to do the same thing so that it no longer feels like a chore?

If you weren't practicing self-care before, how might you begin practicing soul-care now? Where could you find sixteen minutes a day to be alone with your thoughts? Do you need to read that article on sleep hygiene so you can improve your quality of sleep? Do not overwhelm yourself by trying to start a lot of new things at once. Pick one or two soul-care activities to try for now, perhaps ones in an area that you think you need the most work on. Then come back later when you've successfully implemented them as habits and try something new in a different area.

Lastly, consider what things you've been missing out on because you haven't wanted to do them by yourself. How might you change this and help yourself feel more comfortable and confident so you can do the things you want to do regardless of if anyone else wants to do them with you?

DAY 10:
AUTOMATE GROCERY SHOPPING

You've most likely heard of online grocery shopping by now. Perhaps, you've already jumped on this bandwagon and have been ordering things like this for a while. But if you haven't, maybe because you're avoiding the hassle of learning something new, or because it's just one more thing on your list of things to do, we're going to change that today.

I was personally intimidated by doing online grocery shopping at first. I put it off for years. But it was incredibly easy to figure out and set up once I *finally* looked into it. Now, I'm kicking myself for not having signed up sooner, and I think you will be too. Just think about all of the hours you've spent grocery shopping in your lifetime and all of the future hours you could spend doing this chore if you didn't have someone else do it for you. You'd be fighting a squeaky cart, dealing with throngs of annoying people, and waiting forever in line. Now, you can bypass all of that!

In this guide, I'll only be covering how to automate your grocery shopping with Walmart. There are lots of stores now that offer curbside pickup and delivery. However, because I want things to be as straightforward as possible, I've chosen to only give one example and do so for a store that is nationwide and affordable, so it's accessible to everyone. I've also chosen to only cover Walmart because of the many great benefits it offers its customers, some of which I'll go over today.

If you don't currently shop at Walmart, I encourage you to read through today to see if the perks are worth switching stores. If you want to continue shopping elsewhere, that is perfectly fine. However, I recommend you utilize automated grocery shopping from now on. So see if your store offers these services and begin using them.

<u>If you're already doing automated grocery shopping at Walmart, I still suggest you read today's chapter anyways</u> as you might learn something new.

Set Up

Begin by downloading and setting up the Walmart Shopping & Grocery app Walmart's app doesn't currently accept coupons so promo codes are one of the few ways you can save money. Take advantage of these savings while you can. (When you sign up via that link, I also receive $15 off as well. So thank you in advance!)

After you've downloaded the app, set up your profile. If you have multiple Walmarts in your area, choose the one that's closest to you or that you prefer to shop at most.

Next, consider if you'll usually want to pick up your groceries or if you'll have them delivered to your house. Of course, you can always change how you receive them depending upon your needs for a specific shopping trip.

Pickup: This option is free. I recommend it if you have a little bit of time to spare and can work it into your schedule so it's not too inconvenient.

Delivery: If you only occasionally need things delivered, you'll have to pay $9.95 each time, but depending upon your situation or how much time you'd like to save, it may be worth it to you. If this is how you'd prefer to *always* receive your groceries, I recommend you become a Walmart+ Member. Sign up for this or try out their free trial period to see if it's the right fit for you. Their membership will only cost you a few more dollars than a single delivery charge ($12.95 to be exact), but it will give you *unlimited* deliveries. Even better, if you purchase this plan for a whole year, you'll only have to pay the equivalent of $7.56 a month!

Place Your Order

After you're done setting up the app and deciding if you're going to do pickup or delivery, you can begin shopping. Even if you just went grocery shopping and don't need anything right now, keep reading so you'll know what to do next time.

Begin by choosing the day and time you want to receive your order. You can do this by opening the app and on the main "Shop" tab, clicking "See times" up towards the top next to "Reserve Pickup or Delivery." Choose your preferences. Here, you can also change the store you want to shop at if you have several Walmarts in your area.

Next, find and add the items that you want. A lot of this will be self-explanatory as Walmart's app is set up in the same way that many online stores are. You can search, browse, and look at pictures of items. To find something, search for it in the "Search Walmart" section at the top of the main "Shop" page. If you want to read more about a product, just click on it. It'll show reviews, a description, and more images. Once you've found what you're looking for, click "Add", and then adjust how many you'd like. Items that require age verification, such as alcohol, will not be able to be added to your cart and purchased online.

This app is great if you're wanting to save money because it will usually show how much an item costs based on its weight (something we talk about later in the money-saving chapters) so you can compare prices more accurately and save. You'll find this information underneath the item's price.

Another great feature of this app is that you can use their barcode scanner to quickly find and add products that you already have in your possession. From now on, anytime you run out of something, scan its barcode before you throw it away. This way, it'll already be added to your cart waiting for you, and you won't forget it when you go shopping at a later date. To find the barcode scanner, look for the barcode symbol inside the "Search Walmart" section at the top.

While we're on the topic, I'd like to quickly interject that any time you think of something that you want or need to get (regardless of if you have it in-person), plug it right into your Walmart app. Let it serve as a running shopping list.

Want to save by seeing everything that's on sale? Click the search bar at the top once again, and type in "Clearance" or "Rollback". You can also search for similar variations to these words or look up short phrases such as "Clearance under $5.00" or "$1 or less".

After you're done shopping, click the cart symbol at the top right of the page. Look over your items, and then click "Continue to Checkout" at the bottom.

If you're doing pickup, this final page is where you can edit the person who is picking up the order by switching things to their name and email address. This is good to know if someone else has to fill in for you. For example, if you were to get stuck at work, you could send your spouse to pick up the items.

If you're having your items delivered, this final page is where you'll have the option to choose how much you want to tip the delivery person and say where or how you'd like them to leave your stuff. We'll go over those things shortly.

Finally, check out when everything is to your liking. However, before you do so, always verify that you don't already have the things that you're purchasing by quickly looking through your cupboards, etc.

After You've Placed Your Order

Add or Remove Something

What if after you've submitted your order, you remember that you need one more thing? Or what if you place your order, only to realize that you don't need something after all? All is not lost! After you've placed your order, Walmart will give you a certain amount of time, based upon how soon your order is to be picked up or delivered, for you to add or remove things. You can even cancel your order altogether. To edit an order, go to "Account", "Purchase History", and then "Edit items". To put in a request to cancel the whole order, go to "Account" and then "Purchase History" again. Find and click the order, scroll to the bottom, and click "Request Cancelation".

Substitutions

Don't worry about being kept out of the loop of the whole shopping process. <u>You'll be kept well informed with lots of emails, notifications, and texts</u>. Walmart is very good about this. A lot of their messages will be letting you know that they received your order or any additions or edits. One notification that you should look out for in particular is the one regarding substitutions.

Sometimes, in between when you purchase something and when the person shops for you, things will run out. If the Walmart employee can't find an item, they'll mark it as not available, and offer you a comparable alternative. You'll receive a notification about this, and can then approve or disapprove of their suggestion.

Pickup

Before it's time for you to go get your things, make sure there is a clear space for the groceries in your car. We'll cover clearing out and cleaning up your vehicle in another chapter. But for now, if it is very messy, take out what you can or at least move things over to make room.

When it's time for your pickup, or after you've received a notification that your order is ready, make sure to "Check in" *before* you go. This gives the workers some time to pull your refrigerated items out and put them into a cart so they can wheel your things out to you faster without you having to wait a while. The Walmart app will use its software to see how far away you are from the store, but I recommend checking in if you're ten minutes away or less.

After checking in, you can then drive to the store. Follow the signs that say "Pickup" and park where they tell you to in the designated spots that have a sign saying "Reserved" with a large number on it. Depending upon your store, both of these types of signs will either be bright orange or dark blue.

After you park, <u>you should receive a notification to let them know what spot you're in</u>. If you don't, pull up the app and look at the top of the page to see the prompt. This part of their app has been a little finicky in the past, so if you've been waiting for more than ten minutes, call the number that's in front of you on the sign and let them know your name so you can check in.

After that, just sit in your car and wait for the Walmart employee to come to you. They'll ask you to verify the name on the order, and then ask you where you'd like them to load your groceries. They'll put them into the car for you, and that's it. It's that easy!

Delivery

With delivery, <u>you can choose to have the items left at your front door or to sign for them</u>. If you're in an area where petty theft is an issue or if you have temperature-sensitive food, like if you ordered ice cream in the middle of summer, I recommend you choose to sign for them. This way, you'll know when your things arrive so you can bring them inside immediately, instead of perhaps not hearing your doorbell ring and leaving them outside a while.

Also, be aware that Walmart will *automatically* add a tip for your driver. You can edit the amount of it, or remove it altogether, before or up to twenty-four hours after the delivery. I confirmed with my deliveryman that 100% of the tips do indeed go to the driver. So if you want to give them a little something to show your appreciation, you can do so before placing your order by scrolling down a ways on the "Review Order" page to find the section dedicated to this. If you want to offer them a tip afterward, go to "Account", "Purchase history", find and click on the order, and then edit the amount.

Lastly, clear a space on your porch if there is no room for them to place your grocery bags, and sweep it before your things arrive. Your bags will be set down on the ground. So when you bring them inside, any dirt and gravel that they were sitting on will be brought inside as well and transferred to your clean countertops.

Good to Know

Shop Faster

Your first purchase will most likely take the longest as you'll be learning how to navigate the app. But next time, and each time afterward as the app learns what you usually buy, it'll be easier and quicker for you to place your orders.

The app will automatically make a collection of all the things that you've bought previously, even if you've only purchased something once. The collection will include things that you've bought inside the store as well, as the app syncs in-person and online purchases. To find this collection, click "Account" at the bottom, and scroll down until you see "Reorder" in the "My Items" section. Click it to see and quickly browse only the items that you have a history of purchasing.

You can also create a collection of things you buy regularly, instead of things that you might only get occasionally, which is what the previous option gives you. To create your own collection, click "Lists", which is also in the "My Items" section. Then add groceries to that list by clicking on an item and scrolling down until you see "Add to list".

Even with a personalized list, you'll still have to add each item to your cart. That's why I suggest you bypass all of that by creating and purchasing an order _only_ consisting of your essential items. You can then use the app's amazing feature that adds everything that you purchased in a previous order to your cart once more. To do this, go to "Account" again, and then click "Purchase history" at the top. Find and click on the order you want to replicate. Then scroll to the bottom and click "Reorder all".

Verify You Received Everything

Make sure that you lay eyes on every single item as you bring your groceries inside and start to put them away. As you'll read about in the other chapters, I'm a big fan of sharing chores. However, this is my one exception. You need to see everything that comes in so that you can know everything that didn't.

This is one of the drawbacks of having someone else shop for you. Inevitably, there will be at least one or two things missing or forgotten. That's why I recommend you always go back through your order and verify that you got everything you paid for. To do this, open the app, click "Account", "Purchase history", and then find and click the order you just made so you can scan through it.

Refunds & Returns

If you didn't receive everything, don't fret. Getting refunded is _super_ easy, which is yet another reason why I recommend shopping at Walmart.

If you need to make a return, exchange, or if you simply didn't receive an item, follow the same steps as before to get to the order that has the problem. Once on that page, scroll to the very bottom of the order and click "Start a return". From there, select the item. You'll be prompted to say what the issue is, such as if it is missing, past expiration, damaged, etc.

After you've submitted your request, you should receive an email within a matter of minutes saying that they've initiated a refund. I've always received a refund and have never had any issue where they asked for verification or proof of my claims, so don't worry about not getting your money back.

If you need to make a return, you'll have to do so in person. You'll have as little as 30 days to return a few select items. But for most things, you'll have up to 90 days, which is wonderful for those of us who drag our feet when returning things. <u>So if you're thinking that it's been too long to take something back, take it back anyway and just see if they'll accept it</u>.

Groceries, however, are not returnable. Occasionally, when Walmart employees shop for you, you'll receive extra items that you didn't order. I've verified this multiple times, but they don't actually want you to return any food, as they'll have to throw it away. So <u>you get to keep any extra groceries you get for free</u> ! I once received what must have been a whole potluck supper based upon the pounds of spaghetti and chili ingredients I was accidentally given.

The Walmart app is *constantly* being updated, so if you can't figure out the return or refund process because the app has changed, or really for any reason, call their help desk at +1 800-925-6278. I've been nothing but impressed by their speedy and agreeable customer service.

Action Plan

Download the Walmart app and set up your account if you haven't already done so. Determine if you're usually going to do pickup, or if you want to test out having your things be delivered with Walmart+ Membership's free 15-day trial.

I recommend you spend any remaining time that you reserved for this guide to <u>familiarize yourself with the app and begin organizing things to make your shopping faster</u>. Consider making a list and grouping together items you usually buy, or start to add your essentials to your cart for the next time you shop.

DAY 11:
PLANNING & MAKING MEALS

Why You Need to Plan

Did you ever go to the grocery store and fill your cart with food, only to bring it home and not be able to make anything with what you purchased because nothing went together? Or did you bring things home only to realize that you already had some stuff that you just purchased? Maybe you had an idea of what you wanted to make, so you went off of your memory instead of a list. But when you got home, you realized you had forgotten the most important ingredient. Then you had to make a whole shopping trip just for that one item!

I remember back during that time when I was at my worst, I used to open the door to my fridge and see a bunch of food but nothing to eat. Things sat for *weeks* until I finally grabbed a trash bag and threw every rotten, stinky thing away. Then I'd shop whenever I could find the time. This was usually very late in the evening, around when I should have been going to bed. I'd go into the store without a list or a recipe, and just put whatever looked good into my cart. I didn't think about what would go well together or even if I knew how to cook something. A few times, I was so tired after my late night shopping trip that truth be told, I went home and left all of the groceries out on the floor and not put away.

During this time I was failing on multiple fronts. My lack of planning was easily costing me hundreds of dollars of wasted food per paycheck. And because I hadn't considered how I would make meals with the ingredients I had purchased, my husband and I were encouraged to eat out more often, as at least the restaurants and fast food places had food that was put together. Lastly, because I allowed other things to take priority over and didn't schedule time for this essential chore, I was sometimes too exhausted to properly care for the things that I'd spent all of that time going out to get.

Thankfully, that was quite a few years ago, and I've learned so much since then. I've already shared one vital tip with you yesterday, which would certainly have helped me back then. But today, I'm going to share with you even more ways that you can plan for your meals, so you can confidently and quickly perform one of the most fundamental parts of adulting. From now on, you're always going to go at this chore with a game plan.

How to Meal Plan

The Tools You'll Need

First, download the My Meal Plan printable I've created for you. It's been thoughtfully designed to limit food waste, save you money, save you time, and maybe even save some of your sanity as it takes away any stress you might feel surrounding this chore and gives you structure to make meal planning a breeze.

Follow the instructions on the second page of the printable. In a nutshell, you're going to be writing down all of the food or ingredients you have (not necessarily all of the spices or little things) in each section, first the fridge, then the freezer, then your cupboards, etc. Then, you're going to look at everything that you have and consider what ingredients you could put together to make a meal. Work from left to right putting more focus on using up things that will go bad first. To stretch your dollar as far as you can, <u>try to make meals using the things that you have, and only add an ingredient to your shopping list as a last resort</u>. Write any meals that you come up with in the designated section on that printable.

If you're a bit stumped on what meals you can make, check out MyFridgeFood.com (they now have an app as well). On this site, you can list specific ingredients you have, and see what food they say you can make using those same ingredients. Don't list a lot of things though, or you may get some unappetizing suggestions. Perhaps <u>just stick with one main ingredient, such as pasta or a protein, and then add one other thing.</u>

If you're not finding anything to your liking and decide that you'll need to get a few more ingredients anyway, download the Tasty app for some tasty (no pun intended) inspiration and recipes. While you're using the app, <u>you'll still want to try to use up at least a few things you already have</u>. But it is perfect for finding new ideas to try, and it'll make your meal planning process a lot more streamlined.

How will the Tasty app help you and why are we going to use it for meal planning? <u>It integrates seamlessly with the Walmart app</u> that you set up yesterday. Anytime you find a recipe you want to try on the app, it will add all of those ingredients to your Walmart cart. It basically shops for you! <u>It also automatically adjusts how much of an ingredient you need when you change how many portions you're going to make</u>, so you don't have to do any calculations yourself. It has helpful videos showing you how to make each recipe. And you can even favorite recipes, so you can save ones you've tried that you want to make again (more about this later).

Share the Load

As I mentioned yesterday, and as you'll continue to see throughout this guide, I highly encourage you to share chores. Making meals can be a huge endeavor and time-consuming. If there are multiple mouths in your household, there is absolutely no reason why you should be the only one feeding them.

Talk to your spouse or your roommate/s and determine how you can split up this chore to make things fair for everyone. Some people love to cook, and if that's the case, then by all means have the person who enjoys it do it! But make sure that the other person who is not cooking makes up for it in some way, perhaps by picking up chores that the cook would usually do.

If no one loves cooking in particular, then you can split things by having one person cook and the other person clean up, alternating each time. You can also try cooking together. This is a great opportunity for couples to work on their communication and teamwork skills. A third option would be to have each person be fully responsible for cooking and cleaning but divvy up how many meals each person does per week.

There is no right or wrong way to divide things. Find what works for your household. Because I'm home all day, I cook more often than my husband does. We currently have things split so that I will cook and clean up twice a week, while he will do it once.

There are a few additional things you can do to make sharing this chore easier for yourself. First, have everyone be responsible for deciding their own meals that they will make. Second, clearly mark who is responsible for each meal so that no one forgets. And third, share the plan with them digitally or display it by printing it out. This will help you avoid having people pester you asking to be reminded of what they're cooking or what day they're cooking. This will also help you bypass the repetitive, oh-so-annoying question of "What are we having for dinner?" If you display it, then people can see it for themselves.

Set Aside Specific Days

It's very helpful to have a tentative plan for how often you'll shop, when you'll plan your meals and order the ingredients, and then when you'll get your groceries.

First, decide how often you want to grocery shop. Will you shop one time a week, one time every two weeks, or if you have a deep freezer, could you challenge yourself to do it one time a month? <u>Eliminate extra trips where you can, as the fewer times you go shopping, the more time and money you'll save.</u>

This part is going to be tricky for some, but when I talk about going grocery shopping once a week or once every two weeks, I mean that quite literally. I mean not running to the store multiple times because you forgot milk or you need eggs. Do not make all of these extra trips because you need one thing. This is *such* a big waste of time, and it stresses you out having to rush to get stuff last minute. No more! If you run out of something, oh well. Buy more of it next time it's your shopping time and eat other stuff until then.

Next, decide what day you'll meal plan and order, and then what day you'll get your things. As you'll see on the Ultimate Chore Chart (which we'll go over in another chapter on a different day), I've already reserved every other Sunday for you to get your groceries. This is assuming that you'll be spending the day before that meal planning and ordering.

Something that you'll also have to consider is the business of your Walmart. You may find that Sundays are so busy, that you have to order multiple days in advance to reserve the time slot that works for you. You need to decide what days will work best for your schedule and with your Walmart. <u>When you get your chore chart, change it to reflect the day/s you've decided you'll do these activities.</u>

I found it extremely helpful to work picking up my groceries into my schedule by pairing this activity with another activity that I did that was close to the store. Now, I order my groceries on Saturdays. After church on Sundays, when I'm close to Walmart, I swing by to pick up my things on my way home. <u>If you've chosen to do pickup, how could you work ordering</u>

and getting your things into your schedule to make it as effortless as possible ?

Lastly, create a meal schedule by determining which days you will cook on regularly. Anyone else who is cooking needs to decide this for themselves as well. What days of the week are the busiest for you? You'll probably not want to cook on those days, so plan to cook the day prior, and then eat the leftovers on your busy day. Is there a day you usually go out to eat? Keep this in mind when you're scheduling. Do you regularly have friends over on a certain day? They'll probably appreciate having a fresh meal, so plan to cook then.

I don't plan to cook on Saturdays, as my husband and I usually go out for a date. And because I know that we'll both be out of the house for activities on Mondays, I plan to cook on Sundays. This way, we can have leftovers on the day when neither of us will be able to cook.

It may be easy to forget to do things on their specified days when you first begin planning and making meals on a schedule. If you need to, add these activities to your Google calendar and set reminders for them.

Making Meals

Tips for Success

Let's next go over some quick tips which I think will make the whole cooking process easier for you.

Set food out to thaw. This might seem obvious, but it requires forethought on your part. I can't tell you how many times I've gone to start cooking dinner, only to remember that I never set out my ground beef. It really slows things down when you're trying to cook something that's frozen solid. So if tomorrow is cooking day for you, or if you're scheduled to cook later this evening, take some time to think about what meal you're going to make. Either set it out or move it from the freezer to the fridge so it can start thawing ahead of time. You might have already seen that I added a reminder about this in your To-Do List printable just because I think it makes that big of a difference.

Have your sink and/or dishwasher empty before starting so that it is ready to receive all of the dishes you're about to dirty up. This way, anything that gets used can be rinsed and immediately put into the dishwasher. Nothing is worse than spending a lot of time cooking, only to turn around and see a giant pile of dirty dishes that you now have to spend a lot of time cleaning up as well.

Similarly, be sure to clean as you go. I mention this in another chapter, but it's worth mentioning again, as it makes tidying up much less overwhelming. I like to keep a little bag or trash receptacle out on the counter to collect all of the scraps as I cut things up. This way, all of the trash is contained, and I can quickly toss it out when I'm done. Also, there is nothing wrong with wiping down the countertop multiple times while you're cooking. It makes things much quicker when you can pull things out of the cupboard to use, and then put them back without having to wipe each one off because you sat them down on something sticky.

Cook in as large of a container as possible. I thought it was silly at first when my husband brought home a giant pot that could probably feed twenty people. After all, there are only two of us. Yet as it turns out, I love having a giant pot to cook with, and I think you will too. Because it's so large, I can cook in bulk using one container, instead of having to dirty up multiple pots. Also, I always have enough room at the top that all of the spatter from the food stays contained inside its high walls. It makes it easier to clean things up afterward when the stove and surrounding area stays clean. I don't just recommend having a large pot though. Having any kind of large cooking container, such as the largest crockpot, baking tray, or pan that you can get away with, will help you in these same ways.

Be Flexible. Sometimes stuff will come up that you have to do, or you'll still have leftovers that need to be eaten. Instead of insisting upon cooking on the day you planned to cook, or insisting upon making a particular meal you planned to make when other things need to be used up first, roll with the punches. This is why I don't recommend you assign specific meals to specific days. Flexibility is key to making a lot of things work, including meal making. Just push the day that you (or the other person) will cook to the next day or whenever you have time, and cook whatever works best for *that* day.

Make a *Lot*

As I mentioned, I like to cook in bulk, and I recommend you do the same. Despite it just being my husband and myself, I usually make about twelve servings of a dish. My logic is that if you're already dirtying a pot, why not fill it up all the way? If you're already boiling water, why not boil more?

My goal for you is to make enough that you can have food for that day and at least one extra day. If you do this, you'll only need to have a meal planned for every other day. This will instantly cut your meal planning in *half*. Plus, on the days when you're not cooking, the kitchen will remain gloriously clean, leaving you with one less thing to do.

Because we cook in bulk, my husband and I only cook a total of three days a week. We eat leftovers three days a week, and then we usually go out to eat on the final day. We might end up eating leftovers the final day as well if we still have a lot of cooked food that needs to be eaten.

When cooking, I usually just focus on making dinners as the food can be reheated and eaten for lunches as well. However, you can use this idea of batch cooking to specifically make breakfasts and lunches too.

If you want to replicate what we're doing though, because making one meal sounds way easier than making three different meals, be sure to keep a supply of healthy food on hand in case anyone gets bored of eating the same thing. Things like boiled eggs, yogurt and nuts, fruit, a block of cheddar cheese cut into serving sizes (it's cheaper this way), and frozen edamame that can be popped in the microwave are all great ideas. You can additionally keep sandwich-making ingredients around in case you want something else. You'll probably also find that you'll occasionally have multiple different cooked meals to choose from, so you will have a little variety. This is because sometimes you might end up having to cook something, despite still having leftovers, because its ingredients start to go bad.

In my opinion, you can never make too much, so don't be concerned about this. If you have so much leftover that you don't think you'll be able to eat it all, simply mark what the food is and put it in the freezer. Then you'll have a meal that you can reheat another day when you don't have time to cook.

Everything that I've shared with you is just what has worked for my husband and me during this season of our lives. Your situation may be different. Consider how much you'll need to cook for your household. Does everyone eat a lot or could you get away with cooking less? If you easily get bored with the same food, how could you interject some variety? <u>How could you make a meal last as long as possible so that you can save time by cooking as few days as possible</u> ?

Meal Ideas to Get You Started

Here are a few recipes I recommend that are relatively easy to make. Feel free to use them as your meal plan for the next two weeks. And if you like them, be sure to add them to your cookbook (we'll go over how to shortly).

Taco Chili - Throw in some spinach for extra veggies.

Herb & Mayo Salmon - Make sure to get fish with the skin on, and then cook it skin down.

<u>Spaghetti Squash</u>

Coconut Chicken Curry & Rice - To speed up the process, consider using cooked chicken. I also recommend adding some plain greek yogurt to the curry to add creaminess. Make the rice by using two parts water to one part rice. Heat the water with the rice already in it. When it's boiling, lower it to a simmer and cover it with a lid. Leave it on without stirring or lifting the lid for roughly ten minutes or so, until all of the water has evaporated.

Cabbage & Kielbasa (or Bacon) - Get one head of cabbage per two packages of kielbasa. Remove the outer casing on the kielbasa if there is any, and slice it into bite-sized pieces. Chop the cabbage into big chunks, then steam the two together with the kielbasa on top so that the juices can run down into the cabbage. After the cabbage is cooked, add butter and salt if you'd like.

Baked Chicken Thighs & Roasting vegetables - Coat the thighs in your favorite seasoning, and cook them at the same time that you're also cooking another pan filled with a blend of roasting veggies. You can make a blend with frozen, pre-chopped yellow squash, acorn squash, brussel sprouts, and zucchini. Just dump them onto a pan with parchment paper. Drizzle them with oil, and add salt, pepper, and garlic. Then bake them.

Meal Planning in the Future

When I'm meal planning, I usually find that trying to decide what meals I want to make is the part that takes me the longest. To make things as easy and quick as possible, I recommend you do yourself a favor by saving recipes.

I used to find recipes online that I liked, but then for some reason, I never saved them. This inevitably led to me trying a million different ways to bake chicken without ever having perfected the craft or having honed in on what worked for me and my stove (according to my appliance man, every stove is slightly different, so you need to see what works for it). Don't be as silly as I was! If you're not already, save your recipes so you can make them again and again, improving on them as you go.

I won't deny that there is something nice about cooking out of a real cookbook or keeping a folder of index cards with recipes that your grandma wrote down for you. But if you don't have any sentimental reasons to keep something physical around, I highly recommend, like pretty much everything else in this guide, that you go digital. <u>This will clear up valuable cupboard space, and make it easier for you to search for and find a recipe when you're looking for it</u>.

There are a few different ways you can create a digital cookbook. As I mentioned earlier, you can save recipes on the Tasty app. To do this, simply "heart" them. The app will then create and organize a "Cookbook" for you by placing recipes that you've liked into different categories based upon things like dinner, drinks, snacks, etc. <u>This is the most time-efficient option</u>.

You can also bookmark recipes that you find online and then save them to a specified folder. To do this while using the Google browser, first create a "Recipes" folder by right-clicking up on the bookmarks bar, or by clicking to the left where it says "Apps", and then hitting "Add folder". After you've made one, go to the page with the recipe you want to save, and then tap the little star up in the search bar.

My third suggestion is to take pictures of recipes that you have in person, type up recipes that people tell you verbally, and save online links into your Google Keep (like we talked about on Day 2). As I already went over how to do this on desktop, here is how to do this on mobile: Open the Keep app, hit the plus symbol, then the plus symbol again, and either take a picture or add an image. Title it, and then add any notes that aren't written on the recipe that you want to remember next time. Next, hit the three little dots to the bottom right, select " Labels", and then save this recipe under a label specifically for all of your recipes. If you need to make a new label, hit the three dots again, select "Labels", type the name into the "Enter label name" section, and then click "Create".

My final suggestion, and what I suggest you do if you decide you want to stay with something physical, is to create a binder or something to keep and organize all of your 3x5 cards and printed off recipes in. Really anything will do. Just make it work for you.

Whatever you decide to do, I suggest you designate *one* place (or at least try to narrow it down as much as possible) for all your recipes from now on. This will again make it easier to locate a recipe when you're trying to find it.

Action Plan

If you haven't already done so, download the My Meal Plan printable and spend some time filling it out. Write in all of the food you currently have in your house so that you'll already have this done when it's time to meal plan.

Determine how often you will grocery shop (once a week, every two weeks, once a month) and what day of the week you will shop. Keep in mind the busyness of your Walmart.

If you don't live by yourself, talk with those you live with about divvying up the chore of cooking. How often and what days will you cook? And how often and what days will they cook? If you will be doing all of the cooking, what will they do as a tradeoff?

Decide how you'll save all of your recipes moving forward. Will you keep them physical or go digital? If so, where will you limit yourself to keeping your recipes?

DAY 12:
LIVE WITHIN YOUR SEAMS

Why You Should Declutter

A study published in the "Personality and Social Psychology Bulletin," found that women who described their living spaces as cluttered or full of unfinished projects were more likely to be fatigued and depressed.

How would you describe your living space right now? Do the things in your house give you joy or make you feel depressed? Can everything be put away so your space is kept neat, or is it so full of stuff that your home is bursting at the seams?

In this consumerist society, we've been conditioned to believe that more is better, bigger is better, and "he who dies with the most toys wins," as Malcolm Forbes so eloquently put it. We spend our precious days working longer hours, seeking raises, and increasing our debt all to have more stuff and impress the Joneses.

Is that really what you want? Do you want to spend your life in the pursuit of more *stuff*?

What if instead of buying another knick-knack that you already have three of, you saved that money and put it towards that trip to Europe you always wanted to take? What if instead of having to spend more time cleaning because you have to clean around, under, and over all of those doodads, you got rid of them, and then spent that extra time calling your Grandma who you haven't spoken to in forever?

With all you're giving up to accumulate more things, your mental well-being, time, and money, you have to ask, are your things impinging on you living your best life? Do you have stuff or does your stuff now have you?

Everyone deserves to live in a place that is sanitary and *safe*. We'll be covering the sanitary aspect in the next few chapters about cleaning, but the safety aspect can be addressed now. Are you at the point where you have so much stuff that it has become a tripping hazard? If you had an accident, could medics or firefighters get to you, or would your clutter hinder them? When will enough be enough!?

While I'll be doing my best to help you get your home as decluttered and safe as possible, if you think that you or someone you live with may suffer from a hoarding disorder, please seek professional help.

So when I talk about decluttering your stuff, what exactly am I talking about? The word "stuff" may mean different things to different people. So I'll define it here as being anything that doesn't add value to your life, or as Marie Kondo (a decluttering expert who wrote the #1 *New York Times* bestseller *The Life-Changing Magic of Tidying Up*) puts it, "anything that doesn't spark joy."

I'll be referencing Marie's method, also known as the KonMari method, again later in this guide. But today, we're going to be using her decluttering system in part, because so many have found her tactics revolutionary. I'll also be including some points I've gleaned from another expert, Cas the Clutterbug, who I'll be talking about more when it comes to organization.

How to Declutter

Before we begin, Marie recommends that you first imagine your ideal lifestyle. What would it look like if you didn't have all of that clutter? How would you feel emotionally and physically? Get clear about *why* you want to go on this journey of tidying. This is the most important step. After it, you can start tackling your home.

The KonMari method is unique from others in that you declutter by *category*. The five categories and order in which you should complete them are clothing, books, paper, komono (other general things like your bathroom, garage, kitchen, and miscellaneous), and sentimental. We'll be covering a couple of these things in later chapters though. So I recommend that you hold off on decluttering any clothing or paper until you've read through those sections.

Gather everything that belongs in one category and bring it all together in one place. While this part of the process may seem pointless, it'll allow you to visually see how much you've accumulated of a category and give you a new perspective. Marie says that the "shock" of how much you have is necessary so you can begin deciding if you actually need things or not.

Doing this will also help you discover any duplicate or near-identical items. I found out I'd been hauling around multiple copies of the same books and movies while moving from place to place. Doing so also revealed that I had a plethora of shirts that were all the same color and style.

Cas the ClutterBug alternatively suggests that you should declutter by location or section. This way, you can tackle one drawer of clothing or one shelf of your bookcase, instead of all of the clothes you own or all of the books in your house at once. I believe approaching decluttering in this way may be better suited to people who have less time or are prone to overwhelm. But with that being said, I want to caution you that Marie explicitly warns against tidying in this conventional way as it will *not* lead to permanent change.

In her book, she says that "When p eople revert to clutter no matter how much they tidy, it is not their room or their belongings but their way of thinking that is a t fault." The real issue is not stuff but the way you *think* about stuff. She goes on to express that you'll most likely end up accumulating more things faster than you slowly eliminate them. She must know what she is talking about because she boasts of having a *zero* percent return rate for clients who have completed her program and coaching.

Take this idea of doing a little at a time (if you choose this option) with a grain of salt. You may not solve the real problem, and end up with yet another mess to tidy again later. So if you find that you're caught in this cycle of decluttering, tidying, and accumulating, come back to this chapter and give the KonMari method a try!

Both have their advantages, so do whichever you think will work best for you at this time. You may even end up switching up your approach depending upon what you're tidying, as some methods may work better for specific categories or sections.

According to the KonMari method, you should then pick each item up in the pile you made, hold it, and consider if it brings you joy.

This is one area where people often get tripped up, including me. Do staples and tape bring me joy? No. But do I need them for things occasionally? Yes. So I believe that we are supposed to use our better judgment here when it comes to items that serve a purpose.

Besides that, I love how Marie reminds us through this practice that our stuff is supposed to serve us. Our things are supposed to bring us happiness, not wear us down.

So if you get bummed out every time you see an unfinished project sitting there because you haven't gotten around to it just yet, get rid of it. If seeing a shirt you used to wear reminds you of how much weight you've gained, and instead of encouraging you to get fit again, it makes you upset, get rid of it. If you feel guilty whenever you see something because someone got you that item as a gift and you don't like it, get rid of it. And if you feel shame or remorse anytime you see something and kick yourself for having "wasted" money on it, get rid of it too.

If an item doesn't spark joy, add value, or serve a function, tell it "Thank you" for serving its purpose in your life, and set it down elsewhere to be donated. You may find this practice helpful in taking that final step to get rid of something by acknowledging and appreciating the role that an item had. Did it serve you many years and enhance your life, or was its role to simply teach you that you don't need things like it in the future?

If you're having a hard time figuring out what gives you that "zing," start with something that you love and know brings you joy 100%. Compare everything else to the feeling you get when you hold that thing.

Many confuse the KonMari method with minimalism, but it is not. Instead of focusing on what you'll give away, she wants you to focus on what you'll *keep*. If you're unsure about an item, keep it for now, and come back to it another time.

This may only apply to you if you're married, but Marie suggests that everyone should go through their things alone and decide for *themselves* what items they'll keep. She cautions against trying to sneakily declutter someone else's things for them. It's vital for maintaining the trust and respect in your relationship that you do not do this. You never know when something that you view as junk may be meaningful to your partner. Yes, even if they haven't touched the thing in years.

She is convinced that, "quietly [working] away at disposing of your *own* excess is actually the best way of dealing with a family that doesn't tidy ."

Decluttering sentimental items will most likely be the hardest category. That's why it's saved for last, and also why I feel that it's important to give you a little more help in this particular area.

Understandably, things that are special to you will be difficult to decide what to do with. Follow the same guideline as before and keep items that spark joy. If you have multiple of the same item, keep whatever sparks joy the *most*. Marie says that after having gone through the other categories, you'll be more in-tune with how your body feels and will be able to tell for this last part if something truly makes you happy and should be kept.

I'd like to add to this that it is not necessarily an item but the *memories* tied to it that are special to you. And because you can be reminded of those memories through a picture, you don't always have to keep the item itself. Therefore, I suggest that you take a picture of anything that is not worth *physically* holding onto, and then donate it.

While this idea doesn't align with the KonMari method, it is how I was able to finally let go of things that no longer served me. I can look back at pictures of stuffed animals I used to have as a kid if I ever want to. And now, the ones I donated can bring joy to some other little girl, instead of being sadly tucked away in a box somewhere growing dust and cobwebs.

<u>This idea is not about having a photo, but more about having *reassurance*, and being able to satisfy the "what if" question that may be tripping you up in regards to if you may ever want to look at an item again. You'll most likely find though that once something is out of your life, you never feel the need to look it up in your photos, and will instead enjoy the weight lifted from yet another piece of clutter being gone.</u>

I'll go over this again briefly in the chapter about paperwork, and let you know my suggestion for what to do with all of the pictures that you may end up taking of your sentimental items.

After you've decluttered, and before you begin putting things back that you want to keep, Marie says to remove what you don't want and do so without letting others know what you're getting rid of.

The items that spark joy are personal to you, so don't allow others to go through your discarded stuff and question your judgment. They are your things. If you no longer want to be tied down to them, that is your choice.

Personally discard your items if you need to, to prevent others from burdening themselves with things that they were previously fine without, but now, at the threat of them being tossed, may feel compelled to grab.

What to Do With Stuff You're Not Keeping

Donating is always a wonderful option. If you want to save time, many Goodwills will come to pick up items for you. They'll do this for general things, but this option is especially handy when it comes to big stuff like heavy furniture. If you think this would be the best option for you, contact your local Goodwill to see if they offer this service and schedule a pickup.

If you don't have a lot to get rid of, or if you just want to take things to be donated yourself, designate a donation box, bag, or laundry basket for these sorts of things. Then whenever you find something you no longer want to keep, place it in that container. When it's full, put it in your car, and make plans to zip by the donation center to drop it off next time you're out running errands. If you'll forget that the box is in the car, place it in the front seat so it will serve as a visual reminder. When you drop your things off, be sure to keep your container (unless you're donating it too) so that you can begin the cycle all over again. And ask for a receipt for the value of the things you donated so that you can use it as a tax write-off.

Work to cultivate the habit of adding items to this box as soon as you recognize that something is no longer serving you. This system of designating a box for donations and adding to it regularly is how I recommend you maintain a decluttered home in the future.

Pro-tip: resist looking through your donation's box if it's been sitting for a while because you may end up pulling stuff out that you forgot about. And if you need to, put stuff in a black plastic bag so you won't be able to see what's inside. If you forgot about something and haven't needed it enough to remember and pull out, you don't need it. Also, some Walmarts have a donation bin right in their parking lot. So if you do grocery pickup, it may be easier for you to drop your things in the bin while you're already there.

You can also try selling items to recoup some of what you put into them. I didn't put this idea into the financial chapters because it isn't a reliable source of income. And I'm half tempted to not include it here either, as it can be a big waste of time. But I think that if you're willing to put in the effort, only trying to sell items that are worth $50 or more will be the best use of your time.

Selling on Facebook Marketplace is as good of a place as any. While posting in your local community's Facebook group may be a good option if you live in a great neighborhood, I recommend selling in Mommy groups as I believe that they tend to offer a better clientele, and the people will (hopefully) be less flaky and more trustworthy.

If you insist upon trying to sell your clothes, something that may not be worth the time and effort, check out Poshmark or Plato's Closet. If you take any items to the latter, make sure they are in-season, on-trend, folded, and in a reusable bag, *not* a plastic one, so you get the most items approved and more money for them.

If however, the idea of trying to get things donated or sold holds you up in any way, if being surrounded by bags and bags of stuff causes you to struggle or stress, just throw the stuff away! It's all good to want to donate, but not at the expense of your well-being. You are more important than your stuff!

As Kc Davis (author of *How to Keep House While Drowning*) puts it, "You can't save the rainforest if you're depressed." I believe she is also the one who pointed out that donating an item will help someone, but throwing away that item will *also* help someone, *you!*

So again, if you need to, just throw stuff away. You can always get better at donating next time.

How to Organize What You Keep

While the KonMari method works well for decluttering, I find its organization system more focused on being esthetically pleasing rather than functional. And it is even less time-conservative. It may work well for someone detail-oriented, but there are other ways of organizing. That's why I've chosen to now switch from using the KonMari method to ClutterBug for the rest of your journey, especially considering that ClutterBug's approach encompasses the KonMari method.

As the name suggests, Clutterbug does also focus on decluttering. But I think where this system shines is with organization. Cas doesn't believe that there is *only* one "right" way to organize. She says that " Organization

<u>isn't about pretty Pinterest-worthy spaces. It's about having a home that's so easy to take care of that it doesn't get messy. That it stays tidy all the time because putting your things away is just as easy as leaving it out.</u> "

Cas encourages you to tailor your home to your personality and preference. She suggests that people fall into four different categories of "clutterbugs" or are a blend of them. These different categories include the following:

Simple Organizers

<u>Ladybug</u> - These organizers are not detail-oriented or visual. They prefer items to be stored out of sight and like to have large containers to put their things in.

<u>Butterfly</u> - These organizers are not detail-oriented either, but they *are* visual. If something is out of sight, it's out of their mind. So they like to leave their things out or put things in large containers that are see-through or mesh.

Detailed Organizers

<u>Cricket</u> - Like the Ladybug, these organizers prefer having things put away and do not like visual clutter. But unlike them, they like things to be micro-organized, so they prefer using smaller organizing bins. This is the bug that the KonMari method most aligns with.

<u>Bee</u> - These organizers are also micro-organized. But they are visual bugs, so they want their everyday-use items left out.

Which clutterbug are you? If you're not sure, you can find out by taking this <u>quiz.</u> <u>You can also watch this video about The Four Organizing Types and FAQs.</u>

<u>If you live with a roommate or significant other, you'll have to consider what bug they are as well</u>. Remember with Marie's method, the other people in your household will be in charge of decluttering their own things. But they should be in charge of *organizing* their things too. This way, they'll know where their items are, and more importantly, where they go *back* to.

What about items in the house that are shared? How do you organize those? Cas recommends that organizing should be tailored to whoever is the visual or macro-organizing bug. This is because it's *easier* for the non-visual bug to leave their things out rather than it is to try to force the visual bug to remember things that are tucked away (remember if something is out of sight, it's out of their mind). It's also easier to get a micro-organizer to toss stuff into a large basket rather than it is to get someone who doesn't care about the details to take the extra time and effort to file things away in little containers.

Cas believes that if you've organized in the past and weren't able to stick with it, it's probably because you didn't do it in a way that works for you and your household. Now that you know your organizing style, you can put everything back that you decided to keep in a way that'll make things easier to maintain in the future!

To begin organizing, get the bin size and style that you need based on your bug. If you're a Cricket, you might get lots of smaller bins with lids, as you are not a visual creature. See what products fit your organizing style.

Then fit the bins *into* the space that you're trying to organize. According to Cas, it's much easier to organize your space for your stuff, rather than the other way around. In other words, stick to the following method.

The Container Method

With this method, you limit yourself to only keeping items that can *comfortably* fit inside of a certain space. For example, if you have so many kitchen utensils that they don't all fit in the drawer designated for them, or if you have to stuff them in and struggle to get the drawer closed, then you need to get rid of some. The same is true for a basket, cabinet, or any other kind of "container."

Say for instance that you have so many clothes in your closet that you can't hang anything else up. You've reached the capacity of that container. This is when you'd adopt the Exchange Rule (something I'll go over in the section about laundry), which says that if you were to get any more items that go in that container you'd have to swap them out for something already in it because there is no more room for anything else.

Prioritize what you put into the container, adding in the items that spark the most joy for you first or that bring the most value to your life, because anything that's left over after the container is full must go.

And don't get hung up thinking that you have to spend a lot of money on containers, or use any lack of funds as an excuse to put off tidying. Both experts confessed to starting their organizing journeys using cut-up tissue boxes. So use the things that you already have at home. You can always buy pretty containers and make things more aesthetically pleasing later. But right now, your goal is to just get your space more tidy and functional.

Find a "Home" for Everything

The KonMari method encourages you to fold things a certain way and arrange them so that there is a color gradient when you put them back. But designating a home in your house for every one of your items is at the core of its organizational system. And yes, a home may mean inside of a container.

Marie says, " Ensuring that each one of your belongings has its own spot is the only way to maintain a tidy and clutter-free home. Clutter has nothing to do with what or how much you own – it's the failure to put things back where they belong ." Benjamin Franklin had a simpler way of saying this, "A place for everything, everything in its place."

It helps to be able to put things away when there is a place to put them! So if an item doesn't have a home, make one for it. And if there is no more space for it to have a home, then swap the item out for something that you don't want to keep as much (like we just talked about).

Make things as easy as possible to put away or return to their home. Group similar items together. Designate a home for an item that is close to where you use it, or in the place that you'd be most likely to look for it first. If you use an item often, or if it is difficult to move, like a heavy kitchen appliance that you use daily, consider giving it a home on your counter. But if you have an item that you don't use often, give it a place in your cabinet or up on a high shelf. Leave the "valuable real estate," or lower shelves, for things you use more.

After everything has been given a home, Cas highly recommends that you label any containers that you used. I have to admit, I was not on board with this step. But her argument for labeling is that it will help subconsciously get you to put things back. More importantly, if you live with others, no one will constantly be asking you where things go, or worse, dumping stuff wherever. Labels will help keep everyone on the same page.

Learn More

If you'd like to dive into the topics of decluttering and organizing more with KonMari, check out her book or take her tidying fundamentals course. I also found tips and inspiration from her two shows on Netflix, *Tidying Up* and *Sparking Joy with Marie Kondo*. If you'd prefer to follow the ClutterBug's method instead, she offers a 30-Day Decluttering Challenge on YouTube that you can complete in as little as fifteen minutes a day. For further guidance on organizing, check out her free mini-course here where Cas will go more in-depth into the four organizing styles and how to make things work when different bugs live together. She also has a show, *Hot Mess House*, which you can watch on HGTV.

Action Plan

Today, you have a few different options. You can choose to declutter either using the KonMari method, the ClutterBug method, or to combine them in some way that works for you.

If you choose the first option, you might consider waiting to take on such a big project as transforming your whole home until you're done with this guide. If you choose the second option however, go ahead and jump right in this evening, decluttering a single drawer or shelf. Just remember to hold off on the clothing and paper categories for now.

Decide how you'll get rid of stuff you don't want. Will you schedule a pickup from Goodwill, sell a few items, or throw things away this time and prioritize your health and getting your space cleared out?

Keep your clutter to a minimum in the future and don't regress after all your hard work by designating a donation box and adding to it anytime you find an item that no longer sparks joy. How will you organize the stuff you keep? Determine what your organizing style is as well as anyone else who lives with you. Design your new cleared-out home with that style in mind and cater to any macro or visual bugs.

DAY 13:
SET A CLEANING SCHEDULE

Some ladies are blessed with the ability to see a task that needs attention, and then do it. But if instead, you feel like you're always running around trying to "catch up," if you get overwhelmed by messes that multiply before you can even clean up the first one, having a chore schedule will be *life-changing* for you!

Perhaps you already have a chore chart, but it doesn't work for you, or maybe you don't have one and are just winging it. You do chores when you *feel* like it, which is rare, if ever.

<u>Having a cleaning schedule makes sure that everything gets done and done in a timely manner. This way, nothing gets forgotten or pushed off until it's been multiple weeks.</u>

So today let's determine what chores your home needs and what would be a good rotation schedule, so you can determine when and how often chores will be done. Then tomorrow we will go over how to include those who live with you in your new schedule, so you can share household responsibilities and take some weight off of your shoulders!

The Ultimate Chore Chart/Schedule

Unfortunately, I can't just give you a magic schedule that will work for you, as everyone's needs are different. However, I can give you the tools and information you need to create your own.

Understand It

While the majority of the chart/schedule is self-explanatory, there are a few things I'd like to cover just to clarify and make it easier for you to understand.

On the spreadsheet, you'll find seven tabs. They consist of the following:

Example tabs - You'll be using these as inspiration and as guides to see how often chores should be done at the *least*. Look through these tabs to get ideas of what to add to your schedule as there are chores that are generalized and others that will only apply to certain homes.

Guided and Blank tabs - You'll be deciding between these two different templates/layouts from which you can build and personalize your own schedule.

Let's dive further into the Guided and Blank tabs.

Choose Your Template

The Guided templates have generalized chores listed with everything else blank so that you can add who does what, and which days those tasks happen.

All of the Guided (and Example) tabs follow the same breakdown of <u>days assigned to specific rooms/areas:</u>

Mondays - Kitchen

Tuesdays - Living Room, Dining Room, & Hallways

Wednesdays - 1st Laundry Day

Thursdays - Bedroom/s

Fridays - Bathroom/s

Saturdays - 2nd Laundry Day & Outside

Sundays - Errands, Extraneous, & Seasonal

Inside the Guided and Example tabs, you'll find Daily Chores. These are the few, most important things you need to clean or check on every day. Included in the Daily Chores, you'll find the very important Tidies.

The Morning and Evening Tidies are a time for you to zip around your house and gather anything that doesn't belong to put it back in its place. <u>Do what you can in *only* ten minutes or less.</u> Whatever you manage to get done in that short time will still make the house look better than it did, *even* if you don't get around to everything.

I originally called these Ten-Minute Tidies, as it would take me roughly that long to pick up random stuff around the house. Plus, the name is cute and catchy. However, as I did this chore consistently and got better at putting things away as soon as I was done using them, I realized that ten minutes was not necessary.

I've since changed the name to a more general term devoid of any time amount because I want you to determine how long it will take *you*. Start by giving yourself ten minutes, especially if you have a

large house and a lot of space to cover. But if you can, shorten it down so you don't waste time puttering.

These Tidies will help you start your mornings off right by waking up to a clean home because you tidied the evening before. And they will help you come home to a peaceful environment because you tidied that morning before work.

I've seen some women complete their Tidies by filling a laundry basket as they zoom from room to room, putting things that don't belong into the basket, and pulling out things that go in that room. However, you don't need a laundry basket to grab and move what you can carry. Just go in a methodical pattern to circle back to where you began and hit all of the rooms.

In order to determine how often certain tasks need to be done for your household, the "As needed" notations have been removed from the Guided templates, as opposed to what's shown in the Example tabs. Keep this in mind for tomorrow but leave these spaces blank for now until you've talked with those you live with about how often they think a chore will need to be done.

An example of this would be taking out the trash. Depending upon your household, the trash may need to be a Daily Chore. But if it takes a while to fill instead, and you only empty it "as needed," write that into the chart. Then simply check the task daily to determine if it needs to be accomplished.

If you would prefer to create your own chore chart entirely, use one of the blank templates. If you choose this option, use the Example tabs for inspiration, and make sure that you move the Daily Chores over into your new chart. These tasks are vital to not only keeping a well-maintained space but a *hygienic* home as well.

Besides the templates, you also have the option of using a chore app. Check out Chorma for iOS or Nipto: Split household chores & cleaning tasks for Android. There are many other options that you can choose from, but what I appreciate about these two apps is that they automatically remind people to do their chores and then keep track of what has been done. So no one has to be a nag!

The drawback to using these though is that they only come with a few basic cleaning tasks. If you go this route, you'll still need to reference the examples in The Ultimate Chore Chart so that you can edit the app you choose to include any chores that it is missing that are relevant to your home. Also, make sure you transfer in all of the Daily Chores as well.

We'll be progressing with the assumption that you've chosen to use one of the templates in the chore chart. If you chose to use an app instead, you won't need any further explanation as they're pretty straightforward. However, be sure to keep reading as there will be important things that you'll want to know!

Choose Your View

After you've decided which template you want, you'll then need to determine how you want to view your schedule.

If you would like to see all of the days of the month at once, then the YAAG (Year at a Glance) view will work for you. These include a Seasonal section as well. So as the name suggests, you can see all the things that need to be done for the whole year at a glance.

Use the Seasonal section at the bottom of the YAAG - Example tab as a reference to see how many times a year certain chores need to be done.

If you choose any view besides the YAAG (or if you chose to use an app), make sure that when you divide up chores later, you divvy up the Seasonal chores as well by filling out that section in one of the YAAGs so you'll be prepared for when that time comes.

If the YAAG view is a little too much, use the Week View layout for a seven-day overview only. If that's still too much, the Day View template offers the simplest layout by organizing your schedule by, you guessed it, a day at a time.

All three views for the Guided templates have the same information. They are just organized differently.

I'd personally recommend using the Day View, as you may find this to be the least overwhelming when first getting started with a chore schedule. But of course, use the other layouts if you prefer.

Personalize It

Now it's time to add in any chores you need for your home that are not listed and omit ones that don't apply. Look through the YAAG - Example tab to see if there are any additional chores you should add that are specific to your household, such as picking up dog poop if you have a dog, or hiring a chimney sweep if your home has a chimney.

If cleaning every day sounds like a lot, get creative! You could combine both laundry days into one, and then leave the extra day as a rest day. Play with it and find out what works for you. I would caution you against putting in too many rest days though, as you may end up playing "catch up" and getting stressed out! That's why this schedule was specifically designed so that every day, even if it's just a little bit, you're staying on top of things and keeping things tidy.

If you don't like the idea of tackling all seasonal chores for the whole month on one day, you could make your schedule so that you do them on the specific day that applies to their specific room/area. For example, when it's time to wash your shower curtain liner, you could do this extraneous chore on the day marked for extraneous tasks, Sunday, or on Friday when you typically deal with bathroom-related things. You could also make your schedule so that the larger seasonal tasks are broken up and spread over all the Sundays of the month.

Factor into your chart how you'll handle any extra rooms if you have them. If you have a larger home with multiple bedrooms or bathrooms, it is up to you if you want to spend additional time cleaning *all* of them on their designated day, spread them out over multiple days, or simply eliminate them.

You'll save so much time if you don't use rooms that you don't have to. If you have a spare bedroom, close the door and the air vents in that room. Don't clean it unless you have someone coming over to use it. The smaller you can make your living space the better! You only need one bathroom (unless you're keeping separate spaces like we will talk about tomorrow), so close up the others and have everyone just use the same one.

Just like how limiting the amount of space you have to clean helps save time, so does limiting the number of trips you take to do errands. I hinted at this in a previous chapter, but scheduling all errands for *one* day when you're *already* out of the house and around town saves a lot of time!

The way the schedule is set up now allows you to get your groceries picked up, your car vacuumed, and all other out-of-the-house errands done on the *same* day during the *same* trip.

On the YAAG - Example chart you'll see that errands are only set for every other week. This setup is designed to make things easier for you. But if saving all of your errands for one trip every two weeks is too much, make it a weekly task on your schedule.

Sundays are set aside for errands. However, if doing errands on Sunday doesn't work for you, designate a different day (or two) for this chore, especially if you regularly have errands at places that are only open on weekdays.

I recommend your alternative or second errand day be Wednesdays, as that day is already set up to have a lighter chore load. Any time you schedule an appointment or errand in the future, I recommend scheduling it for this day when you have fewer chores, or on Sundays when you're already out of the house. I've gone as far as only scheduling coffee dates with my girlfriends on these two days because that means one less trip for the week.

Another way to personalize your schedule is to assign certain days with specific *tasks*, rather than specific *rooms*.

An example of this would be:

Mondays - Dusting

Tuesdays - Sweeping/Vacuuming

Wednesdays - Mopping

Thursdays - Laundry

Fridays - Deep Clean (Do on a rotation)

Saturdays - Rest/Play

Sundays - Market Day (Errands and Groceries)

If you decide to do something like this for your schedule, <u>remember to still complete your Daily Chores.</u>

A great benefit to this alternative plan is that you only need to carry one cleaning product at a time. For example, one day your whole cleaning task will be vacuuming, so you'll carry it from room to room, vacuuming the whole house. You might not like this setup though if doing all surfaces for that chore seems like a lot of area to cover in one day. This is opposed to focusing on one room, where you'll switch between multiple cleaning tools and products.

While you're designing your chore chart, I know it'll be tempting to fill everything in, but don't fill out who does what yet. <u>We want to respect the other person/people you live with by giving them the opportunity to decide for themselves what chores they would prefer to do.</u>

Also, don't choose which day of the week you will complete a group of chores until after negotiations. This won't necessarily affect you if you're doing a YAAG or Week View, as these are laid out so that any chore can be done on any day. But it will affect you if you're doing a Day View, where the main premise is to have a theme for the day. Leave the section for days blank for now.

How to Make the Chart/Schedule Work for You

Start Small

Now you have a beautiful, organized chore schedule that's primed for negotiations tomorrow and personalized for your household. But looking at all you have to do may be stressful. Or maybe, you're feeling bad because you realize how far off you've been from what you're "supposed" to have been doing. It's okay! We all need to start somewhere.

<u>If doing everything I've suggested seems like a lot, start by only doing the Daily Chores, and then take it one day at a time.</u>

Cleaning is a *marathon*. It's not a sprint. It's better to do a little bit rather than to clean for hours and get so burnt out you don't do anything for a month!

Release the idea that your home needs to be Pinterest-worthy. That's perfection and it's crippling! Your home will never remain perfectly clean, but it can remain pretty good with a little bit of daily work.

If you start by only doing the Daily Chores, <u>slowly add the other tasks</u> as you grow comfortable with your new routine. As these chores become habits, they'll become easier for you and faster to complete.

Skip the Lines

I mentioned earlier that the schedule is set up so that you do errands on Sundays. This is assuming that you work Monday through Friday and that the weekend is the best time for you to get this done. But that's when everyone else is doing their errands too. So how do you make this work without spending a ton of time fighting the crowds?

<u>Do your errands when everyone else is busy</u>, either sleeping in after a late night or while they're going to church. Sunday mornings are usually very slow at stores, or at least much less busy than any other time on the weekend. So take advantage of this slower time!

If getting your weekly fellowship in is a concern for you, see if your church offers different services that will work with this schedule, like a Sunday evening or Wednesday night service. You could also go to the earliest service and then do your errands after, as the majority of the crowd will be going to the later ones.

If it's important to you to keep going to your regular service, see if you can schedule your grocery pickup (if that's what you opted to do) for immediately after, so you can still compile all your errands into one trip. But be warned, you'll probably have to reserve your order a full 24-hours or more in advance as any time slots from midmorning to midafternoon on Sunday tend to be very popular.

Be Flexible

I also briefly mentioned that you should leave the day section blank for now, so that you can first discuss which chores will be assigned to which days. <u>Realistically, having your days be themed may only end up applying to you</u>. And depending on how much you want to make the cleaning schedule work for your household, you may have to be okay with this.

This is because your roommate or significant other will probably want to do their chores when it works for *their* schedule, on the days *they* want to do them. But ultimately, it doesn't matter if they do a chore on a different day than the theme calls for. What matters is that the chore gets done, and is done as regularly as it needs to be.

The Day Views have been set up with themes to make it easier for you to remember what chores you need to do. But <u>don't get hung up on this structure. If it's too much of a hassle, remake your schedule so it isn't themed.</u>

What to Do if You Mess Up or Fall Behind

What do you do when *life happen*s... you catch a cold, work late, or are mentally drained and you miss a day? Don't stress!

If you miss a day of chores, do what you can the next day, or just *leave it* and do it when that chore comes back around next week.

If you're able though, try to always get the Daily Chores done at least. But if you can't, like if you're having a particularly bad day, it's okay. <u>The great benefit of cleaning all surfaces weekly is that everything stays maintained, so occasionally missing something isn't a big deal.</u>

I certainly don't do everything on my chore chart every day. Checking everything off is the goal, but that's *perfection* and not realistic.

If you do slip up and miss a day, it's important to just try again tomorrow.

As James Clear talks about in this article, it's not so bad if you miss a day of a new habit you're trying to create (like cleaning your house). It's when you miss *two* days in a row that things start to become a problem. So it's okay to occasionally miss a day here and there.

In the future, if you do miss something multiple times in a row, maybe that means you need to revisit your chore chart and make it work better for you, or (like we will talk about tomorrow) hand it off to someone else.

Action Plan

Download The Ultimate Chore Chart. Determine which template you're going to use, how you'd like to view it, and then personalize it for your space. Add in chores that are not included and remove ones that aren't relevant. If you don't like any of the templates, download one of the chore chart apps I mentioned and set it up for your use.

DAY 14:
SHARE THE LOAD

You're trying to adult, but there is so much to be done! You can't do it all, as we talked about in previous chapters. But everything that needs to be done can be done, when you *spread the load*. If others live with you, unless they are royalty, you shouldn't be doing everything yourself! So then comes the big question. <u>How do you get other people to help?</u>

Whether you live with a roommate or a significant other, learning how to effectively communicate about chores, and how to share responsibilities so *no one* feels taken advantage of, is key! Even if you're currently living by yourself, these are good things to learn for when or if your living situation changes.

I'm sure it's no surprise to you that the majority of chores fall to women. According to the U.S. Bureau of Labor Statistics' American Time Use Survey, the average woman spends 2.5 hours a day cleaning. While the amount of time men spend doing chores has been increasing over the years (it was at 1.9 hours at the time of this survey), <u>how do you share the chores more equally *today!?*</u>

Before we go any further, I want to quickly address the fact that *both* genders can be messy. I'm by no means saying that men can't be the tidier of the two. Plus, by your own admission, *you're* the hot mess here. But for all intents and purposes, I'll be mostly referring to things in this chapter under the assumption that you're the neater individual.

Communicate

Ideally, have a conversation about responsibilities *before* you live with the other person. This takes the pressure off and <u>prevents both of you from falling into a routine before any cleaning expectations can be formed by either party.</u>

If you're already living together, no worries! You can still work towards sharing the household responsibilities more equally.

Decide upon a good time to talk.

Don't discuss these things when one of you is exhausted from a full day of work, when it's too early and one is still half asleep, or when someone is rushing out the door. <u>Do not approach the topic when you're feeling especially emotional or angry about the situation</u>. Talk about things when both of you are in a good place mentally and can engage in the conversation fully.

If you think things may get heated, maybe plan your talk for when you are out in public at a restaurant so that things can't get too out of hand.

Begin by discussing how important it is to you that your home be clean. Use "I" statements so you are more likely to spark a *conversation* instead of a *confrontation*!

By using "I" statements, you take the pressure off of the other person. You focus on your emotions, and it's difficult for them to argue with you because they can't say that you don't feel the way you do. With these statements, you simply frame your sentences with "I feel...when you..." For extra clarity, you can extend the statement by adding, "because...I would like."

An example of using the basic "I" statement would be, "<u>I feel</u> (insert emotion, not a judgment) upset <u>when you</u> (measurable or observable behavior) leave your clothes on the floor."

The extended version would be, "<u>I feel</u> upset <u>when you</u> leave your clothes on the floor <u>because</u> it seems like you don't care about having a clean home. <u>I would like</u> you to put your clothes into the hamper."

Avoid using "You" statements. "You don't do any work around here!" "You are such a slob." These cast blame and may put the other person into a defensive mode. It may make them feel resentful, and will certainly make them not want to cooperate as much. <u>Pointing fingers and playing the blame game will only lead to a heated conversation, at which point, you won't be able to resolve a lot.</u>

Incentivize

The best way to implement any kind of change in a situation is to come up with a win-win scenario. <u>You want to share the chores. What do *they* want?</u> Remind them of how having a clean or tidy home can positively impact things they care about.

If they tend to suffer from allergies, you could point out that regular dusting will diminish this problem for them. If they like to have friends over, mention how a clean-smelling home will make their guests more comfortable than one that smells like old trash. You could also throw in a few statistics about how having a neat house makes people feel less stressed, if this is an area of concern for them.

If it applies to you, why not also mention that it's been proven in marriages where the chore load is shared that the couple is more satisfied with the relationship and has more sex. In fact, <u>marriages that share the load have sex 6.8 times a month on average. That's .5 more than those who don't</u>. If this won't motivate a man, I don't know what will! Of course, if you do mention this, make sure you hold up your end of the bargain! You know what I mean.

Seek to Understand

<u>Try to understand where they're coming from</u>. Maybe their last roommate always did *fill in the blank,* so now they assume you will too. Maybe their Mom always cleaned off the table after dinner, so now your spouse is in the habit of getting up and walking away which leaves you to take care of it.

Keep in mind that they (most likely) want you to be happy, and for the house to be a place of harmony. No one is *trying* to take advantage of you by making you do the bulk of the cleaning. Give them the benefit of the doubt.

<u>There are almost certainly things that the other person is *already* doing for you that you may not realize</u>. In fact, they may have been doing things the way they *think* you want them done this whole time.

While it's not related to cleaning, here's a funny example. I love bacon in almost any form. Crispy? Sure! Almost raw? Heck yeah! But I don't like my bacon black, and for the first seven years of our marriage, that's all my husband served me. Being the loving wife that I am, I ate what he made me without qualms. But it turned out that he'd been purposely burning the bacon all along because he *thought* that's how I like it!

So ask your partner or roommate how they want things done, and clearly communicate how you do in return so everyone can be on the same page.

Come Up With a Plan Together

For a plan to succeed, all parties need to agree. <u>If you just tell s omeone what to do, they may go along with it for a little while, but they (most likely) *won't* stick to it.</u> So determine who will do what *together*.

A good place to start is to ask them what they think could be done to help the house get clean and then stay that way. By allowing them to input their ideas, you'll make them *invested*. Make them feel *empowered* and not emasculated. After all, wouldn't you be more willing to work on something and want it to succeed if you had a say in it, rather than if someone *forced* you to do it?

After you've discussed things that could be changed or improved, pull out that lovely chore chart/schedule you made yesterday and begin negotiating and splitting chores. You may have already addressed specific chores during your discussion, so edit the chart accordingly.

If you're particularly good at something or enjoy doing it, see if you can negotiate to make that chore yours. "I wouldn't mind cooking all the meals. If I do that, <u>what do you think would be a fair trade-off?</u>"

To make things easier, and the other party more agreeable, consider offering them first dibs. Let them choose which chore they want first, and then take turns. If you're feeling particularly generous, let them choose all of their chores before you.

Put the person who will be responsible for the chore next to it in the designated place on the chore chart.

If you both equally dislike a task, could you take turns doing it? If so, write in "Shared," or something that you will both remember. If not, perhaps you could do the chore neither of you enjoys in exchange for them doing multiple things for you.

Certain chores may take more time than others, so keep this in mind when dividing things up. If someone only has three chores, but it'll take them a total of three hours to do them all, that is not comparable to the other person having six chores that will only take them thirty minutes. It's not about how many chores someone has, but the amount of time they will spend doing them! If someone is faster at doing something, perhaps they should be the one doing it.

Also, keep in mind any mental roadblocks that may hinder someone from effectively doing their chores. There may be things that the other person is not as familiar with or has to learn. How will they be able to feed the dog if they don't know where the dog food is or how much to feed them? How will they be able to shampoo the carpets if they don't know how to run the carpet cleaner?

Consider keeping chores that you are more familiar with for yourself. Or give the other person the responsibility, but be patient and spend some time teaching them. Most importantly, you'll have to be *okay* with their end result as they learn. They'll improve with time.

While you're negotiating tasks, if you're unsure how often something will need to be done, quickly reference the Example tabs on The Ultimate Chore Chart. After all, the other person might change their mind if a task needs to be done multiple times a week versus a single time. Make sure you *both* are clear on how often things need to be done.

When determining which days of the week chores will be completed, keep in mind any days that you usually get home late from work, or days when you have extra activities planned. Plan your chores around your schedule. If you always have a long workday on Tuesdays, don't assign a lot of chores for that day. The same goes for your roommate or partner.

Can you work out a themed day for chores with the other person and your schedules? Are they agreeable to having themed days or do they want to do their own thing? Remember, the point of having your days themed is to help you know what tasks you need to do and when. But ultimately, it doesn't matter what days chores are scheduled for. What matters is that things *get* *done*, and done as often as they need to be.

Once all chores have been assigned and days designated, print the schedule. Put it somewhere visible so that everyone can see it so it can be used for quick reference as well as a reminder.

<u>Consider getting the schedule laminated or put inside of a plastic sleeve so you can wipe it down</u>. This will allow everyone to check off chores once they've completed them. This way, you'll see if the other person needs some gentle reminding if they haven't been doing their tasks, and it'll show them that you've been doing yours!

While I'm not a fan of having any extra paperwork lying around (we'll go over paperwork decluttering in a couple of days), <u>this is one of the few things I recommend you *do* print, as a printed copy that everyone can access and reference will help eliminate any confusion in your household over what has or has not been done</u>.

If you want to keep things digital, send your spouse access to the chart through their email (remember sharing the contents of this guide to anyone who is outside of your immediate family is prohibited and may result in your access being revoked without any refund). You can also switch to using one of the apps mentioned yesterday.

How to Stick to the New Plan

Lower Your Standards

I'm not saying to allow the other person to be a slob. But if you're a perfectionist, be grateful for the help you're getting, and *don't* redo their work.

Recleaning immediately after they do may come across as disrespectful and unappreciative. It is nonverbally saying, "You didn't do a good enough job." <u>The other person may then question why they should even do the chore in the first place</u>, and begin to think that it would save you both the hassle if you just did it yourself. Yikes!

To avoid the above dilemma, consider what chores the other person could do that wouldn't bother you too much if they weren't done "perfectly." Do you need to edit your chore chart and swap some tasks?

For example, my husband is in charge of vacuuming the carpets. If I can't see every pet hair, like I can on hardwood floors, then it doesn't bother me as much if he misses a few.

<u>Wouldn't you prefer to have your spouse or roommate work with you and get your space 80% of the way clean rather than do everything yourself?</u>

You may think that you're letting the other person's work slide, but there are probably some things that your spouse prefers to be immaculate that you are only cleaning to a "good enough" level. For example, maybe your partner is proud of his car, so he likes to keep it spotless. But for you, well, your car is just a means to get to work.

Michel de Montaigne (one of the most significant philosophers of the French Renaissance) said that " <u>A good marriage [is] between a blind wife and a deaf husband.</u> " So maybe practice turning a "blind eye" to things that aren't up to your level of cleanliness if they don't matter in the grand scheme of things.

If things are not being cleaned to the level that you'd prefer and you don't think you're being extreme about it, have another discussion about your expectations, especially if it involves health concerns. Or just swap chores so you can do the thing you're particular about.

Be Open to New Ways of Doing Things

When your roommate or partner is cleaning, be careful of presuming that the way *you* would do

something is the "right" way, and their way is "wrong." <u>Their way may simply be *different* than yours</u>, so be slow to correct them.

While growing up, I always saw my parents use brooms on the hard surfaces and vacuums on the carpet. Then when I got married and asked my husband to clean the hardwood floors, he vacuumed them! I was quick to correct him and tell him how he was "doing it all wrong!" But as you might know, and what I quickly learned, was that his different way was way easier!

So <u>be open to the other individual's different style of cleaning</u>. You may learn something.

Even if they are most definitely doing things "wrong," immediately scolding them might not be the best option if you want them to keep doing their chores in the future! Pick your battles. If it is important enough that it needs to be corrected, *gently* guide them.

Be Appreciative

Some may think that you shouldn't have to thank the other person for doing chores. After all, aren't they just doing what they *should* have been doing all along?

But a sincere thank you doesn't cost you anything, and it makes it more likely that the other person will do their tasks again, as they feel that the work they *are* doing is acknowledged. <u>Why would anyone want to keep doing something when they aren't appreciated?</u>

How can you show your appreciation in a way that speaks the loudest to *them?*

Does your roommate love hot fudge sundaes? Surprise them by bringing home the ingredients for sundaes one day as a "thank you." Is your partner's main love language "Words of Affirmation?" Give them multiple "Thank yous" throughout the day and even some by text. Praise them in front of other people about what a great job they did cleaning "XYZ."

Do the Chores Together

Create a sense of comradery with your partner or roommate by working together on chores. If the other person is struggling to complete a task, doing it with them (not doing it for them) will strengthen your bond and result in appreciation and maybe even reciprocation.

Use each other's momentum. You may find that you get a burst of energy when you see the other making dents in their chores. Use that to get your tasks done at the same time. Why not put on some music and make it a party? You could also put on an audiobook you both enjoy and listen while you work.

What if They're Still Not Doing Their Share?

Do Not Clean for Them

If they don't clean, do *not* do it for them! If they fall off the wagon and start letting their things slide, *leave them* as they are. <u>By picking up their slack you enable them to not hold up their responsibilities in the future.</u> This may be a big reason why your attempts to share chores have failed in the past!

Regardless of how *they're* doing, *you* do what you said you would.

Let the space speak for itself. Sooner or later there will be a visible indicator of who is holding up their end of the bargain and who isn't.

Give Gentle Reminders

<u>Your roommate or significant other may simply be forgetting or getting distracted by life's other priorities</u>, so don't be too harsh on them if something goes undone. They might just need a little reminder.

Try framing it as a question. "<u>Do you have time to do the dishes?</u>" is *respectful* as it doesn't *assume* anything. They might not have the time to do the dishes right then. But if instead, you *tell* them to, resentment and anger may flare up as they may feel like they have to rearrange their schedule to do a chore when *you* say to.

You could also say "<u>Would you mind doing the dishes today?</u>" By adding in the deadline "today," you help ensure that the task won't be continuously put off.

If you have to keep reminding them though, you might consider switching to using one of the apps we talked about.

Keep Your Spaces Separate

You're going through this program and working on becoming the best adult you can be. You're getting your life together, and that includes having a clean home. Just because others aren't doing their half of the chores doesn't mean that you shouldn't enjoy the cleanliness you're working towards. Don't allow their mess to negatively affect your life!

First of all, if they can't get on board, maybe they need this guide. Tell your roommates about it (if you haven't already), so they can order a copy and learn how to adult themselves. Second, <u>one huge way you can eliminate the tension and still feel like things are clean *without* anyone feeling taken advantage of is by designating separate spaces.</u>

An example of this would be his and hers sinks. He can use his own sink, and if it gets messy, he has to deal with his own mess. If he keeps his sink clean, he can enjoy its cleanliness. And the same goes for you. If your bathroom doesn't have two sinks but you do have more than one bathroom, <u>have the person who is the tidiest get the bathroom that will most often be used by guests</u>.

Another example of this would be designating separate rooms for your things. Of course, if you're living with a roommate you most likely already have separate rooms. But if you're married, having things separated like this can be *very* helpful, like the idea of her having a she shed and him having a man cave.

Instead of "nagging" the other person (or having them nag you) to put things away, you can simply tuck items into that person's room and then <u>shut the door</u>. If you and your roommate share a common space, encourage them to put their things into their room so that the common area can remain tidy.

<u>Putting things into peoples' designated rooms allows them the freedom to deal with their belongings *when* and *if* they want to.</u> This will also eliminate any visible clutter for those not responsible for it, so *both* parties feel respected.

Hire Out

Are things still not working out? If you've done all of the above, and you don't want to succumb to doing things yourself, hire out! It doesn't have to cost an arm and a leg.

Teenagers are always looking for a little spare change, so why not ask your neighbors if their kids want a part-time job? You might be able to get some yard work done or have them mow your lawn for way less than it would cost for a professional service to do it. Of course, the work won't be the best, but the chore will get done and it's one less thing for you to do!

You could also ask for help on your neighborhood Facebook Groups.

Hiring individuals on Facebook Groups was one of the big things that helped me when I was feeling overwhelmed with life. They were instrumental in giving me and my house a clean slate so I could get back on my feet.

<u>If you can't afford to pay for help, but need the assistance regardless, see if there is a "Pay it Forward" group near you and post in it.</u>

Wherever you choose to post, either in your local community group, a Mommy group, or a "Pay it Forward" group, if you're honest about your situation and what you're needing, you'll more than likely get very kind responses offering assistance. Perhaps a few stay-at-home moms or ladies in between jobs are needing some spare change and looking for an opportunity just like this!

An example of a request you could post would be, "Hi, I'm going through a program that helps women learn how to adult. I'm realizing that there are a lot of things around my house that I need help with and I'm feeling a bit overwhelmed! Would any ladies be willing to help me organize and declutter? I'd be so grateful!"

When doing this, I recommend discussing any details in private and determining how much you will pay them *before* they start any work.

Any time you pay an individual, whether that be a neighbor's kid or a young lady from Facebook, I recommend you <u>pay them more than what they might receive elsewhere to incentivize them</u>. They'll be grateful for the extra money and want to keep you happy so you keep inviting them back! Plus, if you've been blessed, why not bless others?

I'd aim for around $15 or so per hour if you can afford it. Yes, it's a little more, but it'll still save you from paying a professional $25-50 per hour, which is the national average for house cleaning, or $30-80, the national average for lawn mowing.

You may be able to negotiate a lower amount by having them use your cleaning supplies or tools instead of having to bring their own. You could also try negotiating a lower amount by offering them a lump sum for a project as opposed to paying by the hour. This latter option often works with lawns.

A benefit of hiring an individual as opposed to a professional, besides them charging less, is that <u>they may be willing to work with you or do things for you that wouldn't be on a professional's regular agenda.</u>

When I was feeling overwhelmed with that mountain of laundry I mentioned before, I hired a woman to come over and take all my clothes to the laundromat so they could be washed faster than doing individual loads in my washer. She then hung up all the clothes I wanted to keep and took the rest to donate. This was great because a lot of what I needed help with wasn't just cleaning, but running errands and plain "catching up" on life, things that a regular cleaning service most likely wouldn't have done.

Of course, you always have the option to hire a professional. You may consider doing this if your funds aren't too tight, you can't be at your home when they come to clean <u>(for security reasons I wouldn't recommend leaving someone who isn't a professional alone with your belongings)</u>, or if you'd rather have things cleaned the best they can be and in less time.

If you don't want to hire out, brainstorm ways certain chores could be eliminated.

An example of this would be getting rid of the chore of loading the dishwasher. Instead of having someone take the time to scrub off hardened food on plates left in the sink, and then put the dishes in the dishwasher, have everyone immediately rinse off food and load their plates. This saves a whole cleaning step. <u>Be sure to let those who live with you know though, so everyone can do their part with their dishes</u>. If it means one less chore and no more soggy leftovers on plates, they'll more than likely be down.

You could also invest in a product that will do the chore for you or make it way easier, like a Roomba! If nobody wants to vacuum, or if you can't convince them to vacuum as often as it needs to be done, why not save up and get one, or wait until one goes on sale?

Walmart occasionally offers huge savings on robot vacuums. Though the sale will have ended by the time this guide is live, Walmart is currently offering 50% off a $300 Shark robot vacuum, and it's nowhere near Black Friday. So yes, you can get great deals on these year-round. You have no reason not to save yourself a bunch of time and get one.

Go With the Flow

Things will change depending upon the day and season of life. Your roommate may move out and a new one move in. Your partner may sprain their wrist and won't be able to push the vacuum, or they may be preoccupied with a pending promotion at work. Things will change and you'll need to reevaluate.

Don't be afraid to occasionally revisit and update your chore chart to work for your household (especially if something isn't getting done). In fact, I recommend you revisit your chore chart/schedule in two weeks to see if any chores need to be swapped, shared, or divided up further.

Action Plan

Determine when it'll be the best time to talk to those you share a space with. <u>Today may not be the best day to do it!</u> Brainstorm things you could bring up that may be important to them that you could use to get your point across. Prepare some "I" statements and practice saying them in your head beforehand, so you'll have well-crafted sentences ready for the (potentially) emotionally charged moment.

Remember that sharing the chore load is important for the household and that having this "scary" talk is going to be *so good* for your relationship or friendship. No one will feel taken advantage of anymore. You'll be able to save so much time. You'll feel less stressed, and your relationship will be strengthened as you both openly communicate and work on maintaining your home together.

Determine who will do what chores, and after your talk, print the schedule and put it someplace visible! You got this girlfriend!

DAY 15:
MAINTAIN CLEANLINESS

Oftentimes, it's the little things added up that help us maintain the cleanliness of our home, just like how it's the little things added up that lead to a giant mess.

If you don't want to have to keep battling buildups of laundry, dishes, and dirt give some of these "rules" a try.

Rules for Cleanliness:

Preventing a Mess is Always Easier Than *Cleaning* a Mess

You might think that stuff won't stick when you're cooking, but having a pan lined with parchment paper or tin foil just makes cleaning up way easier and faster. Also, try lining the bottom of your stove with tin foil to catch any drippings, or get this oven liner on Amazon. Pulling out dirty foil to throw away or that reusable liner to throw in the dishwasher, is so much easier than breaking your back trying to bend down and scrub the inside of your oven.

Another example would be putting plastic floor mats in your car (I'll be talking about this again on Day 30). They really are the way to go for hot mess gals like us who spill things constantly.

You could also <u>use car seat covers, put a mattress cover on your bed, slipcovers over your couch, and use a duvet cover too</u>. Anything helps!

Make Things Incrementally Easier

Put extra bags into the bottom of your trash cans so that you don't have to hunt for a new bag every time you change out the trash. Even if the box of bags is only a room away, <u>you're more likely to set up the new trash bag immediately if you have one right there, rather than if you have to put any effort into finding another one</u>. I've gone as far as storing the *whole* box of bags for my kitchen trash inside of it. It's right there when I need it, and it gives me more room in the cupboard. Try it!

Another example would be to put your cleaning materials for particular rooms into those rooms. When you make a mess in the bathroom, you can wipe it up then and there and not leave it to forget about it or let it sit and build up. When you make a mess in your car you can clean it up quickly and not leave it to cause a stain.

One-Touch Rule

Quite simply, put stuff where it goes the first time.

An example would be to leave the washing machine lid open and put your dirty cloths directly into it. This works for things like cleaning rags and hand towels, *especially* when they're wet. Just throw them into the washing machine and it'll allow them to drain. Then they'll already be in the machine when it's time to wash them. You'll just have to shut the lid and turn it on.

A second example would be putting your dishes right into the dishwasher and not putting them into the sink, as I mentioned before. If you put them into the sink, you'll just be creating more work for yourself later. Put them where they go the first time and don't touch them twice.

This rule also applies to cleaning surfaces. Have you ever found yourself pushing stuff around and moving it out of the way while trying to clean? <u>Just take the ten seconds that are needed to put the things away, rather than moving them to one side</u> to wipe and then moving them back to the other side.

Never Leave a Room Empty-Handed

Chances are that there will always be at least one item out of place at all times. So, whenever you leave a room, take something that doesn't belong with you and go put it away. If you do this every time you leave a room, you'll keep things more organized and your space will look tidier.

Apply this rule to your car as well! Do you always have a build-up of fast food bags and water bottles in your vehicle? Every time you get home, carry in as much as you can and dump it into the trash. We'll also cover this again on Day 30 in the chapter on maintaining your vehicle, but you can still work to <u>make this into a habit</u> now and do a little bit every time. Soon enough your car will be clean and *stay* clean.

Clean as You Go

This rule changed the game for me when it came to cooking!

I used to only focus on cooking food while I cooked. I'd tell myself that I would clean up everything afterward, but inevitably, I'd be too overwhelmed with the mess or too tired from cooking to do anything about it. I'd usually end up leaving everything to be cleaned up later. But once I got around to it, it would take me much longer to clean because stuff had been allowed to harden. Also, everything had to be wiped down before being placed back into the cupboards because everything had been splashed with food from the stove.

It would have been much faster and easier for me to have cleaned as I cooked, to use items and then *immediately* put them away before they got dirty, to wipe messes before they hardened, to throw trash away before it accumulated, and to rinse the pots and pans and put them in the dishwasher before they made a giant intimidating pile in my sink.

Since I've adopted this rule, the clean-up process after cooking is *way* more manageable as there is hardly anything left out to clean. I'm also using the mess prevention rule (mentioned earlier) and am now lining trays as well, anything to make things easier!

This rule applies to other things, not just cooking. Where could you begin implementing it to make cleaning up easier on yourself?

Efficiency Over Aesthetic

I used to think that having little trash cans everywhere was unsightly. Maybe I'm the only one, but I just thought that it didn't look very pretty, and so I only had one trash can, the one in my kitchen.

You might be laughing at how difficult I was making things for myself, with rightful reason. This led to massive clutter in all the other rooms, because why would I "waste time" walking a single Q-tip all the way to the kitchen every time I used one? It would have been way easier for me to just have little trash cans where I needed them.

You might find that to be a silly example, but I can almost bet that you have at least one thing you can change in your home right now that is more about looks than efficiency. What could you change that would make things a *little* bit easier for yourself?

1 Minute Rule

This one's pretty straightforward. If you can complete the task in one minute or less, do it now and get it over with. Otherwise, you'll end up with a million little things waiting to be done and it can get overwhelming. If it's only 60 seconds or less, stop procrastinating and making yourself suffer longer. Just get it done.

Action Plan

What rules stuck out to you today? Which ones will you adopt? Remember, not everything works for everyone. *You* have to figure out what works for *you*. But I believe that the more of these that you can build into a habit, the easier a time you'll have keeping your space clean and maintained.

What's one thing you could put a liner or cover on that would prevent or lessen a mess? Do it today or make a plan to get the cover/liner that you need.

What's one thing that you could do to make a chore incrementally easier? What is one thing that you could do to make something more efficient rather than esthetically pleasing? Brainstorm and implement your ideas!

Are you going to work on building the habit of always carrying in your trash from your car? Are you going to start cleaning while you're cooking or putting things away where they go the first time? How could you implement these rules to make your life easier?

DAY 16:
SOLVE YOUR PAPERWORK PROBLEM

You may be in a situation right now where you have so much random paperwork that you don't know what to do with it or even where to begin. You may be leaving everything in a pile on your entryway table or throwing it in a box so you can shove it in your closet later. You tell yourself you'll get to it eventually, but the pile just keeps growing!

There are important documents like bills, sentimental items like photos and letters, some magazines you ordered but haven't even glanced at, coupons that you might need at some point, and a lot of junk mail that you haven't gotten rid of because there could be a good deal in there somewhere.

If any of that sounds familiar, or if you struggle with paperwork in general, today is for you. We're going to be pulling out that box in your closet, or emptying that paper drawer you stuff everything into, so you can face your paper monster head-on and finally free yourself from its clutches.

I'm sure this will come as no surprise that we're going to be using technology to help you address this problem area. With it, you'll be able to toss a lot of paperwork that is taking up valuable space and organize what you hold onto so it no longer clutters up your home.

You already have a pretty good start reducing your paper clutter because you followed the steps outlined for you in the previous chapters, like transferring all of the information from your sticky notes to Google Keep and paying your bills online so you no longer receive paper statements. But there are other kinds of paperwork that we need to go over how to deal with.

Tackle Your Paper Pile

Pull out all of the random paperwork you have and sort it into three piles. These will include important and legal documents, sentimental papers, and the third will be whatever is leftover. Then, follow the instructions below for each pile.

What to Do with Important Documents

A lot of the paperwork in this pile is going to need to be kept, but it shouldn't just be left in disarray. Let's create a new home for it so that you'll know exactly where it is when you need it and so you'll know where to put similar documents in the future.

Get a filing cabinet or file box. If you want to instantly go from feeling like a hot mess to a got-it-together adult, get yourself a filing cabinet. They aren't *just* for businesses. Filing cabinets are for smart, organized individuals, like you!

Once I finally got one for myself, I wondered why I put it off for so long because it makes managing paperwork *much* easier. So grab yourself a cute file box at Target, or if you don't want to spend a lot there are usually plenty of inexpensive filing cabinets at thrift stores.

After you've bought and set up your filing cabinet, place important documents that you *need* to keep into it, and label the files appropriately. Things like birth certificates, passports, house deeds, and college diplomas should all be kept. Charitable donations and church tithes should be kept track of too because these can be tax-deductible.

Speaking of, tax documents need to be held onto as well, but because what you need changes occasionally and is based upon your personal situation, I recommend you talk to a tax professional regarding what documents you need currently.

So what do you do with the rest of the things in this pile that you think are important but that don't necessarily need to be kept? Take photos of them and put them into a specified digital folder so that you'll be able to reference them later if you need to.

Google Drive is not something that we've talked about before, but it is something that you have automatic access to because you have a Google account. It offers a *free* way to store, synchronize, and share files to 15 GB. Because this software works so well with the other applications you now use, and because it doesn't cost a thing, we're going to be using it today and in a later chapter to store the images you take and any other documents you want to keep.

If you have any question in your mind about whether you'll need a paper that is in this "Important Documents" pile again or not, keep the physical copy and make a file for it in your cabinet. But with the other two piles, *especially* the third one, it should suffice to simply take a picture of the paper and file it digitally.

If you want the documents that you take a picture of to appear more polished, in case you ever need to use them again in a professional setting, use the Simple Scan - PDF Scanner App This is a neat app because it offers you a lot of the same functions that an actual scanner would, but at a much cheaper price. You can "scan" receipts, IDs, or any document for that matter. You can sign them, store and organize them, add a watermark, adjust image color, and even fax them right from your phone! I particularly like it because you can set it to *automatically* upload anything that you take a picture of into Google Drive. Unfortunately, this app costs money if you want to use the majority of its features. However, they offer a free three-day trial. So if you have a lot of paperwork you need to upload images of, use this app as it will save you a whole step. Just take advantage of their trial period, upload everything you need to within the three days, and then cancel your subscription before they charge you.

What to Do with Sentimental Papers

In this pile, you may have old papers you wrote for school that you're proud of, artwork you made as a kid, letters from a pen pal or deceased relative, Christmas greeting cards, and pictures that you intended to make into a scrapbook at some point.

Understandably, this stack of paper can be particularly difficult to sort through because you may have emotional ties to a lot of the things in it and want to keep them. However, I want to remind you of what we talked about before in the chapter on eliminating clutter. It is not necessarily an item or piece of paper but the memories tied to it that are special to you. Unless the document is meaningful enough that it sparks joy, or more joy than another similar document, keeping a picture of it will suffice.

Take images of anything not worth physically holding onto that you would still like to remember, and then throw them away. Again, sort these photos into special digital folders for them. These may be titled something as simple as "Memories," or be as specific as you need them to be if you have a lot you need to differentiate between, such as "School Papers from 9th

Grade" and "School Papers from 10th Grade."

Just like you did with the previous pile, put the physical papers and documents you deem important enough to keep into their assigned folders in your new filing box.

What to Do with the Remaining Pile

Now it's time to address your final pile. I think it's safe to say that the majority of it will probably be junk. This one is, in my opinion, the "fun" one, because you can toss things left and right. However, there may be a few things in it that are hard to decide what to do with.

Perhaps it'll be easier for you to get through this pile if you consider the following while doing so. Anything that you allow to stay in your home will need to be *maintained*. You're already spending your valuable time going through all of this paperwork today. If you're struggling to decide what to do with something, <u>ask yourself "Is this *worth* my time? Do I want to see this and have to deal with this *again* next time I sort through all of my paperwork?</u>" If the answer is "No," dispose of it.

Throw away anything that you put into your paper pile that you thought you might want to read or reference later that you haven't in a long time. <u>If you'd wanted it that badly, you would have pulled it out by now.</u>

Take for instance that magazine that I mentioned earlier. You wanted it, you paid for it, yet it's sitting in your paper stack growing dust. Either find a place for it like on a shelf if you collect magazines, make a plan to read it either this evening or tomorrow, or *toss it!*

Toss all of your coupons and sales flyers too. <u>Don't waste your time checking their expiration dates</u>. If you insist on couponing, you can come up with a better system for organizing them moving forward. This way, you'll *know* all your coupons are current.

Get rid of all of the assembly instructions or care instructions that you received when you bought something. <u>*If* you ever need any of them, you'll most likely be able to find them in a document online.</u> If you're hesitant, look up the manual online before you toss it. If you find it, throw away the physical copy. But if you can't find it, keep it, and make a designated folder for this sort of thing.

For warranties, you can take a picture of them and then toss them as well if you feel comfortable, or you can just make a folder for them too.

Put all of the paper that you have to *do* something with into a special "To-Do" folder. We'll go over another idea in a few minutes regarding what to do with these sorts of things in the future. But for now, compile these and keep them separated so you can address them later. Items in this folder might include things like receipts that you need to add to your Budget Spreadsheet (we'll go over this in a few days) and fliers for events that you want to sign up for.

Alternatively, you could take a picture of the paper so that you can get rid of it, and then move the image to a digitalized "To-Do" folder. Afterward, write down what you need to do in your Daily Check-in (or wherever else you're keeping track of your to-dos) and specify where the picture of that paper is being stored in case you need to reference it.

Immediately toss anything that's addressed to "Current Resident." Similarly, anything that says "PRSRT STD" or "Presort Standard," up inside of the little box where the stamp would go usually, is most likely junk as well. It's from some business that is paying the post office to circulate their mail to *everyone,* not just you because you've been "specially" selected. So don't even waste your time opening it up to see what the letter is about or opening up any other kind of promotional mail for that matter.

Also, I feel like it goes without saying, but don't open up anything that is addressed to someone else. That is a federal crime! Instead, mark "Return to Sender" on it and put it back in your mailbox with the flag up. If this is a common occurrence, contact your post office or leave a note for your postman.

How to Dispose of the Trash

Now that you've figured out what you'll keep and what you'll get rid of, it's time to figure out how you'll toss the stuff you don't want.

Recycling is a great option if you have it available to you. But don't let this one step hold you up. If you need to, just toss everything this time and figure out how you can get better at recycling in the future.

Of course, you don't want to throw away paper that has important, sensitive information on it though. You can hand rip, cut up, or swipe a permanent marker through your information. However, these things can be tedious and time-consuming.

Luckily, there are things like this identity protection roller stamp, which is Amazon's Choice for a stamp that rolls over your important information and makes it illegible. <u>If you only have a few documents with sensitive information</u>, or if you don't want to buy a whole paper shredder, <u>this is a good option.</u>

Getting a paper shredder would certainly make the process of catching up and then keeping up on your paperwork easier though. This shredder is particularly handy because <u>it takes care of two things that can be quite a nuisance when trying to shred, documents</u> <u>with staples and credit cards</u>. It shreds paper super fine, which makes it harder for someone to put back together. And it can handle up to nine pages at once, so you can quickly get through all of your paperwork while resting assured that your information is protected.

However, if you have a *giant* pile of paper, the most cost and time-efficient option would be to take it to the UPS store. Because this store is a franchise, <u>prices and options may vary. So check with your local one to see what services they offer and how much they charge.</u>

The one local to me charges $1.49 per pound for bulk shredding. They don't require a weight minimum, but they also don't offer a sliding-scale discount if you bring in more than one pound. Thankfully, they shred things with staples. So you don't have to do any staple-pulling or preparing beforehand. You can just dump everything there and be done with it. This is a nice option because they also recycle the paper they receive.

Stay On Top of Paperwork Moving Forward

We've already gone over a few ideas for how you can do this in the future. These include things like getting a file box so you can have an organized system for things you want to keep, and getting a shredder so you can quickly toss stuff in and not have to worry about your identity being stolen. But there are two other things that we need to cover that will help you keep your paper pile in check.

Create a Routine

The first, I'm sure you're not shocked to learn, is to create a routine or schedule for taking care of your paperwork on a regular basis.

Because I work from home and my dog kindly alerts me every time the mail comes in, I quickly go through it right then and there. But one of my girlfriends, who works out of the home, takes it with her to work every day and goes through it during her lunch. Alternatively, you might have a P.O. Box, in which case you may only sort through your mail once a week when you pick it up.

Another option, and one that I believe may be the best for the majority of women reading this, is to collect your mail daily (especially if your area is at high risk for porch pirates), put it in a designated folder or tray, and then sort through it once a week. This idea piggybacks off of the suggestion I made earlier about making a "To-Do" folder. However, I didn't suggest this at first because I wanted you to start your new paper journey with all documents put away. But after you've caught up on your paperwork and have completed everything in your To-Do folder, designate a space as your "Inbox," and create a special folder for this in your Google Drive as well. If you choose to keep your subscription to Simple Scan, this is where you'll have it upload images to moving forward.

In the future, <u>whenever you get any kind of paper, put it in your "Inbox." Then at the time you've set aside for this, go through everything and place things where they belong, whether things need to be thrown away, filed, or filed digitally and then thrown away.</u>

The reason I suggest you only go through your paperwork once a week is because all of your bills will be automated and digitized in a few days. You'll no longer be receiving these kinds of important documents in the mail, so you won't need to look for them every day. However, <u>if you're expecting something important, by all means, go through your mail and other paperwork more often</u>. But no matter when you'll collect your mail, how often you'll go through it, or how you'll store it until you go through it, you'll still need to decide on a routine that'll work for you. <u>If you need to, add whatever schedule you decide on into your calendar as a recurring event until it has become a habit.</u>

Also, add a recurring event in your calendar to go through all of your paperwork once a year and clear out everything that you can. This might include any new paper subscriptions you've signed up for, files of things you thought you might need but didn't, piles that have snuck up on you, sentimental items you've collected, etc. Clear out the old and make room for all of the new paper you'll accumulate in the upcoming year.

I recommend you <u>do this after you've filed your taxes. This way, you'll be able to verify with a professional which tax documents you can get rid of and how far back you need to keep others</u>. You'll then be able to go through the rest of your paper while resting assured that you're keeping the most important things.

Reduce What Comes In

Now that you're no longer swimming through piles of paper, I imagine that you want to keep it that way. Sure, you need a routine to do so. But it's going to make it so much easier to stick to that routine and keep your paperwork under control if you reduce the amount of paper that comes into your home in the first place.

<u>You can lessen how much paper you bring home by refusing receipts at checkout</u>. Nowadays, a lot of stores can look up your purchase through your card, email, or phone number. So you don't always have to keep a physical copy of a receipt in case you want to return something. We'll go over this more in the financial chapters, but this is assuming that you'll be using digital means to track your spending. If you'll be tracking manually, you'll need to keep the receipts until you've added what you've spent into your budget. You'll also probably want to keep them long enough to additionally scan them into a money-back rewards app.

Other ways you can reduce paper clutter include the following: When someone offers you their business card, don't accept it. Take a picture of it. Be very particular about what you sign up to receive in the mail. Question if you will actually take the time to read a magazine before signing up for it, or consider if it's time for you to end a subscription if you have one already and don't use it. Stop paying for newspapers. If you cared enough, you would look up the news online. Don't take home pamphlets that you get from church. Take a picture of your notes and toss the pamphlet while you're still there. Better yet, save the church some money and don't use their handouts. Take all of your notes on Keep.

When it comes to reducing how much mail you bring into your home, by far the easiest and quickest option is to walk straight from your mailbox to your trash and dump the junk right in. Don't even bring it in the house to pile up.

Unfortunately, this option is not a permanent solution and the junk mail will just keep coming. So if you'd like to solve your problem long-term, there are a few ways you can opt out of receiving *most* of it. However, they take a little bit of effort.

Before we continue though, I want to caution you against signing up to stop receiving mail on any random site, as there are a lot of scams. Do your research before paying for anything.

The options below will not necessarily remove you from the personal mailing lists of businesses that you agreed to receive things from. To stop receiving mail that you previously signed up for, contact that business directly and ask them to remove you.

To read how to reduce *some* of the unsolicited advertising you get, go to this article by USPS. In it, they recommend you register your mail preferences and opt-out service through DMAchoice.org. The processing fee is $2 and it lasts for ten years. This will not exempt you from getting things from local retailers or politicians, but it will certainly help reduce the volume of junk you receive. I found this site through the aforementioned article, and separately through US.GOV (a government site), so I believe it is legit.

In that article by USPS, they also recommend you stop credit cards and insurance offers by calling 1-888-567-8688, or by going to https://www.optoutprescreen.com/selection where you can fill out an opt-out form online. Both of these options will only get you out of their mailing list for five years. For the permanent option, you'll need to mail in a form. The link above takes you to a page where you can do either.

While this doesn't pertain to paperwork, I'd like to quickly mention another way you can reduce unsolicited advertising. Go to donotcall.gov to be added to the National Do Not Call Registry and stop receiving those annoying telemarketing calls. The process is extremely easy, your registration *never* expires, and it's free!

Action Plan

Do what you can this evening to begin sorting through your paperwork, deciding what you'll keep and what you'll get rid of. Get a filing box or cabinet, and make relevant folders for the papers that you'll hold onto. Take pictures of anything important or sentimental that you won't keep, and put these pictures into designated folders on Google Drive. Consider using Simple Scan or another app to make this process of "scanning" and uploading easier.

Go through the remaining pile, tossing what you can and digitalizing the rest. Cancel any subscriptions adding to this pile that you no longer want. Create your "To-Do" folder for anything that you need to do something with, and make other folders for any warranties or care instructions that you insist upon keeping.

Consider how you'll handle any leftover paper. Do you anticipate that you'll have a minimal amount, so you'll be able to cut up all of the documents with sensitive information? Do you think you'll have too much to cut up by hand, so you should invest in a paper shredder? Or do you think you'll have so much that you'll need to take all of it to the UPS store to have it shredded for you?

Lastly, decide how you'll stay on top of your paperwork moving forward to avoid things getting out of hand again. Will you use an "Inbox" tray and only deal with your mail and paperwork on a certain day at a certain time? Or will you instead put things away into their folder or digital file *immediately*? How will you handle the unsolicited mail you receive? Will you just dump all of it right into the trash from now on, or will you sign up to stop receiving it?

<u>If you don't get through all of your paperwork today</u>, that's completely understandable. Just <u>make a plan for when you'll finish the rest and put it in your calendar.</u>

DAY 17:
EMPTY YOUR SINK FULL OF DISHES

Since you read the Introduction, you know my "dirty" little secret. I was horrible at getting the dishes done!

I used to procrastinate emptying my dishwasher, and because it remained full, the sink would start to back up. The larger the pile grew in the sink, the more I put off doing anything with it. Eventually, I was left with a big pile of molding dishes and was too overwhelmed and grossed out to do anything about it.

Since then, I've found a few hacks and implemented some habits which have transformed my sink from an area of dread and shame to an area of accomplishment. Now, my sink is empty and sparkling, and I've found that having it that way has had a positive effect on the whole kitchen. These days, my kitchen is always one of the cleanest rooms in my house. Try out the tips and ideas in today's chapter, and if your sink is a problem area for you, I hope that these will help you as well!

Determine the Root of the Problem

<u>If you tend to be behind on your dishes, why do you think that might be?</u> Is it because you're slow to load the dishwasher, or do you think your problem is unloading it? Is it that you get overwhelmed by the volume of dishes left after cooking a big meal? Is it that you have to hand wash everything because you don't have a dishwasher and you find it all too time-consuming? Do you not have the right tools, so effectively cleaning inside of things is difficult, or do you simply *hate* doing the dishes so you put it off?

After considering things, I realized that the root of my problem was putting clean dishes away. It was the bottleneck that stopped the whole dish cycle. <u>By creating a routine for myself, and building it into my schedule, I was able to make a plan for when I would address this problem</u> and make sure this vital part of a clean and hygienic household happened regularly.

I began by starting the dishwasher nightly during my evening routine. Running the dishwasher before you go to bed gives it the whole night to dry. This makes your job easier the next day as you don't have to wipe down any residual water before putting things away. Plus, running your appliances during off-peak hours can save you money (we'll go over this at a later date).

I then added unloading the dishwasher into my morning routine. If you can't unload the dishwasher before leaving for work, try to unload it as soon as you can after getting home, *before* any new dishes start to pile up. <u>Starting the day with an empty dishwasher allows others to put their dishes right into the machine and *not* into the sink</u> (remember the chore eliminating example a few days ago). Then at night, you can repeat the process by starting the dishwasher after all dinner dishes have been added.

As you may have noticed, running and unloading the dishwasher is already added to your Daily tasks as an "as needed" chore. I recommend that you add it into your routine as well, for the reasons mentioned, but also to make sure it's less likely to get pushed off because it has a specific time assigned to it.

Of course, how often you run your dishwasher will depend upon how many dishes you use and how many people live in your house. Determine a schedule for starting and emptying the dishwasher that works for your household.

If the thing that's stopping you from getting the dishes done is that you simply hate doing them, why are you signed up for them in the first place girlfriend? Use the great chore chart you made and take advantage of all the hard work you put in getting others to be involved in the housework. You don't have to slug through all the chores anymore, so trade this for something you can tolerate more.

If you don't have a dishwasher and have to hand wash everything, I know how time-consuming and annoying it can be! Do you need to divide this task up on your chore chart so that everyone can share it? Perhaps if you cook, the other person can clean, and vice versa.

For some reason, it took me a long time to realize that basic sponges don't cut it when you have to hand wash. I can't tell you how frustrating it was for me to try to get into all those nooks and crannies with inadequate tools. If you're similarly struggling, just <u>get the right tools for the job</u> and make your life easier!

A lot of reusable straws come with tiny brushes to clean them, but if yours didn't, get one! There are also bristled wands for cleaning inside of water bottles, and sponges with a long handle like this one which I love. Bottles with narrow necks used to be my dish nemesis, but having the right tools that fit where I need them to has made *all* the difference!

My point is, if you're having a hard time cleaning something, there's probably a tool out there that'll make it easier for you, *but* if cleaning a certain item is always a pain, just *get rid of it!* An example of this would be one of those fun Star Wars lightsaber tongs that makes noise. They are cool, but they're also tedious to clean because they have batteries inside of them. If this would cause you to push off cleaning it, it might not be worth having, and you'd be better off with a plain pair of tongs instead.

You don't need to stress, wasting time cleaning a single item. It's okay to get rid of something if it hinders you from living this easier life you're trying to create for yourself. If a difficult-to-clean item belongs to someone else, have *them* clean it if they *insist* upon keeping it.

If the issue you're struggling with is loading the dishes, having ones that aren't covered in unknown mushy food will *really* make things easier and more pleasant for you. You can scrape food into the trash with whatever utensil you were using to eat with. Scrape it right off after you're done eating and before you rinse the plate in the sink. This will prevent your sink's drain from getting clogged and keep your dish sponge cleaner. A sponge that washes the dishes should be clean and not full of gunk.

If you don't want to use your utensil and want to have a special cleaning tool reserved just for scraping food off of your plate, try these out. I especially like the notched scraper that aligns with most skillet's ridges. If you've ever tried to clean a skillet, you know how *hard* it can be to get down into the grooves and get out that black ooze that's left after cooking. Cleaning my husband's skillet used to be one of those dishes I put off for *days* because I just didn't know how to clean it effectively. These would have been so helpful, and I wish I'd known about them sooner.

Don't do more work than you have to. If you're always behind and overwhelmed with dishes, don't add more to your plate by insisting on recycling. Of course, this won't apply to everyone, but if you have the *option* to not, and are always behind because of it, *stop doing it.*

I am a big fan of recycling, but having lived in places where it is mandated and strictly regulated, I know how much it can cause a backlog in your sink and trash. Yes, it's good to recycle. But if this is an area that's causing you to struggle, maybe you need to make a compromise temporarily and eliminate the extra work of having to wash out and clean containers before you toss them.

If All Else Fails

So you've tried the ideas above and you're *still* feeling overwhelmed by dishes. Maybe you're in a season of life where you need to say "to heck with it!" and stop fussing with the ceramics.

Remember the rule of Efficiency Over Esthetics? Remember how I said that you need to find ways to do things that work for you? Well, here is an idea that ties in both concepts. Some people might scoff at it, but others may need to hear right now, paper plates are okay to use. It's *fine*. Who said they weren't? In fact, I'm a *huge* fan of disposable cups for hot beverages and will tell you more about them and how they helped solve a little problem of mine later on.

If you're worried about using paper plates because you're concerned about what other people will think of you if they find out, just get out actual plates when people come over. Or better yet, *don't care* and eat off paper plates anyway! I doubt they will mind, and if they do, you don't need judgemental friends like that!

What about cooking meals? Just get those tin foil pans that people often use for potlucks. They work great and are large enough you can cook extra food to have for leftovers.

Do what works for *you* in order to get done what you *have* to so that you have more time to do what you *want* to.

Helpful Tips Moving Forward

If you're sticking to regular plates, make sure to rinse off your dishes immediately after use. No matter if the dishes sit in the sink or get put immediately into the washer, they'll still be waiting a while until the machine runs. This gives things time to harden, so regardless of where they'll be placed, they need to be rinsed off.

It is *so* much easier to spend *fifteen seconds* rising off a dish or rinsing out a pan immediately after cooking, than it is to spend *five minutes* trying to scrub off something that was left to harden, so clean off all solid food from your dishes.

<u>If you don't at least remove solids before adding things to the dishwasher, your machine will have a harder time cleaning your dishes, and many may have to be washed again.</u> This could cause a backup in your sink.

Plus, if you send a lot of food through the dishwasher, that'll gunk up the filters which could result in food particles being left on your "cleaned" items. You'll also have to clean your filters and sump more often.

My poor husband had to clean out *baskets* of unpopped kernels from our filter while I was learning this "no solids rule" the hard way. I guess I thought that there was a drain at the bottom of the dishwasher that just flushed all food away, but there's not. Take it from him, cleaning out these filters is not something you want to have to do more than necessary. *Gag*

By the way, when was the last time you cleaned your dishwasher's filter? If you've never done it, or if you don't remember when it was done last, it's probably time to do it.

Make things easier on yourself and your machine. From now on, any time you dirty a dish, cup, pan, or anything else, rinse it off as soon as you're finished using it.

If you know you're going to be making a lot of dishes, like if you're having a dinner party or are about to cook a bunch, consider running the machine *beforehand* even if it's only partially full. This way, <u>you'll have an empty machine to fit in all the new dirty things.</u> If you often get overwhelmed by a large stack of dishes after cooking, this will help you. Instead of having to play catch up, quickly wash and unload the small amount that's already in the dishwasher.

I know some people will be against this needless wasting of water and electricity. But again, you need to do what works for you. If you know you're the type of person who will get overwhelmed if the dishes get backed up, perhaps this is an area you need to make another compromise in.

While we're still on the topic of dishwashers, I'd like to quickly mention that your machine can wash more than just dishes. Why not take advantage of its great cleaning capabilities (some even offering sterilization) and *efficiently* clean things around your home?

If you have pets, throw their toys in it and don't waste time wiping them all down. You can put your plastic utensil holder, drawer organizers, refrigerator shelves, metal vents around your house, and even solo cups and plastic silverware in it. <u>My mother-in-law uses it to store her dish scrubbers and sponges.</u> I *love* this idea and have adopted it myself because the sponges no longer have to be left on the counter causing visible clutter. Best of all, <u>storing them here ensures that the things that are used to clean are clean</u> <u>themselves</u> because they are washed every time the dishwasher runs.

You can put almost anything that won't be damaged by water or heat into your dishwasher. If you're in doubt though, just look it up online to verify, and then put it on the top rack to be safe.

Action Plan

If you have an issue with getting your dishes done, your homework today is to determine where the bottleneck is in your dish cycle and address it.

Come up with an actionable plan for how you will address this regularly, and add it to your routine. Put this chore into your chore chart as often as it is applicable for your home, whether that means making it a daily task because you go through so many dishes, or leaving it as an "as needed" task. Are there any dishes that are a big pain that you could do without? Toss them if they are yours to do so. If you hand wash, do you have the best tools for the job, or do you need to level up your dish-cleaning game the next time you go to the store?

Lastly, if your sink is crammed full of dishes right now and you're feeling anxious just thinking about how the heck you're going to tackle it, breathe. It's okay. Maybe you need to switch to paper plates for a little while until you can get things under control and develop a better dish-cleaning habit. <u>Be sure to ask for help if you need it!</u> There is no shame in trying to get back on track.

DAY 18:
TACKLE YOUR MOUNTAIN OF DIRTY LAUNDRY

You may recall from the Introduction that my pile of laundry used to be so big it was literally the size of my Volkswagen beetle. *So much!*

After talking to other women about their laundry systems, doing a bunch of research, and through trial and error, I've learned and put into practice many of the following things that I'll be sharing with you. Nowadays, the most laundry I ever have waiting to be done is a single basket's worth. That's quite a difference!

Not having a giant pile of laundry demanding my attention, reminding me how behind I am, and constantly making me feel like a "failure," has really helped me mentally. Plus, only having a single basket of laundry to do at a time has been exponentially less stressful to deal with! If laundry is a pain point for you, I hope you will find the same.

Today, I'm excited to share my hacks and the lessons I've learned with you as laundry is such a *foundational* part of having a clean home and being an adult! <u>Put into practice any of the following ideas that apply to you</u>. Some may not be conventional or the "norm," but <u>don't be afraid to try something new</u>! Remember, what you're currently doing isn't working. Together, let's find a *better* laundry method that *will* work for your household.

Eliminate

When the military called my husband and me to move to Japan, due to a unique series of events, I was forced to downsize from a full three-bedroom house to only *two suitcases*! While this forced minimalism upset me at the time, I now see it as a blessing. It showed me something I hadn't realized, as many First Worlders don't, when you own so much stuff, the stuff begins to own you.

<u>If I had to credit a single thing with helping me get my laundry under control, it would be this, drastically downsizing my wardrobe.</u>

Think about it, you can only wear one pair of jeans at a time, so why do you need ten pairs? I downsized to only two pairs of jeans, both with different styles. It helped a ton! With so few jeans available to me, it gave me no choice but to wash them, because there weren't any more to wear after I'd worn both pairs!

Limiting the number of clothes you have forces you to wash things more often, so why not use this to your advantage to ensure you stay on top of your laundry?

By no means am I saying that you must "go crazy" and donate things that are meaningful to you or that you use daily. Ask yourself if something sparks joy and use your judgment. You don't need to drastically downsize to only two pairs of jeans like I did. <u>Even if you get rid of a single pair, that's still one less item that you'll need to wash in the future.</u>

You may be motivated to jump right into decluttering your clothes, like the KonMari method mentioned the other day encourages you to do. However, I suggest you follow the ClutterBug method instead and do a little bit at a time, at least while you're still going through this guide. A lot of the suggestions moving forward will not even align with what Marie recommends. But I believe that by only doing a drawer today and another tomorrow, the possibility of feeling overwhelmed and things being left messier than they were before may be lowered.

To eliminate extra hanging clothes: Turn all of your clothes hangers so that the hooks face *towards* you. Anytime you take something out, flip the hanger so that the hook then faces *away* from you. After a determined period of time, maybe quarterly like it is listed on your chore chart, donate all of the clothes on hangers that are remaining hung up in the initial position. This is an easy way to see which clothes actually get worn and which ones are just hanging around. No pun intended.

To eliminate extra folded clothes: Keep reading, because you may not be folding clothes in the future. However, if you insist upon it, a trick I came up with uses the KonMari method.

Marie suggests you place clothes vertically in your drawers so you can see what you have to wear without messing your folded items up. Unlike what she suggests though, I don't organize them by color. <u>I organize my clothes by what I've worn most *recently*.</u>

Anytime I put freshly cleaned things into the dresser, I only put them in, in the front. After a few months, I look at the clothing all the way in the back of the drawer. If I've forgotten about an item or wasn't needing it enough that I looked in the back where I can't see, I don't ever wear it. I'll then consider if I should donate it or not.

Limit your sheets to one set per bed. If you only have one set of sheets, you have to wash them once you've stripped them off your bed. Otherwise, you won't have any for that night! Plus, only having a single set per bed means <u>you'll never have to go through the hassle of folding fitted sheets again</u>. Not only will this save you time folding, but it'll also free up space in your linen closet, which is always nice.

Limit your towels to one per person. Each person in your household only needs one towel. If you're a woman with long hair, maybe two. Not only will this lessen the volume of laundry you have to do, but it'll also eliminate folding because there won't be a surplus of towels that need to be stored. Just give each person their own designated hook, and then wash and hang the towels right back up.

Instead of getting rid of extra towels you don't use, you could cut them up to be repurposed as cleaning cloths. Doing this won't cut down your laundry, but it is a good way to be eco-friendly and it will save you money on cleaning supplies. But of course, you could donate them just the same.

Stop Adding to Your Problem - Adopt the Exchange Rule

After you've gotten rid of extra clothing you don't need, be careful not to undo your hard work by filling the empty space back up! If you're a shopaholic and this might be a problem, consider implementing the Exchange Rule: If you bring anything new in, you have to remove something to make room for it.

I stopped buying clothes often because we didn't have space in our tiny house overseas, and I knew I was going to be limited to only two suitcases again when I moved back to the United States. I had to learn to curb my consumerist habit, and it might help you as well to prevent the issue you had before.

I found an easy way to do this by creating and implementing the Exchange Rule for myself. <u>It forced me to consider if I *really* wanted to buy</u>

<u>something new because then I'd have to get rid of something that I already had, had spent money on, and *liked*.</u>

If you do this, try limiting yourself to only so many hangers, one dresser, or only so many drawers in that dresser if you share it. You may recall that limiting yourself in this way is called the Container Method, which we talked about back in the chapter on eliminating clutter.

Stop Being Picky

A few days ago, you read that the way I caught up on my giant pile of laundry was by hiring a local lady through Facebook. But what I didn't mention before, was that even though this helped me get back on my feet, I soon found myself drowning in it again! I didn't have a system for washing and putting things away. Instead, I kept doing laundry the same way I had been despite the fact that that's what led to the pile in the first place.

What eventually helped me was realizing that clean laundry, however it is cleaned, is still better than dirty laundry.

I stopped being picky about how it got done and began washing everything together. By stripping away the extra work and resorting to the most basic of steps, I began to be on top of my laundry regularly.

This is also about the time that I adopted the quote, "Done is better than perfect " as my mantra (quote by Sheryl Sandberg), and even dubbed it my "Saying of the year." It helps remind me that my need for everything to be done well is not always necessary nor realistic. And whenever I find my perfectionism tendencies hindering me, whether with laundry or anything else, I repeat this saying to myself. Keep this quote in mind if you similarly struggle and think it will help you.

Now in regards to you washing all of your clothes together, I know some of you may be thinking, "But what about colors bleeding!?" This problem seems to be a thing of the past with modern-day laundry machines, and that's not just my own opinion. In all my loads of combined colors, I've never had color bleeding occur. The key is to wash everything in cold water. I used to think that hot water cleaned better than cold. Much to my surprise, I learned that hot water actually sets in some stains (except when it comes to whites). Plus, it's harsher on fabrics and can shrink, fade, and damage your clothing. It's more costly too. Cold water seems to be the way to go, so toss everything in, and run it on the coldest setting.

If you're still too hesitant to run it all together, use these color-grabbing sheets and wash with confidence.

I know that some people have strong opinions when it comes to washing their clothes. Ultimately, it'll be your choice if you want to switch to doing your laundry this way. But I encourage you to consider washing everything together if that little bit of saved time and effort is going to be *the thing* that helps you get this part of your life under control.

Using this method doesn't have to be permanent. This may just be something you do for a little while until you get caught up and have a better routine.

Improve Your Stain Removing

How is learning about stain removing going to help you catch up on laundry or get it done faster? Effectively removing stains the first time around will help lessen your volume of laundry because stained items won't keep being put back through the washing machine taking up room from other things.

With so many stain removers out there, which should you choose? Save your money testing random ones and give these tried-and-true stain busters, recommended to me by other women, a try!

Shout: Triple-Acting - My mother uses this for getting out the tough stains that come from living on a farm. It's good for grass stains, animal poop stains, tractor oil stains, and even blood. You name it.

The original blue Dawn dish soap - Dish soap can be used for laundry? Yes. It's gentle enough for ducks, but tough enough to clean oil off of them. Why wouldn't it be gentle on clothing and tough on your stains too?! You can't argue with that logic, nor with its inexpensive price. This is specifically good for spot-treating grease stains.

Dreft Stain Remover - This was recommended to me by a mom friend. If it's strong enough to get baby spit-up off of clothing, it's also strong enough to get out those stains that randomly appear when you're a hot mess woman! I appreciate that this formula is made with plant-based ingredients and that it is hypoallergenic. Surprisingly, it's affordable too.

Regular Tide - Another mom suggested this to me. Instead of using Tide as her laundry detergent, she rubs a dab of it wherever there is a spot that needs attention. She then washes the whole load in a less expensive detergent while the stain gets the extra power-removing strength of Tide.

Tide to Go Pens - According to Tide, 72% of the stains that occur when people are out and about are from food and drinks. That's what they designed these pens for. Unlike the other options, these are small enough that you can carry them with you. They enable you to remove a stain as soon as it occurs, while it's still wet and has the best chance of lifting. Make your laundry easier *later* by not letting stains set up *initially*. These are a must-have for us hot messes!

No matter if you use one of these stain removers or if you have your own you swear by, the part that really matters when it comes to effectively removing stains is that you do *not* pass your clothing through the dryer until the stain has been removed.

I used to pull things out of my drawer and throw them right into the hamper if I saw a stain on them, leading to me doing more laundry than I should have had. I didn't realize heat sets stains, and because those clothes had already gone through the dryer, it would be difficult if not impossible to get their stains out.

To prevent permanently damaging your clothes, look at each item before you toss it into the washing machine. Spray any stain and, depending upon the instructions of the product you're using, allow it a few minutes to sit and work. Wash with cold water if the clothing is not white. After washing, look at the clothing that was soiled again. If the spot remains, pre-treat the item and wash it once more. Repeat until the stain is gone, *then* dry.

Stop Putting in Effort Where It's Not Needed

I used to meticulously fold my husband's and my clothes whenever I did get around to putting them away. I thought I was being a "good wife" by doing this for him, but I often got *so upset* when I found his previously folded items completely disheveled. I felt *disrespected* that he didn't appreciate the time I spent making his things neat.

<u>I never stopped to think about the fact that *he didn't care*, that it was only me who wanted his clothes folded.</u> It didn't matter to my husband, *so why did it matter* to me?

Now, I wash all of our stuff together, but then we each put away our separate things. I saved myself time and even improved our marriage when I stopped folding his clothes. These days, it's rare for me to fold his laundry, so when I do, he notices and appreciates it. Plus, I no longer feel taken advantage of or unappreciated.

<u>Splitting up this chore has been a game-changer as far as helping me always get my laundry *done*.</u> There is just something about seeing a big pile of laundry cut in half that suddenly makes putting away the resulting smaller pile much more manageable.

Would this example apply to your household and help you finally get those clean clothes where they belong? Despite now having someone assigned to this chore, if there are still problems with getting clean clothes put away why not make everyone responsible for their own?

<u>Put into practice what you read in the section about sharing chores</u>. Be sure to communicate with the other person about this idea beforehand, then focus on holding up your half of the equation. Remember, even if it takes the other person multiple days to address their pile, don't put it away for them.

Most importantly, <u>don't correct them on how *they* want *their* clothes put away</u>. If they don't care enough to prevent their clothing from becoming wrinkled, they can deal with wearing the resulting wrinkles.

That example won't apply to you if you live by yourself or with a roommate. But you may be putting in effort where it's not needed in other ways, like by overwashing.

Without knowing what the recommendations are for how often things should be cleaned, you may be washing things more than they need to be, giving yourself extra work. I'm not saying you shouldn't wash something that's visibly dirty or smelly, but certain items, depending upon their material, how they're used, and what they're used for, can go multiple uses before needing to be cleaned.

For instance, body towels *should* only be used when you're clean, so you don't need to wash them every time you use them. According to the American Cleaning Institute, they only actually need to be washed every three to five uses.

Different sites have different suggestions on how often things should be cleaned, but my point is that increasing the number of uses you get out of an item before washing it will lower your volume of laundry.

It never occurred to me to have a set place where my husband and I could keep our clothes that weren't very dirty and could be worn again. Everything was tossed onto the ground. Then I'd scoop it all up and throw it into the dirty clothes pile, thereby making things that were practically clean just as dirty as what surrounded them. I was unintentionally creating *even more* work for myself.

Make things easier on yourself and learn from my mistake. Wear things that you can more than once, but also designate a place for them so that everything doesn't get mixed together. <u>A good place to put these clothes that is out of the way is on hooks that are on the inside of your bedroom door.</u> You can find over-the-door hangers with hooks on them so that you don't have to put any holes into anything.

Make It Easier to Put Things Away

For myself and many other women, the part of the process where the clean clothes get put away seems to be the hardest. Up until that point, the machines do the majority of the work. But when it's time to fold, the whole process comes to a screaming halt! Clothes are tossed onto the couch with good intention to be folded later. Yet, they end up living there for a week or more. Does this sound familiar?

I was so bad at putting away laundry that my clothes didn't even make it to the couch. Most of the time they lived in my dryer! How did I go from living out of my dryer to having everything put away? You just learned a big part of the equation, splitting up the responsibility. But there are some additional ways you can make things *even* easier.

First, there is sorting.

Towels don't take a lot of time to sort unless you have bathrooms with different colored themes or live with lots of people who all have their own special ones. But if you want to take what little time you will spend and make it zero, have all of your towels be the same color. And if everyone in the house has their own designated hook, like was mentioned before, <u>you won't have to sort *or* fold!</u> This method makes putting your towels away so easy that you'll have no excuse not to.

Not sure what color you want them all to be? Having white towels allows you to bleach them and clean them in hot water. This sanitizes and kills the bacteria growth responsible for musty smells.

If you want colored towels though, like I prefer, you can also kill viruses and bacteria with vinegar. Vinegar can deodorize your towels as well, and works as a natural fabric softener. It is so cheap and versatile, I use it with every load I wash no matter what I'm washing. Just <u>run it with the load during the rinse cycle.</u>

Another area where you can save time sorting is with socks. Following the same idea as the towels, if you only have one color and style of sock, there is no sorting ! It sounds basic, but it's brilliant. Want to not fold as well? <u>Just get a designated sock basket or drawer and toss them in</u>. When you want them, grab two. No folding required.

Besides sorting, folding seems to be the other time-sucking culprit. I've already shared a few ways you can avoid it, but what about when it comes to the "regular" clothes like shirts and pants?

The No-Fold Method

 My husband is very on-trend, at least in the mom community. I've been seeing more and more moms, especially those with very young ones, not folding anything anymore. Many have realized that tiny baby clothes just don't wrinkle, so why would they waste time folding something when that's not an issue? You can apply the same concept to yourself!

This, as we talked about earlier, is another area where you may be putting in more effort than is necessary. <u>Underwear, socks, undergarments, tight shirts, and leggings don't show wrinkles</u>. So stop folding them if you want to save time.

If you can handle the chaoticness of this method, stuff these items, and anything else that doesn't wrinkle, into their designated drawers. Wadded-up clothing *will* take up more space than folded items, so here is yet another reason for you to downsize your wardrobe.

Of course, when it comes to things that will show wrinkles, like dress shirts, you'll still need to hang them up. Also, things that are bulkier, like sweatshirts and sweaters, will take up a lot of room in your drawers. I recommend hanging these as well, or just get rid of more things in your drawers to accommodate.

Hang Everything

Speaking of hanging, some people insist upon doing only that. Hanging up everything, while not as fast as stuffing things into drawers, *is* quicker than folding. Some things like socks and underwear will still require a drawer, but everything else can be hung.

If you're moving all your clothes from your dresser into your closet, you may need to switch to these velvet hangers as their thinner design allows you to pack in more and maximize your space. Another benefit to them is that their fuzzy material grips your clothing and keeps things from slipping off their hanger. These are also supposed to help minimize those unsightly shoulder bumps.

Try out one of these methods or combine them, and see how much time you can shave off putting your clothes away!

How to Stay On Top of Your Laundry Once Caught Up

Develop a Routine

Once you finally get caught up, how will you *stay* caught up? Create a routine so that your laundry gets done *consistently* and doesn't have a chance to build up again.

Your chore chart comes set up with two laundry days a week. However, you may prefer to save everything for a single day. As briefly mentioned before, if you combine both days into one, this will free up the other as a rest or chore-free day. This would be the most energy-conscious option, as you'll be washing larger loads rather than lots of small ones.

<u>If washing a week's worth of laundry on one day sounds like too much for you, you may need to take the flip approach and do a load every day.</u> This is more common for those with large families, but I still know women who do a load every day even though they live by themselves. Personally, I can't rationalize running a whole load, albeit on the smallest cycle, just for a single shirt and pair of pants. But if you know you'll be more likely to put away your laundry if you only have to do what you wore that day, maybe this is the approach you should take for now.

You also have the option to leave the schedule as is. I found that doing laundry two days of the week works best for me, as it provides the benefits of having a single laundry day while splitting the workload in half.

<u>If this is a problem area for you, don't give yourself an excuse not to do it!</u> Make sure you don't put it off by limiting time-consuming or stressful things on the day/s when your laundry is scheduled. Your Daily tasks still need to happen, but something like having friends over or cooking a big meal can be scheduled for another time. I try to pair the days when I do my laundry with the days when I don't have to cook and we have leftovers to eat. That way the *only thing* on my plate is getting the laundry done.

Give Yourself a Limit

I know some people find having multiple laundry baskets helpful, whether they are for sorting, multiple rooms, or different people. If this idea works for you, I'm happy to hear it. However, I want to caution you that this method doesn't work for everyone, and could make things worse.

I used to have six laundry baskets, all bought with the good intention of helping me sort my loads. What I found was that these *added* to our problem. <u>They *enabled us* by giving us more space to fill up.</u> Even after all the baskets were full, I still put off doing the laundry because I then felt overwhelmed by how much there was to do! We threw more and more onto the baskets until they overflowed and weren't even used. Thus, our laundry "mountain" was born.

Before, my laundry pile was practically limitless. Now, I've restricted myself to a single basket, and when it's full, I wash the clothes. <u>Giving myself a cap on how much dirty laundry I can have at a time, combined with having a set routine, has helped me stay on top of my laundry</u>.

Having one basket for dirty clothes may not work for everyone. But I do suggest you set a laundry limit in some way so that you never again get so far behind you can't catch up, or so overloaded you don't even start.

Go Back to Sorting?

After you've nurtured better laundry habits for yourself, you may begin to wonder if you should start sorting again. You know that sorting by color is not necessary, but what if I told you that there is another option?

<u>Only try this new method and begin sorting again if you're *consistently* caught up on laundry and no longer feel behind</u>. I washed everything together for months before I convinced myself that I'd developed better laundry habits. I then cautiously made the switch to this. However, some days I still wash everything together if I'm busy and just need to get it done.

Instead of sorting by color, sort by *texture*.

<u>If you're washing a thick, fluffy towel with thin, silky pajamas, do you think everything is going to get cleaned *equally* ?</u> It doesn't matter if the towel and pjs are the same color. What matters is that one fabric will absorb most of the detergent while the other will be left wanting. The items that absorb a lot of detergent will get dingy with residue leftover on them. And the thicker items will rub at the more delicate pieces, leading to early wear and tear on your clothing.

After learning about this method, I changed my laundry system. I now sort all of my clothes and linens by their texture and weight. My only exceptions to this are whites and heavily soiled items.

I sort by these generalized categories:

Heavyweight/Durable - Thicker, bulkier items like jeans, my husband's military uniform, cotton t-shirts, thick wool socks, sweatshirts, and old clothing that doesn't need a lot of tender loving care - This is often my largest load so sometimes I will split this up further keeping the most similar textures together

Lightweight/Delicates - Silky or thin items like my polyester shirts, thin workout shorts, underwear, silky pillowcases

Whites - The only load I run on hot water

Towels - All our towels, hand towels, and cleaning cloths that aren't heavily soiled

Super Dirty - I only run an additional load for this if it is needed, like if we gardened or if I have a bunch of really dirty cleaning cloths

<u>Sorting by these categories allows you to tailor your approach to specific textures</u>, particularly lightweight clothing. Because this load is made of thin, delicate material, I know that it needs very little soap and as little time drying as possible. I may even choose to hang it all to preserve it from the heat of the dryer.

I do occasionally stray from these categories depending upon what I'm washing and the size of the load. If I'm washing our bed's thick blankets, I'll throw in like textures, such as my fleece pajamas. However, just because I'm doing my bed's linens does not mean I also throw in my thin cotton sheets. These will get washed with their own similar textures, like with my cotton shirts.

<u>If this way of sorting appeals to you, try it out! But if you're fine with continuing to wash everything together, why give yourself more work?</u>

Action Plan

If cleaning or putting away laundry is a problem for you, your homework today is to determine what you've been doing (or not doing) that is causing you to have an issue with this chore.

Come up with a plan to solve that issue and catch up on your laundry, whether that means doing a little every day, hiring someone, enlisting a friend, or taking it all to the laundromat on a weekend to get it done and over with.

Determine what you will do differently to stay on top of it moving forward. <u>What ideas from today will you adopt</u>? Will you get rid of extra linens so that each bed will only have one set? Will you try out the Exchange Rule or the No-Fold Method? Do you need to spend some time this evening talking to your spouse about them taking care of their own laundry?

Decide when you will do your laundry on a routine basis, whether that is every day, biweekly, or weekly, and adjust your chore chart to reflect your decision.

DAY 19:
ELIMINATE A POINT OF TENSION

Oftentimes, we repeatedly do tasks the same way we've always done them, ways we learned from our parents, or ways we've seen everyone else do them. We seldom stop to question if the way we are doing them is the *best* for *us*.

Today, I want you to think about one Point of Tension, or POT for short, that is causing some minor discomfort in your life.

A POT might be *something* or some *way* of doing something that isn't the smoothest, that causes you anxiety, extra work, extra time, or that is for some reason difficult enough that you often put it off.

A POT might also be a specific *area* or something that is often referred to as a Hot Spot. <u>A Hot Spot is an area of your home that tends to get messier than others.</u> This might be an entryway table that is right next to your front door where everyone dumps their stuff when they get home.

We're going to work to eliminate a POT of your own to make your life just a little bit easier. To solve it, <u>you may have to question *how* or *why* you are doing some things the way you are and convince yourself that it is *okay* to change what you're doing</u>, that it doesn't have to be done a certain way. <u>You may even have to let go of some of your limiting beliefs.</u>

How to Solve a POT

You may recall in the chapter about washing dishes that I mentioned that there is most likely a product already out there that will make the thing that you're struggling with easier. <u>If you're having an issue with something, somebody else probably did as well</u>! So take heart. Any time you're dealing with a POT, there is most likely a solution. You just have to discover it.

First, consider what area, thing, or way of doing something is causing tension or a bottleneck in your system. Next, consider if there is a different action you could take that would solve that problem. And finally, if you haven't been able to solve the POT yet, see if there is a product that could. <u>I recommend only purchasing something as a last resort to help you</u>

<u>conserve financially.</u>

Sometimes, changing up how you do a POT will resolve it. Other times, you'll need a

different tool for the job. Occasionally, you'll need a combination of the two, a different approach and a new product.

POT Examples & Solutions

I'll give you a few examples of some POTs that I had in my life that while small, still contributed to stress, and were a relief once solved.

The first example involves the Efficiency Over Esthetics Rule. It caused me to question, and then let go of, the limiting belief I had for where I could and "couldn't" keep my laundry hamper.

I noticed that when my husband got home from work, his work clothes wouldn't make it ten feet inside of the door. Our laundry basket was all the way upstairs on the opposite side of the house, so his clothes would just be left on the floor to be picked up later.

What did I do? I swallowed my pride about how nice my front entrance looked, and moved our dirty clothes hamper right next to the front door. This solved the problem!

Doing this also encouraged my husband to use the One-Touch Rule, as he could take off his dirty work clothes and put them *right into* the hamper, instead of onto the floor and *then* into the hamper.

The second example was able to be solved with a different product.

I like to send my husband to work with homemade coffee every day. It's a little way I can show him I love him, and a big way we can save money. (I used to spend whole paychecks getting multiple coffees every day, so I know it adds up! You'll learn more about this when we talk about budgeting another day.)

The issue I was having was that my husband would forget to bring home his travel mug until a week or more had gone by. By then, the remaining contents would be so gross I'd barely want to clean it! Plus, he didn't go to work with coffee all of those days in between when I was waiting for him to bring it home. This also led to minor friction in the relationship, because I was constantly reminding him to bring home the mug.

I solved this POT by finding and getting these super cute disposable to-go cups made for hot beverages.

Despite having to repeatedly buy these and not using something reusable, we are still able to save money when compared to him buying coffee every day. These cups hold up quite well, and can even be used two or three times. Now, if he forgets to bring home his cup, it isn't a loss. If it is left to sit, it can just be thrown out. There is also no more pressure on him to bring his travel cup home.

Let's address the entryway table Hot Spot I mentioned earlier for the third example.

You could cover the top of the table with cute decor so that there is no room for junk to be dumped on it. This is what I do with mine, and I haven't had a problem. You could alternatively implement some sort of organizational system right there so that everything could be put away. You could also designate a dump bin where everything could be contained and moved out of sight. If you choose this option, make sure you come up with a routine where you regularly empty that bin and put stuff away. As a last resort, you could simply remove your entryway table.

The fourth example is yet another thing that I'm embarrassed to admit, but one that I hope you can learn from.

For a long time, I struggled with cleaning my cat's litter box. I despised this chore. It's gross, dusty, and smelly! This was something that I put off and got overwhelmed with more often than I'd like to share. However, I knew that I needed to solve this POT for my cat, my sanity, and the sanitation of my house.

Solving this problem took a lot of trial and error. I tested out many different litters to see which ones made cleaning easier. I tried different containers, liners, scoops, and even an automated litter cleaning box. I tried it all. <u>What eventually ended up solving it was a combination of different actions *and* products as well as me remembering, once again, the Efficiency Over Esthetics Rule.</u>

Having the scoop close to the litter box and not hidden away out of sight, like I tried to make work for so long, made all the difference. Now, I have a good setup with the right litter, box, scoop, routine, and placement of my scoop which all help me stay on top of this regularly.

What will make all the difference for you? Where could you remove friction and make something as easy as possible? Let's find out.

Action Plan

Now it's your turn. What POT could you solve today? Can you use any of the other things you've learned to help you? What limiting beliefs or habits of doing things a certain way that you've always done them might be holding you back?

You only need to eliminate one POT for your homework. But feel free to repeat this exercise in the future as many times as you need to, to make your life easier!

DAY 20:
PAY YOUR BILLS

You might recall when reading through the Introduction of this guide that I mentioned how my water bill was turned off because I forgot to pay it. I had to take my dogs' dish over to a neighbor's house to ask them for water so my pups could drink. It was mortifying and completely avoidable.

Today, we'll be discussing how to pay your bills, or more specifically, how to use autopay so that you can avoid the same cringe-worthy experience I had. And if you have had a service turned off before, how you can avoid that from happening *again*.

But why would you sign up for autopay when having a paper bill is better? <u>You may think that paying your bills manually gives you more control over the situation by letting you see exactly how much your bill is and if there are any extra fees</u>.

I understand your reasoning because I used to think the same thing. However, when my husband and I paid our bills manually, it *didn't* lead to us finding any hidden fees. Instead, it lead to us losing out on savings that we would have had by getting the paperless and autopay discounts. We also ended up *wasting* money by paying late fees and fees to turn things back on.

<u>Being signed up for autopay can actually save you money, save you time, and take one more thing off of your plate</u>, or at least it did in our case. It really makes life easier and is something that I think is *especially* important for us hot mess gals who can easily forget things. Getting your bills paid is *not* something that should be forgotten, so why allow room for you to drop the ball? And why, when you already don't have enough time to do everything you want to do, would you spend your time doing something that you *don't* need to?

Of course, it is your decision whether you will automate your bills or not. However, let me remind you once again that what you've been doing hasn't been working. So <u>give this a try if you've been unsuccessful with getting your bills paid consistently any other way</u>. If your bills are already automated, keep reading, because you'll still have some homework to do later on.

Pay Your Bills

Before we get into *how* to pay your bills, I think it's very important to take a second to discuss *when* to pay them. No matter what process you want to use to get your bills paid, I recommend you <u>try to move them (at least the most vital ones) to the beginning of the month or to whenever you have a paycheck.</u> This way, you'll be able to make sure your bills are paid first. <u>You might not have enough money to do something fun with after you pay them, but at least you'll have a place to stay and the essentials taken care of.</u>

<u>If you're paying a mortgage, see if you can scrape together enough to pay a whole extra payment one month ahead</u>. If you do this, you'll have created a safety net for yourself just in case you fall on hard times and can't pay one month for some reason.

With Automation

Unfortunately, <u>I can't walk you through how to sign up for autopay (or even how to sign up for service in the first place) as every company is different</u>. However, there should be prompts on every service provider's website that will guide you. If you're having issues, call the company so they can walk you through the process.

To begin, go to your service provider's site and follow their prompts to create an account. Despite having received service from them in the past, you'll most likely still have to do this if you've never logged into their site before. Then follow the prompts to sign up for autopay.

When it's time for you to enter your payment method, use your credit card if the company allows you to. This is because if you ever need to, <u>disputing charges to your credit card is easier than disputing them on your debit card or disputing charges pulled directly from your bank account.</u>

Now that your autopay is set up, how do you see how much your bill is every month? <u>You can look at the digital copy of your bill through your provider's site</u> where they will list all of your expenses, including any additional fees. <u>You can also sign up to receive emails from them where they will let you know the total of your bill.</u>

Alternatively, you could look through your bank statements at the *end* of the month (assuming that you have enough money to pay all your bills beforehand) to see which service providers pulled money out and how much they pulled. If you do this, you'll avoid having to log into every company's website to see how much they charged you. Plus, you'll be able to see all of your utility expenses at once. This will make it easier for you to then log how much they were into your budget, which is also something that I recommend you do at the end of the month (we'll talk about this in the financial chapters).

Another way you could view your bill is by opting to *continue* receiving paper statements from your provider and *not* signing up for paperless. However, if you do this you'll miss out on any paperless discount that your company might offer.

With Your Bank

So what do you do if you're still not fully convinced that you want to automate your bills? Have your *bank* pay them! While it won't do this automatically, it will notify you when it's time to.

This is a great option if you want to still feel a little more in control, but don't want to risk forgetting a bill and having to pay a late fee. With this option, you can verify that you have the funds to pay a bill before paying it. If you don't, you may be able to delay it a few days before accepting and sending your payment through the bank. Even better, this is often at no additional charge to you!

If you're interested, contact your bank to see if they offer this service. Certain banks like Chase offer rewards for paying your utilities through them! You can save up your points to get cash back, gift cards, trips, and merchandise like iPads. So this might be worth it to you to check out.

Save Where You Can

After you sign up for an online account, have a look around each of your providers' sites or call them to see if they can offer you a lower deal. See if you're also eligible for any discounts, such as if you get a military discount or an employee discount if you work at certain places.

As I mentioned, they might also offer a paperless discount and a separate autopay discount as well. So be sure to ask for these! By signing up for paperless with my internet company, I was able to save $2 per bill. While that's not a lot, it adds up! Plus, when you sign up for this you're being eco-friendly and reducing the clutter that comes into your home, so why wouldn't you?

Your electric company may be able to offer you additional savings. So take this opportunity to find out if they have any kind of time advantage energy rate plan.

This plan allows you to save money by switching the time of day when you run your appliances. Where I'm currently living, in Prattville, Alabama, ninety percent of the day is priced at 6.9540 cents per kWh. The other ten percent is priced at more than *four times* the amount (26.9540 cents per kWh). Considering the vast price difference between the peak and non-peak hours, as well as having the convenience of running your appliances the majority of the time, this plan is worth looking into!

If you decide this plan is right for you, use your company's economy hours to tailor your cleaning schedule. At my electric company, economy hours for the summer are all weekend long and weekdays before 1 pm and after 7 pm. Using these hours as an example, you could switch doing your laundry from Wednesdays and Saturdays to Saturdays only. And instead of starting your dishwasher whenever it is full, you could start it right before going to bed (like I suggested you do).

After talking to my electric company at length, I learned that this plan is better suited to women who work outside of the home. This is because those women can turn down their AC when they go to work, so the biggest energy user (the AC) is running less during those peak hours. Because I keep my AC running all day long to keep myself comfortable, it is not a good plan for myself or anyone else who works at home.

If I hadn't taken the time to call my provider and hash out which plan was right for me, I would have switched to the time-sensitive one and ended up paying more (because the peak hours cost more on that plan)! This is again why I suggest you call your provider and get clarification on whether something is right for you or if you can save in any way. I'll talk about even more ways you can save money on your bills in the finance section. But I'll briefly mention here, as it is worth mentioning more than once, that you should occasionally reevaluate the companies that you get service from and compare them to other companies to see if you're getting the best deal.

If you're unsure what companies service your area, go to https://www.inmyarea.com/utilities to find them using your zip code.

<u>My internet provider recommended that I call them every *three months* to see if they have a better deal, and to do so for all of my other providers as well</u>. While I don't always stick to this suggestion, I do think it's a good idea to reevaluate at least one time a year.

I also found out in another call with a different provider, that some companies will remove a discount from your bill after a certain period of time and start charging you more. <u>To prevent your discount from expiring, you need to provide proof that you're still eligible for it</u>, at least when it comes to certain military discounts.

To address this issue, verify that you're getting all of the discounts that you qualify for, and to make sure that you're still getting the best deals, set a reminder in your calendar to call everyone you receive service from and see if they can offer you anything better than what you're currently receiving. Have this reminder repeat on a yearly (or quarterly) basis starting today.

Action Plan

Today, set up autopay for all of the bills and services that you have or set up payments with your bank.

Call your providers and ask them if they can lower your bill, give you a discount, or if they have any other plans that you can switch to. If you've been with a provider for a while, look into other companies that provide the same service and compare deals. If you already have autopay set up for everything, just focus on this step and the next two.

Make a plan to check your bill statements monthly and look for any discrepancies. Also, be sure to add that reminder to reevaluate your providers into your calendar.

DAY 21:
AVOID "DECLINED" EMBARRASSMENT

I remember going through a McDonald's drive-thru with my two roommates a decade ago. One of them turned to me and said, "Eat up. This will be the last meal we have for a while." I remember it distinctly, but not because going hungry was a rare occurrence at that time.

For months I'd been going multiple days without eating while waiting for my paycheck to come in. I guess this time stood out to me in particular because I'd never heard someone say those words out loud, "We won't be able to afford *to eat*." We can't afford a basic human necessity. I hope you've never had to experience this level of poverty. Thankfully, that time in my life is long past.

Recently, my husband and I fully paid off our home after only owning it for six years. A week after, we bought and paid for a car in full. We are both still in our twenties. To most people, either of these would have been quite a feat and something to be emulated, but I'm not telling you this to boast.

I'm telling you this so that you know I've lived with and without. I've been where you are right now, and there is hope for you! I'm also telling you this so that you know that my financial advice is sound and backed by proof.

Through these experiences, I've learned that being financially "fit" is one of the most *crucial* pieces to not just adulting, but adulting *well*. So let's get started and turn you from a broke hot mess to a financially savvy woman!

Why a Budget Is Important

Have you ever gone to buy something only to swipe your card and see those gut-wrenching words, "Card Declined?" It's embarrassing and frustrating! You might have to ask a friend to "cover" you, or ashamedly walk out of the store leaving behind things you *need*.

It was times like this when I wondered, as you may wonder yourself, "If I work all the time, why don't I have money?!"

Are you currently living paycheck to paycheck like I was? You're not alone. A startling 78% of people live this way.

You may think that if you were to just earn a *little* more, get a raise or a second job, it would solve your problems. Unfortunately, that's not the case. Of those who make $50,000 - $99,999 a year, 28% *still* live paycheck to paycheck. Even 10% of those who make $100,000+ live this way as well.

It turns out that after a certain threshold, it doesn't matter how much money you make. You could make $80,000 a year, but if you spent all $80,000 you'd still be just as poor as someone who makes $30,000 and spent all $30,000.

What matters is how much you save. So how do you keep from spending all your money so you can start saving? You budget.

I know for a lot of people, my old self included, having a budget sounds *restricting!* "I don't want to be told what to do with my own money," you may be thinking. "I work hard for my money, and if I want something I should get it. *I deserve it!*"

Contrary to what you may think, a budget, when designed correctly, can be *freeing*.

Picture this scenario where you live a better life *because* you budget:

Imagine that you're out running errands and see a nice pair of boots you want. Because you're a good budgeter, you have money set aside just for things like this. The money for these shoes is going to come out of a category called *Fun Money*. You can spend the money in this category however you want, on things that are indulgences like eating out, getting your nails done, or buying clothes.

You've budgeted $100 a week for your Fun Money, and because these boots are $89 you buy them *guilt-free*.

A little bit later, you see a cute bag in another store. "This bag would match the shoes I just bought perfectly," you think to yourself. You check their tag and see that they are priced at a point that would cause you to spend more than your $100 limit since you already used up the majority of it.

Even though you know you have more than enough money in your account to buy the bag, you stick to your budget and don't buy it, but not because anyone is *imposing* this restriction on you. Because you have self-discipline, and because you care about your future well-being, you stick to the budget *you* have given *yourself*.

After your errands are done you begin driving home, but along the way, your car blows a tire! Not only are tires expensive, but you'll also have to pay for towing and any damages incurred. Thankfully, you're prepared.

You've been diligently putting money into another category in your budget, your *Emergency Fund*. Every month, you've put a determined amount into this savings fund to be used in a time of need.

Because you budget, this week's tire emergency is not going to cost you next week's Fun Money and enjoyment, or worse, cause you to not be able to pay a bill! And because you *stick to* your budget, you have money when you need it.

Having a budget will help you be more in control of your life, and give you peace of mind knowing that you'll be able to take care of yourself when something happens. By keeping a closer eye on your money through a budget, you prevent it from dwindling away on frivolous things and instead spend it *intentionally* on what matters to you.

What Tools to Use

Now you understand why having a budget *and* sticking to it is so important. But where do you begin? There are many different tools you could use to set up a budget and track your spending.

Some of the top budgeting apps are:

EveryDollar: Dave Ramsey, a financial guru credited with helping millions of people get out of debt and live financially free, came up with this app. I've used it for years and love it. It's the app that helped my husband and me pay off our house early.

The Free Version:

Pros: It's free! It has a basic, easy-to-understand layout, and is almost completely customizable.

Cons: You have to input everything manually which is *very* time-consuming.

The Premium Version : Ramsey+

Pros: It automatically pulls in your transactions from your bank account for you. You get access to all of Dave Ramsey's helpful financial guides and his famous Financial Peace University. You also get to file your taxes for free with Ramsey SmartTax!

Cons: You still have to manually move and match up the pulled-in transactions into the categories they belong in. It costs $11 per month.

TrueBill: I only found this app recently, but I'm loving it. It does a lot of the things that the premium version of the EveryDollar app does except it doesn't cost you a penny!

The Free Version:

Pros: It's free! It automatically pulls in *and* categorizes transactions for you, saving you a ton of time. It also allows you to connect multiple different banks and even investment accounts. It has helpful graphs to let you know how you've been spending, and it has an impressive amount of notification options, so you can choose to be notified if an account is low on funds for example. This app's claim to fame is that it can negotiate your bills to be lower for you, though it does take a portion of any savings you get as payment. It even lets you know what subscriptions you have, which is super helpful when you've been paying for things you forgot you signed up for. It's beginner-friendly, though it is a little more complicated than EveryDollar.

Cons: You can only budget *two* categories, so it is ridiculously limited in building a customized budget. It only updates your information one time a day, so the amount of money it shows may be inaccurate. You also can't edit the names of transactions.

The Premium Version:

Pros: You can choose the price you pay down to as low as $3 per month. It's fully customizable, and it can cancel those subscriptions it found on your behalf! You can also sync it whenever you want to get a more updated, accurate picture of your finances.

Cons: It costs money.

You Need a Budget (YNAB): This app is <u>great for helping people who are in debt stop living paycheck to paycheck</u>. It helps you keep your spending in check because when you overspend in one category, it forces you to pull from another, showing you the real-life consequences of not sticking to your budget.

Pros: You can try it free for a little over a month, or get it free for a whole year if you're a student. Similar to the premium EveryDollar app, YNAB can pull in your transactions automatically but then it requires you to categorize them. However, this app will "learn" your categorization preferences so it will begin to auto-categorize things for you in the future. You can set up the app to notify you any time there is an action needed, which keeps you hands-on with your budget and makes sure you don't forget about it. You can categorize, reorder, and customize however you'd like.

Cons: It costs $12 a month, or $7 a month on a yearly plan. It also only offers automatic syncing to bank accounts in the United States or Canada. This app is more complex and detailed than others, so it'll take some time to learn how to use it.

YNAB's website offers a lot of helpful material at no cost to you, including these free workshops. Even if you choose not to use their app, I still recommend checking out their educational resources.

Mint: This app is very similar to Truebill, and even some of its graphs are the same.

Pros: It's *completely* free! Like TrueBill, Mint pulls in your transactions automatically *and* categorizes them for you. It also lets you track multiple different banks and investment accounts.

Cons: It doesn't offer as many different notification options as Truebill. It doesn't allow you to rename bank accounts for clarity, and it doesn't allow you to change the names of the main budget categories, though you can create new personalized subcategories. Also, there is a long list of default categories that you have to sift through every time you want to manually categorize a transaction. Similar to YNAB, it only supports linking to banks in North America.

Choose a single app or experiment with multiple to find one that works for you. There are plenty of other apps out there that you could look into as well. What's important is that you <u>find a setup you like so you're more likely to use it.</u>

If you don't want to use an app, this Budget Spreadsheet I've created for you is a great alternative. In this spreadsheet, you'll find an example budget, a guided template, and a blank template.

Even if you *do* want to use an app, I still recommend you use this spreadsheet in *addition* to it as this is the only way I've found to be able to see an overview of your total spending for the whole year (unless you use YNAB). <u>This will give you a better picture of how you're doing overall, as opposed to scrolling through a single month's spending at a time.</u> This will also make it easier to see spending trends so you can adjust your budget or behavior.

This Budget Spreadsheet has been thoughtfully designed so that it calculates your total income, expenses, and differences between them automatically. However, <u>there is one thing that it can't do, auto-populate your transactions. This is why I recommend you use this in accompaniment to an app</u>.

Download an app of your choosing, the Budget Spreadsheet, or both. Now it's time to set them up and break down your finances.

How to Set Up Your Budget

Depending upon what tool you chose, the majority of the setup will be done for you. Let's go over the basic steps together though so that no matter what you're using, you'll understand how to set up a budget. The process will be roughly the same whether you're married or single. However, if you're married, plan to do this *with* your partner. We'll talk more about how to shortly.

First, put down your take-home pay, that is the total amount of money deposited into your account *after* taxes have been removed. If you have any other jobs or ways you make money, include those amounts too. To make things easier and err on the side of caution, round numbers *down* to the nearest dollar. This will be your income section from which the other section will be subtracted.

Second, put down your expenses. The Budget Spreadsheet and most apps come with generic expenses listed for you. You can use these as a starting point. Look through your bank statements from the last month to see if there are any other things you regularly buy or pay for that need to be added to your expense list as well.

Then, determine how much each of these things cost you, going back a few months for reference. Don't guess amounts. Look at your bank statements, and to make things easier, round numbers *up* to the nearest dollar.

<u>Budget for the highest amount you've paid for something in the past or leave extra as a buffer.</u> This way, you're covered for any spending fluctuations.

For example, if you have a car you'll need to budget for gasoline. Don't just budget a random amount for it. Look at your past bank statements and find out how much you've paid for it in the past. Let's say how much you spent fluctuated between $76 to $85. Go with the higher amount or leave a little cushion. You could put down $85 or even $90 a month for your gasoline budget.

Next, think ahead to expenses that only happen occasionally. If these expenses are large, or even if they're small but you'd like to make them more manageable, create sinking funds for them.

<u>A sinking fund is a fund that you add to slowly and consistently over time to save up for something</u>. It's basically a financial goal with its own savings account. This is a great way to be prepared for large purchases or costly events. By splitting up the total cost over time, you lessen the financial burden on yourself when that big expense comes around. Some examples of sinking funds would be a pet's annual checkup, Christmas, or a house remodel.

Create sinking funds for any expenses you'd like to save up for that will only happen once or that happen yearly. Designate separate savings accounts for each and don't just lump them all together into one. Having a separate account for each goal is helpful so that you can keep the amounts clear, and so that there won't be any blurring or confusion about how much money a certain financial goal has.

Work these sinking funds into your budget by dividing up the total cost of the items or events by the number of months left until they come around. Some have been added to your Budget Spreadsheet already, but if you're using an app, you'll have to enter these financial goals manually.

Refer to the Budget Spreadsheet's example tab to see how the sinking funds are laid out, and for general inspiration.

While you're looking at the Budget Spreadsheet, let's go over a few last terms so that you'll better understand what things are if you plan on using it, and why things are set up that way.

FUN MONEY (also called an Entertainment budget): As mentioned earlier, this is a budget for spending however *you* want. This is your money for *fun* ! No one else gets a say in how you spend yours, just like how you don't get a say in how anyone else spends theirs.

Make sure to add this category if you're using an app and it's not included.

CONSUMABLES : I highly recommend you make your budget so that groceries and all other household items that get used up, like toiletries and cleaning products, are lumped together into one category. This makes checking out of a store way easier as you won't have to make multiple purchases and hold up the line. You also won't have to go back through your receipt to try to total up different budgets later (assuming that everything is some sort of consumable).

If you do decide to group them together, make sure to set aside more money for this category.

Your Budget Spreadsheet is already set up with a Consumable's budget, but if you'd like to keep your household products and groceries separate, set up your personalized budget to be that way. If you're using an app it will probably separate these things for you, but again, it may be in your best interest to change that.

MISCELLANEOUS : When you first get started budgeting, you're probably going to forget to include an expense here or there. This category is the thing that saves us hot messes when we have a brain fart ! As you become more of a budgeting pro you won't need this as much, but when you first get started it's nice to have just in case. Be careful not to pull from this when you've maxed out your Fun Money though!

This category is also already in your Budget Spreadsheet, but it may not be listed in your app depending on the one you chose. If it's not listed, I reco mm end you add it in as well.

There are many different ways you could set up your budget. Move categories around or rename things however you see fit. Make your budget personalized and laid out in a way that makes sense to you.

Now that you have your income and expenses written down, and your budget nicely organized how you want it, you'll be able to see a clear picture of your finances. But this is not accounting for any extra money you'll need to start building a better future for yourself.

You'll also need to set aside *additional* funds every month, which is why it's imperative that you bring home more money than your expenses consume. This extra money will go towards saving up an emergency fund, and then later, paying off your debt. We'll go more into those shortly, but for now, how much extra do you need? I believe a better question would be, how soon do you want to achieve financial security? Plan to set aside however much you can afford. The more you set aside, the faster you'll be able to create a safety net for yourself and work towards a debt-free life.

From now on, whenever I mention your expenses, this includes all those bills and things you just totaled up, as well as this extra money that will go towards improving your future.

If you're "in the red," and are currently spending more than you make, you'll need to find a way to lower your expenses. Luckily, there are many ways you can. We'll go over them in-depth in the next couple of days.

If you instead make more than you spend, congrats! You're already a step ahead. You'll still want to plan those extra dollars you have into your budget though because <u>if you allow loose money to sit unbudgeted, it's going to disappear on random things</u>.

That's why it's so important that you budget, or create a plan, for *every single dollar*. In a well-balanced budget, your income minus expenses should equal zero. Every dollar needs to be given a "job," and in this case, your extra dollars' first job will be building your safety net.

If you're single, you can skip this next part and jump right into learning about building that safety net in the form of an emergency fund.

How to Set Up a Budget with Your Spouse

Financial problems are one of the top reasons why couples get divorced, at 41%. So you both must be on the same page with this.

Talking about your finances with your spouse may be stressful because it serves as a reality check. Being realistic about your situation and determining if you're making ends meet or if you're instead drowning in debt can be upsetting! For men especially, who often bear the burden of the provider, this can be a *very* touchy topic. The details of your finances need to be brought to light though so that corrective action can be taken.

Figure out a time when the two of you can get together to make a budget, and follow the steps outlined above. <u>If you think this might become a heated conversation</u>, like mentioned before, <u>plan to have this discussion while out in public</u>, maybe over dinner at a restaurant.

One of you may be more mathematically inclined than the other. Regardless, I recommend you *both* partake in making it for two key reasons. Similar to getting the chore plan to succeed, <u>your spouse will be more likely to want the budget to succeed when they helped create it</u>. Plus, getting everyone involved and <u>seeing the numbers themselves will help them understand *why* they need to stick to the budget</u>.

This last part is crucial. If your partner is going to stick to the plan long-term, they need a better reason to cut out their double latte a day than just doing it begrudgingly because you, "Said so."

While you're planning your budget together, ask questions and keep the communication open. A good way to start would be by asking, "How much do *you* think would be an *appropriate* amount to allot to XYZ per month? " This way, you won't impose your opinions on the other person, and it will also keep the focus on spending realistically as opposed to setting superfluous limits.

This won't matter with things like bills, as you won't have a lot of say in how much they cost you. But when it comes to things like your Fun Money or any of the other nonessentials, amounts can be adjusted or cut, so they need to be discussed and have limits set for them.

Because opposites attract, oftentimes one person in the relationship will lean toward spending and impulsive buying, while the other will lean toward saving and being frugal. The saver may need to compromise by not being as "tight wadded," and allow for more freedom when planning the budget. The spender, on the other hand, may need to compromise by "reeling it in," and understanding that while they can still spend, they'll need to be a little more disciplined. To create a budget that will work long-term, you both will need to compromise and find a happy medium.

After you've set up a money plan you both agree on, determine who will be in charge of tracking the finances and updating the budget in the future. One person may be fine with tracking everything, or you may choose to split up who tracks what.

For example, since I'm the one who grocery shops, I'm in charge of that expense. I'm responsible for finding ways to lower the cost, tracking what I spend, and updating the budget accordingly.

You and your spouse also need to agree on a cap for large expenses. It can be difficult when one wants to buy the other an expensive surprise gift, but you both must come to an agreement on a limit and stick to it. <u>If one of you wants to buy something that exceeds that cap, you need to discuss it before purchasing.</u>

<u>This is not a way to control the other person. It is a way to show *respect* and *preserve* a balanced budget</u> without someone "blowing" all of the money on one thing and leaving nothing for the rest of the month. Or without someone trying to make a purchase, only to find the account completely drained without them knowing.

If you're worried that once you've created a budget one or both of you won't stick to it, hang in there as we'll be going over that in a few days as well.

Set up an Emergency Fund

Having an emergency fund ensures that your bills and other expenses will be taken care of because you won't have to use the money you would have on those things to pay for the emergency.

Having this buffer is important not only for preparedness but also because <u>it helps you be able to think through things more rationally</u>, as opposed to making impulsive decisions because you're in a place of desperation.

In the example given earlier, an emergency fund would also allow you to <u>take better financial action</u> and purchase a tire that would last longer, even if it was more expensive. This would be opposed to getting the cheapest tire you could afford, even if you knew it was a waste of money because it was poor quality and wouldn't last long.

<u>A good amount to aim for when first starting an emergency fund is $1,000</u>. I know that may seem like a lot right now, but saving for this needs to be a *priority* because you don't just need to be prepared for *if* an emergency will happen. You need to be prepared for *when* it will happen.

Make a plan to put whatever amount you determined you can set aside earlier (any extra money not going to a bill or another expense) into this account every month until you reach $1,000. <u>If you spend less for the month than you budgeted for, throw those unused dollars into this account as well to save up even faster.</u>

This money is not to be touched under any circumstances, except of course, in an emergency. A trip to the ER, a pet getting sick, a last-minute flight to see a dying loved one, a broken fridge, or a car towing would all be good reasons to pull from this account. Use your judgment, and don't "borrow" this money to pay for other things.

<u>If having the money sitting there will be tempting, move it to a place where it'll be harder for you to get to.</u> You could move it to an account linked to a specific card, and then not carry that card around with you. If you do a lot of your purchasing online, take the funds out in cash. Put the money in an envelope, and then tuck it out of sight. You could also see if a trustworthy friend or parent would hold onto it for you.

Ultimately, it'll be up to you to exercise some discipline and not touch that money if you want it to accumulate and be there for you when you need it.

I've already added an emergency fund to your Budget Spreadsheet, but if you're using another tool to budget, add in this crucial savings fund if it's not listed.

Pay Off Debt

After you've saved up your emergency fund, then you can start on the next step in your financial journey, becoming debt-free.

"The rich rule over the poor, and the borrower is a *slave* to the lender ." - Proverbs 22:7

Perhaps you're feeling that way right now, like a slave to your debt. You may be scraping together enough for minimum payments each month, but you know you have *years* of debt ahead of you. You may feel defeated, and accept that this is just the way things are. "This is the price you have to pay to get an education," you tell yourself. "This is the price you have to pay to get a good car, and I have to have a car to get to work…"

Luckily, paying off your debt is possible. You *can* do it with just a little discipline and a plan.

Plan to use the extra money that was previously building your emergency fund to next pay off your debt. And again, if you have anything left over at the end of the month, put it towards your debt as well.

You may be thinking, "Why use that extra money when I already have the minimum payments budgeted for and covered? I'll just pay the minimum, and it'll eventually get paid off. I should use this extra money for something fun instead!"

In the past, you may have thought that way. But I'll let you in on a little secret the credit card companies don't want you to know. Paying the minimum will only drag things out, costing you more money in the long run.

Credit card companies want you to stay in debt. Unless you pay your balance in *full*, your interest will pile up, meaning if you only pay the minimum payment, you'll end up paying interest that's *on top* of your old unpaid interest ! That's why you should be paying more than the minimum on your debt.

Now for the big question. How do you go about tackling your debt? Use this tried-and-true technique.

The "Debt Snowball" method:

Work to pay off the *smallest* debt you have while paying the minimum amount on all the others. Throw as much money as you can at it until it's paid off.

Move onto the second smallest debt. Use the money that would have gone to that first debt in *addition* to the minimum payment you were already paying on this second one. Throw as much money as you can at it until it too is paid off. Meanwhile, continue paying the minimum payments on the remaining debt.

Continue the process until you're done.

With this method you'll pay off bigger and bigger debts, faster and faster, thus creating a "Snowball" effect.

While you go, focus on paying things off that *lose* their value over time, like cars or electronics, as opposed to a house which typically goes up in value.

Check out the Budget Spreadsheet's Example Budget to see the "Debt Snowball" method in action, and how things may look for you while working to get out of debt.

In January, our fictitious woman put her extra money towards her smallest debt, while paying the minimum amount (her Expected Expense) on the others. In February, she spent more than she had budgeted for, as is visible by the Monthly Total being highlighted in red. Despite overspending in other areas, she still made the effort to at least pay the minimum payment to avoid fees and penalties. However, she'll need to be more conservative in the future if she wants to get out of debt sooner rather than later.

For this process to work, you'll first have to stop adding to your problem. You can't get out of debt if you continue to borrow. So stop using your

<u>credit cards</u> while you focus on paying them off.

If you're so far in debt that you can't see a way out, you still have options. It's called Credit Card Counseling.

There are nonprofit organizations out there that will put you on a Debt Management Program. They'll go through your current finances, set up a budget, cut unnecessary spending, and determine an amount that you can afford to put towards your debt. They too will suggest that while you're getting out of debt, and while they work with you, you stop using credit cards.

They'll stand in as the middle man for you so that you won't have to get those calls from the creditors anymore. They *may* even be able to get some fees waived and negotiate lower rates for you. You'll send them a lump sum, and then they'll pay all of the different companies you owe on your behalf.

<u>These services typically don't cost anything, or if they do, it's very little</u>. They offer free advice and may charge a small fee if they put you on the Debt Management Program. However, they may waive that fee if you can't afford it.
While these services specialize in credit card debt, many counselors can advise on other forms of debt too. If this sounds like the best option for you, check out the National Foundation for Credit Counseling for nonprofit financial guidance.

How to Avoid Going *Back* into Debt

After you pay off your debt you're going to feel liberated. But <u>be careful, it's easy to fall right back where you were</u>, especially if you haven't completely broken your bad spending habits.

Don't start racking expenses back up on your credit cards once they're paid off. If you can't help yourself, you might need to get rid of your credit cards permanently. Whatever you decide to do, don't undo all the hard work you put into getting out of debt!

In the future, instead of taking out a loan or putting something you want on credit, save up for it. From now on, if you don't have the physical cash or the funds in your bank to buy something, <u>you don't have the money for</u>

it. Be prepared by looking ahead for things that you'll want or need. If they are large purchases, consider creating sinking funds for them, like we talked about earlier. Make use of the great budget you just built, and create a plan to start saving up regularly *now* so you won't feel the need to go into debt over what you want/need later.

Saving up for something won't just save you money in interest, or help you live less stressed by being debt-free. By saving up and having the physical cash to purchase something, you'll most likely have a better shopping experience, enjoy faster customer service, and you may even get a lower price!

This is how my husband and I were able to buy a car without taking out a loan. Because we had cash in hand we had saved up, we were able to "slip in" and get a car that was technically already "sold" to someone else. We also received a discount for buying it fully right on the spot.

What's Next?

There's so much more to learn about budgeting and finances, but we only have so much time, and you've got a lot to do already. Once you've accomplished all this and would like to learn more, or even if you need more help than what was discussed today, I highly recommend you take Financial Peace University by Dave Ramsey.

I'm not sponsored by him, but I know his teachings have helped so many people, including myself. If you don't have the money to take his course, check with your local churches. I was able to take his course for free when my church purchased the program and offered it in group sessions. You can also get his program for free when you sign up for his app's Premium version, as I mentioned earlier.

Even if you choose not to purchase any of his services, his site still offers a lot of free tools you may find useful. Check them out!

Action Plan

I'll leave you with this Chinese idiom, "When you ignore money, money will ignore you." So don't ignore your money!

Today, decide which tools you'll use to track your finances, and then set up your budget.

If you're married, set up a time to sit down with your spouse and create your budget together. Also, determine who will track the finances in the future. Will one person be fully in charge of the budget, or will this responsibility be split up? If it will be split, decide who will track what.

DAY 22:
CUT EXPENSES PART 1

One of my favorite quotes by Dave Ramsey, and one that I say to myself often is,

"If you will live like no one else, later you can live like no one else."

In other words, if you want to save money or pay off debt so you have a better future, you're going to have to live *uncomfortably*. You're going to have to cut things that you'd *like* to keep, and maybe do things that you *don't* want to do. But don't worry, this is all just temporary.

Yesterday, you designed a killer budget. You looked at your income and expenses, and perhaps for the first time were able to see a clear financial picture. Whether you're making more money than you spend or spending more than you make, we all could use some tips to cut costs and live more frugally. That's why today and tomorrow we're going over ways to cut or at least lower your expenses.

A good place to start is by looking at the expenses you've already listed. If you're using the Budget Spreadsheet, you may have noticed that there are asterisks next to certain expenses. <u>These asterisks signify things that you can cut if you need to save money</u>, so refer to these if you need some guidance on where to begin.

Besides going over ways you could cut or lower those expenses you already have, I'm going to dive into other ways you could save as well. The more of these tips you apply to your life, the more you'll save!

Minimize One-Use Items

This may be a little confusing because in other chapters I encouraged you to use disposable items if you feel overwhelmed, need to save time, or need to take one more thing off your plate. However, I'm sure it comes as no surprise that repeatedly buying something will cost you more money than purchasing something once. So it'll be up to you.

If your finances are tight and you could spare a little time, consider using more reusable items. Of course, buying things that are meant to last *will* cost you more upfront, but they'll still save you in the long run.

Besides switching to the more obvious reusable items, like exchanging paper plates for ceramic plates, what other reusable things are out there? There are plenty of others, you just have to look. Take for instance this revolutionary new Period Underwear which replaces expensive period products and will eliminate your need to buy tampons and pads ever again.

The average woman will use an insane 9,120 tampons in her life! That's so many one-use products that are going to take *years* to break down in landfills. Plus, think of how much all of those tampons will cost you, and how quickly these panties will pay for themselves.

Instead of wasting money repeatedly buying dryer sheets, get these dryer balls. They don't only help reduce static, like dryer sheets do, but they also help reduce wrinkles. They even cut down on your machine's drying time by 10-25%, saving you money on electricity as well. Even better, these dryer balls are renewable and eco-friendly as they're made out of wool.

You could eliminate one-use K-Cups and get refillable K-Cups, or if you don't have a Keurig, a reusable coffee filter. Yes, they make those. You could get these reusable baking sheet liners that replace parchment paper and cooking spray, or similarly these reusable cupcake liners. There are even reusable sandwich bags that are thicker and can be washed in the dishwasher. According to their listing, one of these can replace up to 300+ disposable plastic bags.

You could also get these Silicone Stretch Lids which replace both plastic wrap and tin foil. Unlike those items, these lids provide an airtight seal that preserves your leftovers longer and stretches your dollars.

If you're feeling adventurous, you could get a bidet. This will replace toilet paper and give you as clean of a tush, if not cleaner.

One switch that helped me save *tons* was changing from using costly Clorox wipes and disposable floor cleaning pads, to cloths. Even things like paper towels added up in comparison to washing and reusing rags. You may recall in the laundry section that I mentioned repurposing excess towels as cleaning cloths. You could do the same with old t-shirts too. Or just go out and buy some cloths and stop using one-use items to clean.

While trash bags aren't necessarily reusable, my neighbor came up with this frugal idea. When his trash is full, he carries out the whole bin and then dumps the loose trash into the trash can. He keeps reusing the same trash bag until something sticks to it or until it starts smelling.

Invest in Good Quality Products & Maintain Them

It's tempting to buy cheap alternatives, but when getting something reusable, why not spend a little more and <u>get a high-quality product that will last a long time</u>?

For example, you could get an inexpensive piece of furniture from Walmart made out of particleboard. But will furniture made by a company that sells everything and that is known for having the "lowest" prices really hold up? How many more years do you think a solid wooden piece built by a company that specializes in good quality furniture last?

Even more importantly, once you own something, maintain it ! Use a cell phone cover on your expensive device to protect it (I'll cover this in more detail and give you my recommendations in a later chapter). Take your car to get regularly serviced and don't wait until it breaks down.

I feel like in this day and age we've developed an "if it breaks I'll just replace it" mentality. I know I've certainly been guilty of this. But more often than not, it's cheaper to keep something in good condition or running well, than it is to replace and buy a new one. So <u>take care of what you have</u>. This way, you'll get your money's worth out of it.

Stop Buying Brand New

I feel like it's important to next mention that investing in something that's built well does not mean you have to spend an arm and a leg. You can enjoy having nice quality things *and* not break the bank. You just need to thrift.

If you're not thrifting yet and are still paying full price for things, you're missing out! There have been so many times where I've found name-brand clothing with tags still attached. Once, I even found a purse worth a couple of hundred dollars! It blows my mind how much people will spend on things and then discard them. Let their loss be your gain.

Besides clothing, you can find brand new or gently used appliances, furniture, and building materials at thrift stores. The Habitat for Humanity Restock is an *excellent* source for these things. This nonprofit organization sells the items they don't use when building homes for the needy to the general public. When you buy from them, you support their mission and the community as the proceeds go back into the organization.

With so many second-hand stores out there, there's no need to go shopping to buy something brand new, unless of course if it's underwear. So save your money, have fun checking out all the unique things you'll find, and thrift instead of shop!

Use What You Have

I credit my parents with the saying, "The cheapest thing to buy is the thing you already have. " While I didn't always like hearing this, you can't argue with their logic.

Instead of buying the newest and greatest cell phone simply because it came out, stick with the one you have that's already paid off. Keeping and using what you have is not always the most *fun*, but it is the *frugal* thing to do.

If you received something as a present, use it before you buy something new. I know your Aunt Linda might not have your preferred taste in things or know what style you like, but if you have something sitting in your house, either regift it, use it, or use it up. That's one less thing you have to buy.

The same goes for products that you've bought, used once, and then stuffed in the back of your cabinet to forget about. You already spent money on them, so use them! And of course, use up every drop before buying a replacement.

If you have leftovers, eat them! We talked about the value of making extra food for leftovers in order to save time, but what's the point if you let them go to waste? If you spent money on groceries and time making food, why wouldn't you eat it?

Ask For What You Want

I know this idea may be tough for some, but if you can muster up the courage to ask for the specific gifts you want, you may be surprised to learn that the people buying those gifts are glad you told them!

You see, when it comes to things like Christmas, your birthday, or an anniversary, <u>your loved ones are going to spend money on you *anyway*</u>. You'd do them a *disservice* if you didn't have this discussion with them because <u>if they got you something you didn't like or wouldn't use, it's a waste of their money</u>!

Instead, ask for what you *do* want, what you *can* use. Tell the people who usually buy gifts for you that yes, gift cards are okay and even *preferred!*

Do you want to save money on dates with your spouse so that you can use those freed-up funds to pay off debt? Ask everyone to only get you restaurant gift cards this year. If you prefer to receive experiences, ask for Groupon activities in your local area.

Is there something you want or need that's more expensive? Wait until Christmas or another holiday and <u>ask everyone to chip in on that one thing</u>. Then you'll get what you want/need without having to break your budget, and everyone else will be happy because they helped get you what you wanted.

Skip a Year of Giving

If you're going through a period of financial hardship, consider skipping a year of giving.

You need to first care about your four walls and bare essentials. If you can't afford to pay the electric bill, then you do *not* need to be buying presents! <u>If the people in your life truly care about you, they will want you to make sure that your basic needs are met *more* than to receive gifts from you.</u>

So what do you do? Send an email to everyone you regularly get gifts for and explain that things are tight right now so you won't be giving gifts this year. If you want, you could add that the reason why is because you're trying to prepare a better future for yourself by tackling your debt. Or you could say that you're opting for a less consumerist approach, and you're instead choosing to focus on the real reason for the season.

You may find that people are actually *relieved* to hear this, and some may even join you in not exchanging gifts as gift shopping can be such a stressful and expensive endeavor.

You could consider offering other alternatives. Instead of giving gifts, you could send a heartfelt, handwritten card. So few people receive letters these days. This would be an inexpensive and super meaningful gift you could exchange with your family and close friends.

Set a Limit

If you can afford to buy presents, make sure you create a sinking fund for them, if you haven't already, and give yourself a limit per person *not* per holiday or event.

By giving yourself a limit per person, you're more likely to stick to your budget, instead of breaking it to try to make up for any accidental overspending on one person and underspending on another.

Figure out how many people you usually buy gifts for, and multiply that by a reasonable amount you think you could spend on each person. Then, like with the other sinking funds, divide by how many months there are left until that day comes.

In 2020, Americans on average spent $998 on Christmas gifts. To save up this much, you'd have to set aside approximately $84 a month. Plan for this amount or whatever amount you determine you'll need for gifts. If there are any other birthdays, anniversaries, or holidays you typically buy gifts for, start planning and saving up for those now too. Again, make sure to set a budget limit per person, or set a limit per couple if that's easier.

If $84 a month is too much right now, but you still want to get your loved ones something. I especially love the woman's suggestion to fill a mason jar with ingredients for a recipe. You could then handwrite the recipe to give with the jar for a more personalized touch.

How My Husband & I Saved Big

Yesterday, I mentioned that my husband and I were able to pay off our house in six years, but what I didn't mention was that <u>more than half of the value of the house was paid off in a single year</u>! What did we do differently that last year that allowed us to make such a drastic change in our budget so we could wipe out our mortgage? A few things.

One huge saver I mentioned earlier is that I switched to using cleaning cloths. For years, I cleaned everything with expensive Clorox wipes or paper towels. Now, I only keep a few of these around for really gross messes, like bacon grease, cleaning the toilet, or pet accidents. But these one-use items really add up, which is why I use my microfiber cloths for everything else. Switching to cleaning cloths was *life-changing*, as was my "discovery" of cleaning vinegar.

For a long time, I thought that cleaning vinegar was just some low-grade product that wouldn't hold its own when it came to killing germs and cutting grim. Instead, I bought toxic, super-strong cleaners that came with a costly price tag. Once I finally gave vinegar a try, I saw it *was* effective, and as a bonus it was inexpensive. Now, I use vinegar to clean almost everything ! Check it out and see if switching to this cost-effect and environmentally-safe cleaner would work for you. <u>If you do end up switching to this, make sure that you verify that it is safe to use on something before you clean with it</u>. Vinegar is very acidic and can damage certain materials.

Another big way I saved was by cutting back on personal care by finding cheaper alternatives or by doing things myself.

For example, I used to be religious about getting my nails done. A pedicure would cost me $60 not including a tip. Now, I paint my toenails myself. Getting my fingernails done was a different story though. I continued to get my fingernails done professionally because I thought the only way I could get the long acrylic nails I love was through a salon. Then I discovered our beautiful press-ons_and began enjoying salon-looking results at home.

I also used to get my hair dyed all the time, but my hair and bank account suffered because of this. Now, I've learned to embrace my natural color and have let my hair go back to its original brown. By learning to embrace my natural looks, I've developed a new love and appreciation for who I am. I finally see the beauty that I have without feeling the need to change myself in some way. While I may choose to dye my hair again simply for the fun of it, eliminating this one thing has saved me hundreds.

Another thing that helped me save was that I learned how to cut my hair. However, I wouldn't recommend this to everyone as I know that not everyone is artistic. Plus, some hair cuts can be pretty difficult. But if you want to try this, there are lots of tutorials on YouTube to guide you. And if you want to save money on your spouse's haircut, buzz cuts are super easy! Just invest in clippers that come with different guide comb lengths. One key thing to keep in mind if you decide to cut your hair or your spouse's is that <u>you can always cut more, but you can't get back what you've cut</u>. So always take off less than you want to be left with!

The last way my husband and I were able to save, and what probably provided the biggest difference, was that we cut back on how often we ate out. Before, we went out to eat daily, sometimes even multiple times! I used to buy at *least* one coffee a day. Then I'd usually buy lunch from the little café that was close to my work. And then, if it had been a long day, I'd also stop by a fast-food restaurant on the way home.

No wonder I never had any money. <u>I *ate* it all!</u>

"Eating" all of the money seems to be a common issue nowadays when I talk to other women or couples my age. It's just *so easy* to zip through a drive-through when you're tired, when you "don't have time," or when you're so overwhelmed with everything that you can't do one more thing. *I know.*

The thing that helped me the most in changing this was creating a routine, and building in or finding the time to prepare our food and drinks beforehand.

For example, I found that I only need about a minute and a half to fill our coffeemaker's filter with grounds and get the water filled up. That amount of time was usually how long I *wasted* waiting for something in the microwave. Previously, I had just stood there playing on my phone. Now, while I wait for the microwave, I prepare the coffee so it's ready to brew the next morning. I've created a habit of doing this, and we rarely buy coffee anymore.

<u>What little change do you need to make to your days, to your routines, so that you too can start making and preparing your meals and drinks at</u>

home ? If you need to, go back to when we talked about routines to see where you could find some extra time and build in this habit. Are you cooking enough so that you have leftovers for lunch, or should you set aside time on the weekend to bulk cook lunches? When could you premake your coffee or other drink? Could you squeeze things in somewhere like I did? Do you need to wake up earlier so you have time to prepare things, or would working this into your evening routine work better for you?

My hope is that after our time together, you'll have the time, the routines, the encouragement, the money, and the know-how to be able to do all the important things you need to do and want to do. And you'll be able to cook more for yourself or your family, and not eat out as much. When you do, you'll save drastically.

One last thing I'd like to mention while we're talking about eating out is that when you occasionally do, perhaps for a date or a special occasion, eat before you go to the restaurant. This way, you'll be less hungry and less likely to order a large meal. You might be able to fill up on an appetizer or just get dessert!

Save On Groceries

Of course, there are other ways you could save on food besides cooking more and eating out less.

Buy Generic

Brands have paid lots of money to get in front of you and establish familiarity so that when you see their products on the self, you recognize them and are more likely to buy them. Unfortunately, you as their customer are left picking up their advertising tab.

Generic brands are often made and packaged in the same factories as their more expensive counterparts. Sometimes the *only* difference between the two is that they have different labels! The reason why this is not more commonly known is because there are non-disclosure agreements. They don't want you to know so you continue to buy their more expensive products. It makes so much sense!

If you're still skeptical about giving up name-brand food, have a friend set up a blind taste test for you, and have fun seeing if you really can tell the difference between the two. Or check out all of the hilarious taste testing videos out there. They prove that most people can't tell the difference, but your wallet will!

<u>Buying generic brands will save you anywhere between 15-30%</u>! Even if you don't do anything else, this one change will have a big impact on your budget.

Stop Buying Convenience Items

This is another area where you're going to have to choose if you value saved money over saved time, but you're going to be paying for that time dearly.

Single-serve items that are portioned out, or food that is cut up and pre-seasoned will almost always cost you an arm and a leg more. Plus, the pre-chopped foods require more chemicals to preserve them, yet they still don't last as long as something that doesn't come cut up. I recently compared the price of prepared rice cauliflower to cauliflower florets. There was a startling $6 difference between them all because one bag had been run through a food processor for thirty seconds.

So <u>chop or portion food yourself</u>. Yes, it takes time. But depending upon how much money you save, it really could be worth it!

Order Online

Another reason I recommend you order your groceries online is that besides saving you time, it also saves you money!

It's easier to stick to your budget when you shop online because you can see your total tally up as you go. This way, you know if you're under budget or if you need to remove some items from your cart. Not only that, it helps lower or even eliminate impulse buying as you won't be in the store to see and pick up items, and therein lies the key. A study performed by UCLA found that <u>you're more likely to buy something after only a *single* touch because it increases your attachment to it.</u>

So if you want to cut costs and not be tempted to get things you don't need, don't go inside the store. Shop online.

Only Buy What You Need

Contrary to what many think, it *is* possible to eat healthily and not spend a ton. Things like beans, potatoes, and eggs all offer a lot of nutrition and are very affordable. In fact, white potatoes provide almost your complete nutritional needs with the exception of a few vitamins and minerals What are some foods you love that are healthful but also inexpensive?

<u>Anything that isn't adding value to your diet, that isn't nutritious, can be eliminated</u>. I'm talking about snack foods, desserts, and condiments. I know this idea may sound crazy, but things like chips are not necessary for you to live. You'll be fine going without your favorite ice cream for a few months. You'll save money, and your body will appreciate this temporary break from junk food.

Likewise, <u>anything that isn't water can be eliminated</u> as well. Things like soda, wine, and juices are all nice but not essential. Your body will receive all the hydration it needs with plain water. But if you must have some kind of flavoring, tea bags aren't too expensive.

Reduce or Eliminate Meat

Protein is usually one of the most expensive things to buy. <u>By building a meatless dish into your regular meal plan</u>, like having Meatless Mondays, <u>you'll save a lot</u>.

Buy In Bulk

You probably already know this, but just in case you don't, oftentimes stores will reward you for buying more by reducing the cost of an item per weight. This means that even if a small bag of rice has a lower price than a larger bag of rice, you may be paying more for what you're getting. However, this isn't always the case. That's why it's very important to <u>look at the price *per weight* in order to compare prices *effectively*</u> and see which is actually cheaper.

Take Advantage of Sales by Buying More & Freezing the Excess

I highly recommend you get a deep freezer so you can buy a bunch of something if it goes on sale. You can then freeze what you don't immediately use, and have a discounted stockpile.

Items are often put on sale when they are about to go bad, but if you freeze them, you push out their expiration date and extend their usability. Don't let discounted food scare you! The store is not going to sell already expired items that could get a customer sick and get themselves in legal trouble. In fact, it's illegal for stores to sell perishable food that's past its expiration date. Those discounted items are simply good food at a great price.

So what food can you freeze? Check out this in-depth article with lots of freezing dos, don'ts, and to find out how long different perishables will last. Did you know that you can freeze wine? I didn't either! Read the article to learn what else you can keep in the freezer, so you can go to town next time there is a sale!

Buying a bunch of an item that is on sale will help you save in the long run, but it might make you overspend in the meantime. What are you supposed to do? Spend less on your groceries next time you shop. If you're in the middle of the month, it's fine to take a little from next week's Consumables budget. However, I don't recommend "borrowing" from a future month as you could end up owing yourself indefinitely. If you need to, spend less in another area of your budget for that same month to make up the difference.

Incorporate What's on Sale

Follow the order of meal planning we talked about before. Build your meal plans using up what you already have. Then consider how you could incorporate what's on sale, and often also in season.

Pretend for instance that it's fall, and you have all the ingredients you need to make a pie besides the fruit. Would it be the best financial decision for you to plan on making a blueberry pie? Not really. Blueberries would be $5 a pint since fall is not their season. But you could plan on making an apple pie. They'd be getting harvested around then and would be on sale due to their overabundance.

Plan Your Meals

We went over this before, but because this is not just a time saver but a huge money saver as well, it's worth repeating.

Going to the grocery store without a plan and buying whatever looks good or what you *think* you could throw together, more often than not leads to wasted food or a full fridge with "nothing" to make. Instead, meal planning lets you be intentional about what you get, so you *know* the food you're spending money on will get used.

Just Ask

A great way to save, but one that people often forget about, is to ask for a lower price.

I can't tell you how many times my dad embarrassed me while I was growing up by asking someone if they would give him a bargain. I was always worried the other person would feel *insulted* by this. But in hindsight, the worst thing they could have said was "No."

Apply this to your own life! You'll never know if you don't ask. Just ask if you can get what you want at a discounted price.

The other day I was in Kohl's and asked a woman at customer service if they had any deals or coupons they could apply to my purchase. She readily whipped out a store coupon for me. No coupon clipping was required, and I didn't have to spend time hunting online or looking through their store's app for discounts. I simply asked.

Action Plan

What changes are you going to make *today* so that you can live life like no one else *later*?

Go through your budget and eliminate all unnecessary expenses. If you're using the Budget Spreadsheet, look for the asterisks to know what things can be eliminated.

After you've cut everything that you can, see how you can use the tips you learned today to lower the expenses you can't cut or that you're choosing to keep. Are there a few reusable items you want to switch to? What limit will you set for gift-giving per person, and how much do you need to start saving now? Are you going to buy more generic brands? What habits of yours do you need to change?

Don't worry if your budget is still not balanced after doing all of this as we'll be going over even more ways you can save tomorrow.

DAY 23:
CUT EXPENSES PART 2

Buy the Year Subscription

We already went over how you can save money with groceries when you buy in bulk, but people forget that the same concept applies to things other than food.

<u>Many subscription companies offer bulk discounts when you buy their services for the whole year</u>. This is another area that while it costs more upfront, can save you BIG in the long run. For example, with YNAB's budgeting app you learned about in the first finance chapter, if you were to pay for a year's subscription instead of the monthly one, you'd save a whopping $60 while getting the *same thing*. Getting the year's subscription is a no-brainer!

If you subscribe to any services, see if they offer a discounted annual rate. If they do, save up for them so you stay within your budget when you purchase them.

Cancel Subscriptions You're Not Using

Everyone knows you should cancel subscriptions you're not using, but no one talks about how easy it is to forget that you subscribed to something in the first place, especially those 99¢ phone apps. It's hard to remember all the little things you're subscribed to, let alone know how to cancel them. Or what about those subscriptions that you *have* tried to cancel, but they're such a pain that you've decided to leave them and keep paying?

You should absolutely not be losing money to things you don't use, or worse, forgot you signed up for. Thankfully, there are things you can do.

First, I'd recommend you <u>download the app</u> Truebill that we talked about previously, at least temporarily. Truebill will show you all of your subscriptions, and they'll even cancel them for you on their premium version. But because you have to pay to "unlock" these cancellation services, I recommend you take note of what subscriptions you have with their free help and then cancel them yourself. According to one of the cofounders, an average user of Truebill saves $512 a year, so this app really can help you find and cut back on those subscriptions! Give it a try.

To solve your other issue, what do you do if you've tried to cancel a subscription but the company keeps making you jump through hoops? Call your bank and have them put a *stop payment* on that company. While you're at it, see if you can start a dispute to get money back for all of the months of service you paid for but didn't use. You're even more likely to get that lost money back if you can prove that you've been trying to cancel with them for a while.

I had to do this with my old gym and was able to get back multiple months of payments. Once I learned this was an option, it was so easy to stop playing "runaround games" with the gym and just go straight to my bank to have the issue quickly resolved.

Lower Your Bills

We went over how you can lower your utility bills previously. Hopefully, you did the steps suggested then so that your utilities now cost less. But if you haven't called and asked for a discount yet, follow the suggestions mentioned in that chapter today so you can start saving.

Besides doing those things, how else could you lower your bills?

Downsize Your Home

Now I'm not saying that you need to go out today and find a new place, but the next time you switch apartments or look for a new home, consider the square footage. There's a reason why tiny homes are so popular right now, and why more and more people are changing to this way of living. They've figured out that less space means fewer utilities used, aka money saved.

Downsize Your Car

If you're struggling to make ends meet, you don't need the newest, prettiest vehicle out there just because it makes you look "good" or feel "cool." <u>A car is just a means to get you from Point A to Point B.</u>

If you still owe a lot on your vehicle, it may be in your best interest to trade it in for something older, smaller, and cheaper. This way, you'll be able to reduce or even eliminate your car loan, and it'll be one less debt for you to pay off. Read how to trade in your car with a loan for a cheaper car if this is something you think you should look into.

Be Conservative

You wouldn't leave a fridge door open, would you? So why would you leave a light on when you leave a room? Get into the good habit of turning off everything as soon as you're done using it. During the day, open up the blinds and take advantage of the free sunlight. Doing so will also give you the added benefits of feeling energized and getting Vitamin D.

If you go extended periods between using a device or appliance, why not unplug it? Even if something is turned off it still draws power. This <u>standby power equates to 5-10% of your bill</u>, according to the Lawrence Berkeley National Laboratory. You may find it revealing to learn how much watt usage the devices you have plugged in are consuming with their Standby Power Summary Chart, and next time you switch something "off" consider if you should just unplug it.

The Department of Energy says that <u>adjusting your thermostat 7-10% for only eight hours</u>, like while you're away at work, <u>will save you 10% or approximately $83 on your heating and cooling costs per year</u>. How much more could you save by leaving it at that adjusted temperature the other sixteen hours of the day? So put on another layer in the winter, and turn on a fan in the summer to watch the savings roll in.

Switch Companies

It's easy once a bill is set up to forget about it, but don't get lax in your spending. Like we talked about before, it's important to reevaluate your providers (at least once a year) to see if they are giving you the best rate or if another company could give you a better one.

<u>Even if you're satisfied with what you're getting it's worth comparing and shopping around</u>. For years, I did my banking through USAA, but then I heard about a local mortgage company. By switching to them I was able to save $100 *per month*. I'd been perfectly happy with my mortgage cost through USAA, and had even thought I was getting a great rate! But you never know if someone else may provide better service at a lower price.

Speaking of switching companies, did you know that there are cell phone providers out there that run off of the same big networks you know about but at *half* the cost ? Here are a few:

Airvoice : Runs on the AT&T network. Lets you choose how much data you want, and costs $70 down to just $20 per month. It includes unlimited talk, text, and even international SMS. It also offers a Pay As You Go Plan as well.

Ultra Mobile : Runs off of T-Mobile's network. Its costs vary depending upon how much data you want and how long you want your contract to be. Their least expensive option for the yearly plan is $10 for 250MB, but for $30 more you could get their unlimited yearly plan. If instead, you'd prefer a short commitment, they additionally offer single-month plans at a slightly higher cost.

Visible : Runs on Verizon's network. For $40 you get 5G with unlimited everything. This service offers additional savings with Party Pay, where you can get your costs down to as little as $25 a month when in a group of four or more. The cool thing is, you don't have to be family members with those in your party! It could just be you and your roommates saving together.

There are even more small phone companies you can check out, such as Hello Mobile (T-Mobile), (T-Mobile), Google Fi (runs off of T-Mobile and U.S. Cellular), Tello (also T-Mobile), and others. See if any of these would suit your needs more than what you're already using.

One common theme I've found with these cell phone providers is that they give you the option to bring your phone or buy a new one through them. I love that they allow you to bring your current phone when you've already paid so much for it. But unfortunately, they seem limited as far as compatibility goes. For example, my phone is just three years old but it's too old to qualify. Because of this, if you want to use one of these services you may have to get a new phone through them. But at these low prices, it's worth checking them out!

Regardless of if you switch to one of these companies or stick with your current provider, comb through your bill. Make sure you're aware of *every single thing* you're paying for. And if you're not sure what a charge is, ask.

I'm embarrassed to say, but despite all the times I called my phone company over the last three years to discuss my bills and their fees, I somehow glanced over the fact that I was paying to have a mobile hotspot. I didn't even know what that was! Once I finally took the time to ask their customer service, I found out I'd been paying an extra $10 a month for something I don't use/need.

So comb through that bill girlfriend! You may be paying for international calling, location tracking, device security, or having a mobile hotspot like I was without even knowing it.

The same goes for your other bills. Double-check to see *exactly* what you're paying for, and have anything you don't use be removed from your plan/bill. Are you paying any extra hidden fees, like for instance a $2 paper delivery fee? Switch to ereceipts. This is another reason why it's important to track your budget, so you notice any bill fluctuations and can address unexplained charges.

Drive Less or Rideshare

Remember how we talked before about consolidating all of your errands into one trip to save yourself time? Well doing everything when you're already out, instead of taking lots of little trips here and there, will also save you money with gas.

Alternatively, you could take public transit if your city offers it. I love this option because then you can do something else while someone drives you around. It's like having a chauffeur! You could read, catch up on sleep, or even do a craft like knitting while someone else takes you wherever you need to go.

You could carpool as well. Does anyone you work with live near you or on your way to work? You could take turns picking each other up and driving. Carpooling is illegal in some places, like California for example, but if you're in a place where it's not, why not save on your gas and upkeep when you already have to drive to that location?

You can use Waze Carpool to help you find people who want to share a ride. It allows you to filter them by gender, star rating, if they're a coworker, or if you have mutual friends. Waze charges the rider 54¢ per mile and you receive part of that. It's not a way to make money per se as you don't get paid a lot and are limited to two carpools a day, one "to work" and one "from work," but it will certainly help reduce your car's expenses. Also, the money you receive is not taxable as it's not classified as an income.

Go On a Free Spree

What can you get for free? I bet it's more than you think!

If You Want to *Do* Something for Free

Look on Facebook Events, or just type into Google "events near me" to see what activities are going on in your local area.

If You Want to *Get* Something for Free

There are a few different places you can look to see what people are giving away.

You can look in Facebook groups, such as your local community's group or specific ones related to the item you want. For example, if you love LuLuLemon but you're not wanting to spend any money, you go find LuLuLemon Facebook groups dedicated to buying, selling, or *trading*. Then you could swap something you already have for something new to you. There are also book swap groups, plant swap groups, and more. Just type in the item you want in the search bar to see if there is a Facebook group for it.

If you don't have anything to trade, you can still get things for free by searching in the Facebook group section for "Buy nothing groups near me." These offer a random assortment of items that are completely free with no strings attached. Currently, in one of my local groups, a licensed stylist is giving away free haircuts to the community. There is a king-sized mattress and bed frame, a grill, clothes, and boxes full of vegetables that are up for grabs as well.

These buy-nothing groups are a great way to save money and also help keep waste out of landfills. You'll find things that need to be repurposed, need a little tender loving care, or that flat out don't work. But if you have the skills or know someone who does, you can get these items at no charge to you and fix them up to work again.

Other places you could find things being given away would be Facebook Marketplace's *Free Stuff* tab, Nextdoor, and Craigslist.

Of course, you could go to a library to get books for free. But did you know you could borrow other stuff from there too? Most offer videos, video games, and board games for starters. Some even offer free classes or activities, and the supplies for those activities are often free as well! Both the Berkeley and Oakland public libraries go above and beyond what you'd expect from a library. They have a bunch of tools that you can borrow for any masonry, electrical, plumbing, landscaping, or carpentry project. Check out your local library to see what free goodies they'll offer you!

For free digital books, there is 1Lib which claims to be "The world's largest ebook library." However, I prefer a similar app that additionally offers audiobooks. Libby has allowed me the ability to multitask by "reading" at the same time I take my daily walks. Now I'm "devouring" books that I could never find the time for. While this app's selection is nowhere near as large as Audible, you can't beat free! They make it easy to get a library card so you can start reading right away, and you can even get multiple cards for multiple different libraries.

If You Want to Get a *Service* for Free or Free *Things* as Well

Barter! It's a shame that bartering is becoming a thing of the past because it's a brilliant way for both parties to "win." My parents barter their homegrown beef for monthly chiropractic services. No money is exchanged, but both get what they want!

There are lots of things to do or get for free if you look hard enough and are *creative*. Other things you could do would be to play board games or video games that you already have. You could invite a friend over and make coffee for you both at home instead of going out for coffee. You could go hiking. You could borrow a friend's kayak instead of buying or renting your own. You could have a date with your spouse by cooking together instead of eating at a restaurant.

I encourage you to see what else you can do or get for free before pulling out your wallet.

Make It Fun

Why not instead of feeling like you're limiting yourself, or feeling that you're restrained by a tight budget, you make it fun? Think of your frugality as a *challenge* !

Go on a No-Spend Challenge for a week or even a month if you can! During that time use up the household products and food you have, making the most of what you've already spent money on. Don't make any purchases and give your bank's transaction feed cobwebs. Just be sure to not stock up beforehand as that defeats the whole purpose!

While you're doing a No-Spend Challenge, why not try out some of those suggestions just mentioned and see what fun things you can do or get for free?

Couponing & Couponing Apps

At first glance, couponing seems like a great way to save money. However, there are some drawbacks and things to keep in mind if you want to pursue it.

First, there is the fact that you have to find, clip, and pair up deals which can *really* eat up your time. If your job pays you $15 an hour, and you spend thirty minutes looking for coupons, you'll have to find enough coupons to equate to $7.50 in savings to make it worth your time.

You also have to be careful not to fall into the trap of buying something you normally wouldn't simply because you're "saving." It's the same kind of thing as buying something because it's on sale. You may get 40% off on an item, but that's *not* saving if you bought something you wouldn't have otherwise. That's *spending* 60%.

So if you're careful to only coupon for things you were *already* going to buy, and if you're okay with spending some time on it, doing this may be worthwhile to you. However, if you're feeling overwhelmed with all you have going on, perhaps you should steer clear of couponing for now as it's just one more thing to do on your already full "plate. "

If you do decide to coupon I suggest, like almost everything else in this guide, that you only use digital versions. This will prevent paper clutter, and eliminate the tedious and time-consuming task of having to cut them out by hand.

Check out these free digital couponing and money-back apps available to you:

Fetch Rewards : This is my favorite app because it doesn't take that much time to use. However, what it makes up for in speed, it lacks in savings. I've been using the app for five months and have only saved 5,000 points, the equivalent of $5. If you buy generic brands, like I do, this might not be the best app for you as it takes so long to build up any sizable amount of money-back. However, if you buy name brands you'll get more points.

I love this app in particular because it offers a digital receipt scan. You only have to press one button and the app does the work for you, looking through your emails for receipts and even backdating a bit. It then adds credit to your account *automatically*. If you have physical receipts, you can get credit for them as well by taking pictures of them through the app. Fetch Rewards also has a low minimum amount needed for withdrawing. Only $3 is required.

If you're interested in this app, sign up via my referral link above or use code "AUPNE " to earn an extra 2,000 points for free. When you do, I'll receive an extra 2,000 as well. Thank you!

Ibotta : This has an app and a Chrome extension, which makes it very handy to save on all of your devices. With Ibotta, you'll build up a larger amount of savings and do so faster than some of the others on this list. However, a high $20 minimum is needed to withdraw. And despite this being a digital couponing software, it still requires you to sift through a bunch of coupons and "clip" each one individually.

Be cognizant of your time when using this app because it's very easy to chase pennies. They offer 10¢ back on any receipt, and occasionally require you to watch a short video ad to "clip" that 10¢ coupon. Personally, I don't think that's worth my time, nor yours! If you really want to save, use this app when purchasing something expensive or a name-brand item. For example, Zyrtec is offering $4 back right now. While that's not huge, it's nothing to scoff at, especially if you were going to buy it anyway.

One very cool thing I like about Ibotta is that it occasionally has *free* stuff ! At the time that I'm writing this, you could get this mascara for free if you found a participating store and bought it at or below the money-back amount. But again, be cognizant of your time. While free is certainly tempting, if you weren't already planning on going to the store that offers the free item, it might not be worth your time nor gas to drive all the way there.

Other things I like about this app are that it allows you to scan items if you're at the store in person, so you can quickly see if an item has any coupons for it. Also, this is one of the few apps that offers coupons for alcohol, which is nice if that's something you regularly buy. And lastly, even if you forget to use the Ibotta app before shopping, you can still redeem your receipts up to one week later. The next app is not so generous.

To start using Ibotta. New users who sign up using my links will receive a $10 referral bonus once they've completed their first qualifying purchase. I'll get a small kickback as well at no charge to you. Thanks again!

Rakuten (Formerly Ebates) : This has an app and a Chrome extension as well. It kind of serves like a credit card in that you get a small percentage back depending upon where you shopped and what you bought. For example, if you spent $100 at Target, and you bought something in a specific category that Rakuten was offering 1% cashback in, you'd get $1 back.

You can receive money once you have at least $5 in your account, but your cashback is only released every three months, not whenever you reach that minimum amount.

This app shows promise, but I haven't been successful with getting it to work when making purchases from my cell phone. They do offer "Missing Cash Back" claims where you can write in to have them give you credit that failed to be added to your account. But the process is time-consuming and not worth doing every single time you purchase something, especially if it's only a few cents you'll get back. However, it does appear to work well on desktop, at least for myself. And when it does work, the cents add up!

According to their customer service, the app will be more likely to work if you first make sure you don't have anything in your cart on the site you want to shop at. Activate the software and "Start a Shopping Trip" *before* shopping.

How do you "Start a Shopping Trip?" If you're using your phone, click on the app, and then find the store you want to shop at *through* the app. Click the store and begin shopping like normal. If you're using a desktop, go directly to the site you want to shop at, and simply hit the Chrome extension.

Honey : This is a wonderful Chrome extension that works at checkout. When activated, it'll scan tons of coupon codes to see if one will work for your purchase. Within the first month of having it, it saved me hundreds on a video software program. I was surprised that it was first able to find coupons for such a little-known company, and second, that it saved me *so* much *so* easily! I highly recommend getting it.

If you're interested in saving money with Honey, sign up via my referral link above. It's free!

Coupons.com, a great source for digital and printable coupons, now has an app ! This app is unique because it has Manufacturer's coupons, which can often be "stacked" or used in combination with other coupons. It works very similarly to Ibotta in that you must individually find and "clip" your coupons, except that this app needs a little more work on your part. It requires you to submit your receipt and additionally scan the products you want to redeem an offer for.

As an easier alternative, the app can link to certain participating stores with loyalty cards. This way, you can connect the two accounts and receive cashback automatically. You'll receive this cashback within one week, and as no minimum is required, you can withdraw it at any time.

A lot of these apps can be used together to provide you with even more savings! For instance, Coupons, Ibotta, and Fetch could all be used on the same purchase. However, some apps cannot be, such as Rakuten and Honey.

There are many other money-saving apps out there, such as Swagbucks, Shopkick, Checkout 51, and more. I haven't used these other apps myself though, so I can't give feedback on them. But if you're interested, check them out.

If you'd like to start couponing, but want to save time finding and pairing up deals yourself, I suggest you watch a dedicated Youtube channel. Make sure they are a channel that uploads *weekly*, so you can see all of the *current* offers, and how best to coupon for them. Before you do your grocery shopping, you could watch their latest video to see if any of the deals they talk about are things you were planning on getting. Then you'll be able to see which one or multiple of the money-back apps you should use in order to save the most.

There are tons of couponing channels dedicated to this. There are Coupons with Alysia, Couponing with Kayla, and Bree the Coupon Queen for starters. So find one you love, or watch multiple, as some couponers may go over different deals that the others didn't cover. If you're serious about starting to save money with couponing, consider adding the step of watching their latest video to your grocery shopping routine before placing your order.

Get Your Money Back

We just went over how you can get money back with couponing. But what about the original way to get money back, returning things?

I remember when I was going through that chaotic, stressful period of my life I mentioned before, that I ordered something online, but it didn't fit. Despite it being brand new with the tags still attached, I threw it in the trash. I was so overwhelmed with everything else, I couldn't fathom taking the time to return something, even if it meant I was "throwing away" money.

This may be obvious to some, but others may need to hear it. Throwing something away like I did, or perhaps what is more common, stuffing it in the back of the closet to never be used, is a *waste* of your hard-earned money. If you spent money on something and you're not happy with it, return it! You're going to feel like such an adult and be so proud of yourself when you finally take back that item that's been waiting months to be addressed.

I know you might not have the time, the desire, or the energy to go about little annoying tasks like making returns to get just a few bucks back. But once I finally overcame my aversion to this, and began doing it regularly, I felt like I was *making* money when I returned things. Even if I just ended up with store credit, it was like having a discount or a sale the next time I went shopping, because past me helped pay for present me's purchase.

I found the easiest way to ensure you return something is to put the item and its receipt into the front seat of your car, so it'll serve as a visual reminder. Don't put it into your trunk where you might forget about it. Having the item and receipt in the car will remove any excuse that you forgot to bring them, and it'll be easier for you to zip them back next time you're out running errands.

Another way you may be "throwing away" money, or at least leaving it on the "table," is by failing to price match. Yet again, here is another reason why I recommend shopping at Walmart. You may have heard that if you find an identical item from another store that is priced lower than the same product at Walmart, Walmart will often match that price. But did you know that you can price match something you've *already* bought? Depending upon what you've purchased, you may be able to get a price match up to 30 days after buying it.

This is an incredible opportunity to save big time! I purchased my robot vacuum, who my husband lovingly named Marty, for $450. I did a lot of research determining which vacuum to get and was proud of myself for finding such a nice quality one at such a low price. However, when I went to send his link to someone after she commented that she was interested in buying him as well, I was dismayed to see that his price had dropped drastically. If I had just bought him one week later, he would have cost me $300 instead. All it took was a short 14-minute call, a request to price match, and $150 was returned to my account!

So next time you make a big purchase, why not check back on that item later to see if the price changed? You may have better luck with this if it's around a holiday, as there may be a sale going on. If there is a significant difference, like mine was, call in and claim that money back!

More Saving Tips

We've gone over quite a few different ways you could save money, but if you want even more ideas or would like to learn other ways you could be financially savvy, here are a few resources:

If you'd prefer to watch, check out these YouTube channels: Frugal Fit Mom, Debt Free Dana, Mindy Mom, and Under the Median.

If you'd prefer to read, visit The Krazy Coupon Lady's site. This place is a goldmine for couponers and women learning how to score some savings. Here are a few good books as well, the first one being the book that helped my dad grow multiple successful businesses: *The Complete Financial Guide for Young Couples*, *Rich Dad Poor Dad*, *Your Money or Your Life* (the book that started the F.I.R.E. - Financial Independence, Retire Early movement), and *The Total Money Makeover*.

Action Plan

By this point, your financial situation is probably looking pretty different compared to how it was before. Update your budget to reflect any changes you've made.

How are things looking now?

If you still spend more than you make, go back and keep eliminating or lowering expenses. Stop subscriptions you no longer use, and if you're unsure what you have, download Truebill. Do you need to call a utility company, switch to one of those phone companies, or change a monthly subscription to a yearly subscription?

Make sure you're including in your expenses the extra we talked about you needing before, so you can save up for your emergency fund, and then later pay off your debt. Remember, the more you can set aside, the sooner you'll be able to accomplish these important financial goals. So cut, cut, cut those expenses!

DAY 24:
MAKE MORE MONEY & STICK TO YOUR BUDGET

You've probably heard the adage, "A penny saved is a penny earned." But I would argue that it should be "a penny saved is *two* pennies earned" because saving money is easier than making money.

Cutting back on your expenses is going to be where you make the most difference, but if you've cut everything that you can and still don't have a balanced budget, you may have an income problem. <u>If you think this might be the case, how could you increase your take-home pay</u> ?

Ways to Make More Money

We'll be going over a few side hustles you could pursue, but the truth is that for most people, these will not bring in a lot. <u>Depending upon how much you need to make, getting a whole other second job may be what you need to do</u>. Again, you may have to be uncomfortable for a little while, but it will not be forever.

Thankfully, needing to make extra money doesn't mean that you can't enjoy yourself while you're doing it. Think of something that you're good at or that you like to do. Chances are someone out there is willing to pay for it. Why not get paid for your passion? If you love baking or cooking, could you sell your food? If you like keeping things neat and orderly, could you be a part-time home organizer?

If you love dogs, use Rover and get paid for walking other people's pooches. You could offer daycare services in your own home, or you could pet sit and watch dogs in their home. If you want to make the "big bucks," you could even open up your home for overnight boarding.

Want to not do anything and make extra money? Professionals will wrap your car in a business' ad for you, so <u>all you have to do is drive your regular route to work</u> ! You need to drive at least 50 miles per week to qualify, but assuming you meet that requirement, that's 50 miles you could be getting paid for. You get to choose how much of your car you want to be wrapped. And depending upon what you chose, you could bank between $174-452 a month. That's easy money!

Another similar option is Stickr.co. See which car wrapping company is right for you.

You could "double up," and use your wrapped car to deliver groceries, fast food, or people ! I'm sure you've probably heard of Uber Eats, DoorDash, Instacart, Uber, and Lift. If you have a free Saturday, why not download one of these apps and make money, instead of sitting around watching Netflix? The important thing to keep in mind with any of these services though is that <u>you need to have a fuel-efficient car</u>. Otherwise, you're not going to be left with enough money to have made it worth it, after you've filled up your tank.

If having flexibility and making your own hours is something you like about those apps, you'll love Amazon Flex. It promises an impressive $18 an hour minimum! All you have to do is deliver packages for Amazon, which includes an array of options such as Amazon Food, Amazon Locker, Amazon Prime, and Amazon Restaurant. Depending upon the package you're delivering, you may simply scan a barcode and place the package somewhere, or you may need to wait for a customer to get it from you in person.

You've probably also heard of Airbnb. Well, why not put your spare bedroom to work making money for you? <u>You do *not* have to have the nicest house to list it.</u> I've stayed in some subpar locations on the "bad" side of town. But I'm proud of those people who listed their spaces regardless because they were able to make money and work towards a better future for themselves. You could do the same!

I was blown away when I went onto Airbnb's site and saw that if I rented out just one room with a queen bed I could make $789 a month! How much more could you make in your area, and how much more if you had two spare rooms?

Another site where you could rent out an extra room is Vrbo. This site is geared towards vacation rentals, but it's essentially the same thing.

If you have free space in other areas like in your backyard, driveway, garage, basement, attic, closet, or also an extra bedroom, you could rent it out with Neighbor.

Not sure how much to charge? Their app will give you a ballpark suggestion based on what you're wanting to rent out, the size of the space, and your location. Regardless, you still have the freedom to charge *whatever* amount you want!

And don't worry about renters ditching their stuff or failing to pay you. Neighbor guarantees you'll be paid, and they'll even step in to pick up the tab if your renter stops. Not only that, they'll hire a 3rd party to come and move the items out for you. So <u>you'll never be left with someone else's junk or have to get rid of it yourself if they bail</u>.

I've been very impressed by their customer service. It's evident that this company cares about you as the property owner and your experience with them. Plus, they offer a fantastic way to generate cash flow. <u>Simply clean out an area, measure it, and list it.</u> Then that space will bring in money monthly while you do *nothing* but let stuff sit there.

Not going anywhere this weekend? Have a vehicle you're not using? Rent out your car with <u>Turo.</u> Doing so has become such a lucrative endeavor that some people are now buying cars for the sole purpose of renting them out on this site. To qualify, your vehicle can't be older than 12 years and needs to have less than 130,000 miles on it.

Do you enjoy giving your opinion on things? Get paid to do just that! Companies want to hear from people like you about your user experience with their website, apps, and prototypes. And UserTesting will pay you $10 per twenty minutes for that feedback. <u>All you have to do is answer questions or complete surveys</u>. You can even get paid to test "real-life" experiences like doing unboxings. If you really want to reel in the "dough" though, participate in video conference calls to make up to $120!

If you have a degree in something, see if you can market your skills. For example, if you have a degree in education, you could offer tutoring on <u>TutorMe.</u> If you're interested in proofreading, editing, or designing, you could be a freelancer on <u>Fiverr</u> or <u>Upwork.</u> You technically don't have to have education or even prior experience to sell on these sites, but it does help.

Don't have a college education? If you'd love to teach but only have your GED, you could tutor on <u>Tutors.com.</u> On Fiverr's Weird Services, you could make up a random activity and see if anyone pays for it. A gentleman is currently charging $15 to dress up in a flag suit and dance. He has been hired for this service 24 times so far! What fun, odd thing could you do to make some extra cash?

And of course, there's always the possibility to get paid more where you already work. Ask your boss if you can pick up extra hours. Also, be sure to visit PayScale to see what other people with your credentials, experience, and education are being paid in your local area. If you're on the low end, see if you can negotiate a raise in addition to getting those extra hours.

With today's technology and apps available to you, there are a plethora of ways to make extra money. You just have to be willing to put in the time. I know it might not be the most fun thing to go work more when you've already worked all day, but you're doing it for a better future. You're working so that your future self can live less stressed and be debt-free. You're working just a few extra hours so you can have the security of knowing you're covered in case of an emergency. It's worth it! So throw your big girl panties on and get out there.

How to Stick To Your Budget

Now that your finances are (hopefully) balanced, let's go over how to keep them that way. It's all fine and dandy to set up a budget, but in order to make a difference in your life, you need to *stick to it*. So that's what we're going to go over now.

It's important to note though that mess-ups are inevitable. You're not always going to budget perfectly. When you do mess up, what matters is that you figure out why you strayed from your plan, make adjustments, and get back to it as soon as possible.

The Envelope System

If you know you're going to struggle with one particular category, or just struggle with the whole budgeting idea in general, the Envelope System may be for you.

To do it, simply withdraw the total amount of money you've planned to spend for the entire month. Then fill envelopes with that cash, each envelope serving as one of the categories in your budget. Proceed to make all of your purchases throughout the month only using that cash. When the money in an envelope is spent, that's it for that category until next month.

But what do you do if most of your transactions are electronic? Isn't cash a little archaic? My husband came up with a brilliant idea to limit his spending for his Fun Money. Create a new checking account specifically for the category you're having an issue with. Set up an automatic transfer to move the amount you've budgeted for this category into it monthly. Then differentiate the debit card for this account from your regular one, so you'll know which one to use when buying something.

While this separate checking account "hack" will work, it kind of takes away from the whole reason why this system is effective in the first place. There's just something about seeing physical cash leave your hand that is more painful than swiping plastic, and more effective at getting people to cut down on their spending.

Despite the Envelope System's success rate, there are some drawbacks to it which I'd like to mention. Because of these, and for convenience's sake, I recommend you switch back to a digital budgeting system later.

The biggest drawback I've found is that you have to manually tally up totals. This can be a bit time-consuming, and if you're bad at math or forget to write down a purchase, your count may be off. Another problem I have, at least for us klutzy hot messes, is that it's easy to accidentally leave or drop an envelope somewhere. That potentially could be a lot of money to lose, and you'd have to do without until the next month. Lastly, carrying a bunch of cash makes us women *even more* of a target!

Regardless, considering how helpful many have found the Envelope System to be, I recommend you give it a try if you think it'll work for you. Just be careful with how you carry the cash and be smart about not showing it in public.

Stop Tempting Yourself

If you can't exercise discipline, remove temptations and avoid going to places where you know you'll be prompted to break your budget.

For example, if you know you're more than likely going to buy something if you go into a certain store, don't go into it! If you can't help but go on a shopping spree whenever you walk through the mall, don't go there. If getting your favorite store's magazine with all the latest styles is going to be too much, unsubscribe from it. And unsubscribe from their emails too. Even overspending at thrift stores or yard sales is still overspending, so simply don't go if you can't hold yourself back.

Wait Before You Buy

Impulse purchases can get the best of us all at times. A way to minimize them and keep yourself from making a purchase you'll regret, is by giving yourself some time to "cool off" and think clearly. Instead of buying something right then and there, wait a while and think about it. My husband can confirm that I often like to "sleep on it" when it comes to decisions, and that especially includes making large purchases.

Of course, you don't have to "sleep on" every purchase you make. Simply set a limit for yourself that you think is reasonable, and then if you're tempted to spend more than that, give yourself at least 24 hours to think it over. After that time has passed, get it if you still want it and if it's within your budget.

You Can't Buy Happiness

When you buy something your body releases dopamine. Unfortunately, some people get addicted to this "feel good" hormone, and that's when shopaholics are born.

It's often joked about how retail therapy is cheaper than seeing a psychiatrist. Politicians encourage us to shop to keep the economy "healthy." We feel societal pressure to keep up with the Joneses, and we're constantly bombarded with ads that imply, "you'll be happy *if* you buy this." Excessive shopping has become increasingly accepted, and in some cases even encouraged. But the effects of dopamine from all this purchasing are short-lived compared to the effects shopping sprees have on your bank account.

<u>If you find yourself often buying things when you know you don't have the money or don't need what you're getting, could there be an underlying problem</u> ? Are you trying to fill a void or distract yourself? Are you unhappy with your life and trying to find some way to create joy or

excitement? More stuff does not equal happiness. Perhaps seeing a therapist to help you uncover why you feel compelled to shop would be beneficial for you.

<u>The next time you want to splurge and break your budget, stop and ask *why* you need to get what you're getting</u>. Is it because you need it, want it, or just because you love shopping?

How to Get Your Spouse to Stick to the Budget

It's easy to feel frustrated or get angry at your spouse if they don't stick to the budget. They helped create it, so why can't they stick to the financial limitations they gave themselves?

When discussing finances, it's imperative that you do *not* verbally attack, blame, or accuse your spouse if they don't stick to the budget. This will only serve to put them on the defensive. And it will eliminate any chance of having a healthy, constructive conversation about how things could be improved. Instead, <u>make talking about the budget as pleasant of an experience as possible</u> so they don't flat out refuse to talk about finances in the future.

My husband and I budget $400 per person, per month for our Fun Money category. One month a while ago, I calculated that he had spent $800+ on video games. Instead of becoming angry, I used this as a learning opportunity to ask him how much he *thought* he had spent. I then showed him the actual amount. By approaching this as an eye-opening experience and joking about it, rather than scolding him like a child, he was able to realize just how much his video game spending had gotten out of hand.

If a similar over expenditure happens with your spouse, be sensitive with how you approach it. Again, occasional slip-ups are inevitable. <u>Be forgiving and understanding with them, just like how you'd want them to be with you</u>. When you're married, an argument doesn't lead to one person "winning" and the other "losing." <u>You are a partnership. If one person loses, you both lose</u>. Remember that the other person is not your enemy. Focus on solving the problem, the financial issue, rather than attacking the person you love. Focus on the actions, not the person making the actions.

When first getting started with a budget, <u>it may be hard for the spender in the family to cut back</u>. They may simply love shopping, and have a hard time restraining themselves. Or they may just not realize how much they've spent, and break the budget unintentionally. If this becomes a regular problem, it may be helpful for them to carry around a visual reminder of how much money they have left. A fantastic way to do that is with the Envelope System mentioned earlier.

I've found it helpful to set a goal together. If you and your significant other want to go on a vacation, encourage them to stick to a budget that allows for a vacation sinking fund. If they overspend their Fun Money, that "extra" money has to come from somewhere. The bills still have to be paid, so where will that money come from? The vacation fund.

If you were trying to quit smoking, but your partner continued to smoke, it would be exponentially harder for you to succeed. Similarly, getting a better grasp on your finances requires a *joint* effort. You both need to work on building better money habits together. If one person continues to spend without restrictions, they'll undo any progress the other has made.

Like is mentioned in that article, if your spouse refuses to be fiscally responsible, you may need to seek counseling. Remember, disagreeing about finances is one of the biggest reasons for divorce. So it would be in the best interest of your relationship to meet with a counselor and see if there are any underlying issues that are causing the discord.

Another option is to again, take Financial Peace University. This is a great way to get your spouse to understand why budgeting is important in the first place. It's also helpful in explaining and showing how to do it properly, so both of you can be on the same page and attack your debt with a united front. Best of all, Dave will help get your spouse on board the budgeting "train" for you, so you won't have to nag.

Look at Your Budget Often

Last but most importantly, revisit your budget regularly. Do you want to enter in transactions every time you buy something, on a weekly schedule, or all at once for the whole month?

If you're using an app that automatically pulls in your transactions for you, you'll still need to look at things occasionally to see if transactions have been categorized correctly and to see how you're doing with your spending. When do you plan to do this?

Determine a time when you'll regularly look at your budget, and put this into your calendar or put a reminder on your phone. I recommend you check it at *least* one time, preferably around the end of the month. This way, you'll be able to see if you have any extra money left over, so you can use it to build your emergency fund as we talked about. You'll also be able to determine next month's budget, and see if you need to increase any limits or eliminate any expenses. Furthermore, you'll have new insight into your spending habits, and you'll know if you need to slow down your spending in any particular area.

Action Plan

If you've lowered your expenses as much as possible but are still "in the red," how could you increase your income? What passions or skills do you have that you could profit off of? Would it be in your best interest to spend this coming weekend cleaning out an area in your home so you can list it on Neighbor? Or should you spend it filling out a profile on Rover so you can start walking dogs after you get home from work?

How will you set yourself up for success and make it easier to stick to your budget? Do you need to go withdraw funds from your bank so you can give the Envelope System a try? At what limit will you wait 24 hours before purchasing something? Should you and your spouse set a goal together so that they will be more likely to stick to the budget?

Make a plan for when you will regularly check on and update your budget. Add this to your calendar or set a reminder.

I've thrown a lot at you the last four days so it's okay if you don't get to address every expense, bill, or subscription. If you don't though, plan to come back to what you missed another time. Don't leave any expense "stone" unturned as you could be leaving money on the table without realizing it.

DAY 25:
TAKE PRIDE IN YOUR APPEARANCE PART 1

John Molloy, author of the book *Dress for Success*, conducted a study in Grand Central Station in New York City. He walked up to strangers and asked for 75 cents under the ruse that he had forgotten his wallet and needed money to take the train home. For one hour he performed this experiment while wearing a suit and tie. Then he did another hour wearing the same suit but *without* a tie.

It was such a subtle difference, but can you guess when his results were better? While wearing the suit by itself he collected $7.23, but by adding the tie, he comparatively collected a whopping $26!

People Judge You on How You Look

It only takes people 7 seconds (though some studies claim even less) to form their first impression of you.

According to clothing psychology, if your clothes are sloppy, wrinkled, stained, or mismatched, people will assume that you're also sloppy. That means that if you dress like a hot mess, people will assume you're a hot mess!

People make snap decisions about others based on how they look. John Molloy's study indicated, as well as many others have, that how we look impacts our lives. For instance, <u>95% of the determination to hire you for a job depends upon your clothing</u>, according to the American Personnel Consultants (those who hire for large companies).

Let me be clear, <u>I'm not saying that people shouldn't like you for you</u>. But it's important to be aware that how people perceive us, based on how we look, plays a direct role in the quality of our life. Caring about how you dress and how you present yourself is important!

For a more in-depth understanding of how to dress yourself to be perceived in a way you would like to be seen, such as more professional or more attractive, check out this fantastic article: Fashion Psychology: What Your Choice in Clothes Say About You

Take Care of the Essentials

While basic hygiene won't win you the award for personal appearance, it's vital, and can sometimes be forgotten when pushed to the side in place of more urgent matters. I'll be covering some topics that might seem obvious to you. But because not everyone is raised the same, and because I've met full-grown adults who didn't know these things, I'll be covering a few fundamentals.

Skin

Let's start with the most basic part of good hygiene, showering. When we shower, we do so to remove dirt and odor-causing bacteria. Use soap, and wash your *whole* body with it. Yes, I mean in between your butt cheeks, in your armpits, and getting the bottom of your feet as well.

I bet you probably already know that. You most likely have the whole showering thing down and may shower daily or even several times a day. Taking showers is a *good* thing. However, I want you to be aware that more, in this case, is not necessarily better.

Longer, hotter showers can dry out your skin. And washing your hair excessively may cause your body's sebum production to kick into overdrive, resulting in greasy hair. Plus, when you bathe too often or with too harsh a soap (like an antibacterial one), you wash away your skin's natural layer of oil and "good" bacteria which is there for your protection.

<u>Experts agree that one shower a day is fine, but it's not *necessary*</u>. How often you actually need one depends upon your body's natural production of oil and shedding of skin, as well as your lifestyle habits, like if you work outside or exercise daily. The average person only needs to shower two to three times a week.

So the next time you're about to hop in the shower, <u>consider if you're just showering out of habit because you love feeling warm water on your back after a long day, because daily showers are the societal norm, or because your body actually needs to be cleaned.</u>

When I started paying attention to my body's needs and how long it took for my hair to get greasy, I cut back from taking multiple showers a day to only a handful a week. Doing so cut my water bill. My hair and body products last longer, and I spend less time styling my hair. Now, I only need to style it a few times a week instead of every single day, which is a *huge* time-saver!

Moving on, don't be afraid to use deodorants that are stronger (like men's) or apply them multiple times throughout the day if you need to. There is no shame in being smell-free! And to prevent any smelly mishaps, always be prepared by having extra deodorant around. I keep one in my bathroom, in my car, in my purse, and when I used to leave the house for work, in my locker. Baby powder is another option that's good for controlling odors in other places, like your feet.

<u>When it comes to odor in your downstairs region</u> ladies, keep in mind that <u>certain smells are normal.</u> Simply wearing cotton underwear (not what's the cutest or the cheapest), and allowing things to "breathe" is good practice. So is avoiding any douching.

Your vagina's natural acidity kills bacteria. You don't need to use any soap inside, and in fact, that could be harmful as it disrupts your vagina's delicate balance of pH. If this is an area of concern for you, see a gynecologist. Oh, and if your man is telling you that you smell, or that you need to wash down there, take him to the gynecologist too so they can talk some sense into him.

Hair

When you wash your hair, make sure you're only using shampoo on your scalp. It's not supposed to go on the ends of your hair. The conditioner is supposed to go on the ends, but it's not supposed to go on your scalp.

If you don't have time to wash your hair one day, you can stop it from looking greasy by doing a quick touch-up with dry shampoo or baby powder. You can also hide the grease temporarily by wearing a cute hat. Just please do this sparingly. This hack is not intended to let you go a week without washing!

If you have issues with dandruff, don't resign to a life of flakes! Avoid wearing dark-colored clothing while resolving the problem. Get a dandruff shampoo, or see your doctor for a stronger prescribed one if you need it. There are also scalp detoxes that help remove any buildup of products and dead skin.

Everyone has their own opinion when it comes to body hair. But <u>if you prefer to be hairless, I encourage you to come up with a routine for removing it</u>.

I had a habit of pushing off shaving, thinking that I'd do it whenever I *felt* like it. Unsurprisingly, that time never came, and I ended up looking like an ape! Your routine might be to shave every time you take a shower. Or you may decide to only shave twice a week so that things look maintained, but so that you don't spend exorbitant amounts of time keeping yourself hairless. I wish I'd learned this sooner, but <u>shaving facial hair is okay.</u> I always thought that shaving my lip hair or eyebrows would result in thicker, darker shafts. But that's just not true.

It wasn't until I learned that certain celebrities shave that I realized it was fine to do. In fact, your makeup will apply smoother and your face lotion will have an easier time absorbing if you use a razor to get rid of those baby hairs. Shaving also lightly exfoliates the top layer of skin, which will make your complexion look more luminous.

Of course, using a blade or tweezers is completely up to you. But if you find the idea of shaving easier, and would prefer something painless, now you know it's okay to do. So you have no more excuse for having a womanstache !

Mouth

Having worked as the Air Force's version of a hygienist, something that I hinted at previously, I can tell you that flossing is, in fact, important! <u>The bacteria responsible for bad breath live underneath your gums</u>. When you floss, you allow air in underneath, which kills this anaerobic bacteria.

If you have any odor on your tongue, you can scrape it off with this <u>stainless steel, easy-to-clean tongue scraper.</u>

Of course, brushing your teeth is super important too. I once met a person who thought that mouthwash replaces brushing. No, it does not. Brush your teeth two times a day for two minutes. Also, make sure you're *only* using a soft or extra-soft bristle brush. And don't brush back and forth. You want to brush in gentle circles aiming the bristles at your gumline.

If you're like me, you're probably dying to know the secret, best way to whiten your teeth from an insider. Well, the whitening strips that work the best, the ones that all the hygienists and dentists I worked with use, are Crest Whitening Strips.

Nails

Cleaning under your nails and keeping them well-kempt is important, not just for looks, but also for hygiene. Think about how gross it is when you see a man with black fingernails! If you work a labor-intensive job where you often get dirt underneath your nails, or if you have any length to them, get a nail brush. They're inexpensive and make cleaning under your nails easy.

Having chipped nail polish doesn't look, well, polished! It also harbors bacteria. If you want to have your nails done, consider getting acrylic, gel, or making the effort to repaint them when you need to. You could also wear light colors that don't show chips as much or just go bare.

A less expensive option to acrylic and gel nails are press-ons. I already introduced you to these beautiful Coffin Nails back on Day 22, when I revealed how I save money. I like these nails in particular though because they are so versatile. Color Street strips work on them, I can paint them, and they *don't* chip.

These are light and thin so they feel very natural. Best of all, they last two, sometimes even three weeks! Since I started wearing these, I haven't gone back to a salon.

If you're new to the hygiene scene, or perhaps even if you aren't, I've probably given you a few ideas for things you can work on and improve. What routines can you come up with for incorporating and practicing good personal hygiene if you don't have any already?

Your Size Plays a Role

You can absolutely be stunningly beautiful and confident as a bigger gal. But as much as I'm here to let you know your worth and cheer you on when you love yourself and your body, I'm also here to share the realities of the world we live in. It's unfortunate that we have to talk about this, but the reality is that obesity discrimination exists. Obesity Discrimination is when overweight individuals are less likely to get hired, are paid less, and are less likely to get a promotion. Staggering still, obese women have even lower rates than obese men. This negative bias, or fatphobia, extends beyond the work center though.

As sad as it is, your weight, either being a "normal" healthy weight or overweight, plays a factor in how you're treated and the quality of your life. There isn't enough room to go in-depth into this topic and spend multiple days discussing it in our short time together. But because it is so important for your quality of life, and mainly for your well-being, I'll spend the rest of today going over a few tips.

I previously shared some keys to success with you in the chapter called Soul-Care. If you need a refresher, go back and reread that section. Now, I'll share a little bit more with you.

If you suffer from obesity, I've personally been there, and I understand what you're going through.

Losing weight is a *journey*. A saying that helped me get into the right mindset was, "You didn't put on your weight in a few months, so why do you expect it to come off in a few months?" Be patient with the weight loss process. Those who lose weight gradually and in a controlled way tend to be the ones to keep it off.

Do Everything in Moderation

Completely cutting out a food group, which many crash diets encourage you to do, may work temporarily. However, that *won't* work long-term. Instead, seek to eat a more balanced diet where you still eat the foods you love, although sparingly, while also eating healthier options.

It's very important to exercise in moderation as well. Taking rest days and rotating which muscles you work out is *vital* for preventing injury and for building new muscles. Don't go out and run ten miles after reading this chapter when you were a couch potato yesterday. Be gentle with your body and ease it into exercise, slowly building up your strength and endurance.

Make Small Changes You Can Stick To

What incremental changes could you make to improve what you eat or how

<u>much exercise you do?</u>

You could decide you'll park at the end of the parking lot from now on and walk further into work every day. You could take the stairs everywhere you go instead of the elevator. Anytime a paper needs to be delivered to another section at work, you could walk it there in person. When a recipe calls for beef, you could swap it out for turkey. And instead of having two tablespoons of sugar in your coffee, you could have just one.

No change or swap is too small. The smaller a change you can make, the more likely you'll be to stick to it for the long haul.

Expect to Fail

If you don't stick to the changes you make, or rather *when* you don't, don't beat yourself up! Falling off the wagon is inevitable.

I know it may be tempting to throw in the towel when you feel like you messed up your diet and eat whatever you want because "the whole day is ruined." But that's not the case. You don't have to wait until next month, next week, or even tomorrow to eat healthier. <u>You can start over again right now.</u>

When you mess up, do *not* try to make up for your mistakes. Punishing yourself isn't going to help you reach your weight loss/health goals. Trying to make up for eating something unhealthy or too much of something may lead to even worse problems, such as a cycle of starving and binging (called Bulimia).

A healthier approach, and one that could lead to a lifestyle improvement instead of a temporary diet fix, would be to move forward and learn from what went wrong. Instead of punishing yourself, <u>figure out *why* you couldn't stick to your new healthier lifestyle. Plan what you'll do differently next time.</u>

Get Help

If you don't know where to start in your health journey, getting a professional's help is a great place. If you're new to exercising, it's good to have someone there to correct your form the first few times, so that you don't accidentally hurt yourself.

If you're interested in losing weight, toning, or gaining muscle, my dear friend Dani at Fit Bird Fitness offers online coaching for women, specifically for those who are abuse survivors, though you don't have to be to use her services. If you want to get your health in check, I highly recommend her as I've seen firsthand just how much care, attention, and time she puts into every single client. She genuinely wants women to heal not just their bodies, but their minds as well, and relearn self-love for themselves.

Her plans start very affordably at only $10. And you can choose to work with her for as little as a month. If you want a more hands-on approach though, she offers progressively in-depth options as well. So you only have to pay for what you want/need.

I encourage you to get help, either through one-on-one coaching, an online at-home program, or in-person at the gym. Even if you don't have the money for a trainer, there are *free* Youtube videos you can watch where people will do the exercises with you, encourage you, and some will even have timers on the screen to help you count down.

The channels I recommend you check out for workouts are MadFit, HASfit, and Love Sweat Fitness. For direction on dieting, I recommend heyitsjuliana as she has lots of sound advice, straightforward approaches, and applies humor and realism to her videos.

Apps are another direction you could pursue, though not all of these are free options. I love the tough, fast-paced workouts from Sweat. This is a good app if you want to do high-intensity workouts in as short of a period as possible. There is also BodySpace by bodybuilding.com. I recommend this app for any beginners looking to build muscle because it offers helpful videos and breakdowns of how to do exercises properly when lifting weights. And my favorite app is MyFitnessPal. This one is good for keeping track of what you eat.

Find What Works for You

I mentioned before that I intermittent fast. By listening to my body and paying attention to what made me feel my best, I realized that I am a volume eater. I like to eat until I feel satiated. When I don't intermittent fast, which is essentially just restricting *when* I eat, not how much, I will mindlessly snack the entire day.

Intermittent fasting is not for everyone, but why not see if it's for you? A bonus to it is that it saves on dishes and the number of times a day you have to cook!

Some people will argue that intermittent fasting is the wrong way to go about things and that the "correct" way to be healthy is to eat three square meals a day. Others will tell you that the best way to be healthy is to instead eat six tiny meals. Some say to eat lots of snacks. Other people say to not eat any. So what is actually the best? The best way to eat is whatever way works for *you*, not your best friend, favorite celebrity, or what's on-trend.

Consider playing around and trying out different eating patterns, times, and macro (fat, carb, and protein) amounts to see what makes your body feel its best. Maybe you need to eat fewer carbs and more filling fats, like with Keto. Or maybe a lot of fat upsets your stomach, so you'd do better eating less fat, but having more meat or beans for protein.

Another thing you can experiment with is seeing what kind of exercises leave you feeling your best as well. Again, find what works for you. Consider that you'll be much more likely to want to work out in the first place if you choose to do things that you enjoy rather than things you'll dread. That may mean running for a short distance or walking for a long distance. It may mean doing a high-intensity workout or just leisurely going for a bike ride. Maybe it means picking a sport back up that you used to play in high school or trying out an adult league with some girlfriends and learning something new.

Do It for You

I'd like to end today on one last very important note. Whether you're taking these tips and applying them to improve your already healthy lifestyle, or if you're using these in hopes to become the healthy woman that you want to be, please, whatever you do, do it for *you*.

There is a startling percentage of people out there who think they are doing the right thing by letting you know their opinion about your body. Perhaps you've been told by a stranger that you'd be prettier if you "filled out" because being a "string bean" isn't womanly. Or maybe well-meaning family members have thought they were helping you by letting you know you'd gained weight as if you weren't already aware.

If someone ever does this to you, perhaps it's time to make use of those boundaries you learned about. And if you need to, you can always point people to this study that proved that <u>weight shaming leads to *increased* weight gain</u>. Your doctor aside, no one should be telling you what to do with your body. What ultimately matters is that you are *healthy* and *happy* with how you look.

Action Plan

Today, feel free to dive further into any of the articles mentioned or look up your own to <u>educate yourself on why taking pride in your appearance matters</u>. How can you give a first impression that matches the kind of person you *are*, instead of how you *might* be coming across?

Do you need to focus a little more on basic hygiene? Should you get that tongue scraper so you don't scare anyone away with your bad breath anymore? If you shave, what is your shaving routine going to look like so you stay on top of things?

<u>If your weight is a concern to you, or if you'd just like to be at a better, healthier place, do you need to spend this evening downloading any of those apps</u> or checking out Fit Bird Fitness if you think you'd do best with a personalized plan for eating and working out? What is one small change you could implement for the rest of your life that would be a better option than what you're currently doing or eating?

DAY 26:
TAKE PRIDE IN YOUR APPEARANCE PART 2

The Clothes We Wear Affect Us

What you wear does not *define* who you are, but it does have a direct psychological impact on *how* you behave.

There was a study performed by researchers at Northwestern University that showed that by simply throwing on a doctor's lab coat, <u>individuals were instantly able to perform better on tests by 50%</u> compared to those who didn't. That's a staggering difference!

This is called Enclothed Cognition. How can you use it to improve your life? Dress better for others, but also *yourself!*

Yes, I mean <u>even if you're staying at home.</u> Get out of your pajamas. Get out of your sweats and put on a nice outfit like you're going to the office. You'll have more energy, you'll feel more put together, and you'll be in a better mindset to get things done, rather than if you were to keep lounging around in loungers. Plus, if you have a significant other, they'll appreciate you putting effort into your appearance.

How to Dress for Success

Clothing

Dressing better begins at the store. If you know you won't take the time to iron your clothes, try to fill your closet with things that are wrinkle-resistant. Natural fibers like cotton and linen wrinkle easier than synthetic fabrics like polyester and nylon.

<u>A great hack for getting out the wrinkles that do appear is getting a handheld steamer.</u> Never again do you have to walk out of the house looking frumpy. With one of these, you can transform a wrinkled shirt in less than a minute. You can also smooth out curtains and other wrinkled linens. There are less expensive options out there, but I like this handheld steamer because it kills 99.9% of germs, so you can use it to sanitize your couch and dog's bed as well.

If you don't want to spend money but still don't want wrinkled shirts, lightly spritz your clothing with water and throw it in the dryer for 5-10 minutes. Remove it as soon as it's done and immediately put it on or hang it up.

If you have a pet, I recommend keeping lint rollers handy to remove their hair from your clothes. I have an emergency roller in my car just in case I get somewhere and my cat's white hair is showing all over my black leggings. If this is a common issue for you, consider switching your clothing color of choice to something that works *with* your pet's hair color to make it less noticeable. My sister-in-law has done this. She has a black dog and usually wears all black.

If you find lint rollers wasteful, we offer an eco-friendly version of them in our boutique. These use static electricity to get off pet hair as well as lint and dandruff, so they can be used over and over. By never needing to buy another lint roller again, these wands pay for themselves. They also come with a free mini travel wand so you can carry it in your purse and always be pet hair and lint-free.

Another great tool is a depiller. This is a must-have item if you like to wear a lot of sweaters, but it's still useful for any kind of clothing or fabric to remove the fuzzies that appear over time and keep things looking fresh. This one, which I got for myself, currently has over 80,000 ratings on Amazon. So it really is an essential household product. If you get this item though, just be careful to never use it on a garment where there is a snag, as it will cut the fabric and leave a hole. Alternatively, you can use this sweater comb, which doesn't require a battery and is small enough that you can also carry it in your purse.

Next, let's talk about proper fit. Jeans that are so long they drag and get ripped up and dirty, or dress shirts that are so tight they pull at the buttons don't look good. Buy clothes that fit your body type from the start, or take things to the tailor. Going to the tailor's is not an outdated thing. It is something that classy women, like you, do. So take the garments that need some help to be altered. Even clothing that is too tight or short can sometimes have its seams let out to accommodate you.

Having clothing that fits you well will help your outfits look polished and will also help you feel more comfortable in them. Life is too short to feel *stuffed* into something that doesn't fit. Plus, when something doesn't fit, it

<u>usually doesn't flatter your body either</u>. Baggy clothing can make you look shorter than you are. And wearing things that are too tight, like a bra, may make you appear lumpy when you're not.

That's not to mention enclothed cognition, which we just went over. <u>What kind of subliminal messages are you feeding yourself when you insist upon wearing clothes that don't fit?</u> "I'm so big I can't button my jeans. I must be fat." Not necessarily. You're just wearing jeans that aren't your size.

Additionally, having something that you have to keep adjusting, that itches you, or that distracts you, is taking away your attention from more important things that you're doing throughout your day. It's just clothing. If something doesn't fit, doesn't make you feel good about yourself, or is uncomfortable, get it altered or get rid of it.

We must also talk about the arch-nemesis of us hot messes, clothing stains! Doesn't it seem like whenever you're wearing a white shirt that your coffee is drawn to it like a magnet? <u>I recommend being prepared for those oopses by carrying stain fighters in your car, purse, desk, and wherever else you can think of</u>.

We already went over recommendations for stain fighters in the chapter about laundry. If you need a refresher, go back and reread that section of Day 18. But something that I didn't mention is that the Tide to Go pens do *not* contain bleach. So you don't have to worry about using them and immediately needing to wash your clothes, something that previously made me hesitant about them. There are also individually wrapped Shout Wipes, which we did not cover, but that you may find to be even more portable friendly as they are disposable and smaller than the pen.

There are many other options for stain fighters out there. Whatever you get, just be sure to carry it with you, as clothing mishaps are bound to happen, and walking around with stains is not the best look.

<u>The final tool I recommend you get for keeping your clothes looking on point is a snag puller.</u> This is another must-have item, especially if you're klutzy like me and catch your clothing on everything. Be sure to get the deluxe version of this, if you get one, so that you'll have one tool for thicker garments like sweaters and sweatshirts, and the other for fixing pulls in fine-knit clothing.

Shoes

Let's not forget about what you wear on your feet. Keep your shoes clean. If they're scuffed or damaged, can you do anything to repair them or remove the scuffs?

If you want to appear instantly more fit and tall, consider adding heels to your shoe collection. <u>Wearing heels can flatter your legs by making them look more *toned* and *elongated*</u>. You don't have to wear towering heels though. Something with a height of only two inches like booties, wedges, or clogs are still easy to walk in and can be very flattering.

You could also opt for an optical illusion of making your legs look longer by wearing pointed shoes or nude colors that match your skin tone. Of course, keep function in mind. Is there a shoe that you could wear that blends style *and* comfort?

Makeup

Every woman is going to have her preference when it comes to makeup. Of course, you should not wear makeup if you don't want to.

If after reading this chapter you decide you do want to add it into your routine though, or if you want to improve your technique of what you're already doing, there are tons of *free* makeup tutorials on Youtube. You can also go to Ulta, Sephora, or these other stores to receive one-on-one makeup consulting personalized for you (some are free and some charge).

Find a simple look that you like and that you can do fast. Consider practicing it to reduce how long it takes you to do. Previously, when I left the house for work, I was able to do my makeup in just ten minutes.

<u>What is the least amount of makeup that you need to feel put together so you can skip the rest and save time getting ready</u>? For myself, it is mascara, winged eyeliner, and lip gloss.

If having winged eyeliner is one of your important makeup products as well, this Winged Eyeliner & Eyeliner Stamp we offer in our boutique is phenomenal. It literally stamps on a cat-eye look, so <u>your wings are done in seconds and symmetrical every time</u>.

Hair

When it comes to your hair, I encourage you to do the same thing. Find looks that look good on you and practice doing them, so that in a pinch, you can throw your hair up in a tried-and-true style and know you'll look fabulous.

<u>Whenever you're looking for information on how to do something with your hair</u> (or almost anything else for that matter), I highly recommend that you <u>ask someone who is</u> (or was) <u>in a similar situation to yourself.</u>

For instance, if you have short, thin hair, ask someone who also has short, thin hair how they style it, assuming that their style is something you want to replicate. It wouldn't make much sense to get advice from someone who has long, thick hair, as they wouldn't know best how to work with what you've got, unless of course if they're a professional.

This is how I discovered a tool that has honestly changed my hair game. I took the time to ask someone who has similar hair to my own how they were able to get a certain look that I'd been trying to emulate. She introduced me to this curling wand. If you have long, thick hair like mine, and are wanting to get effortless curls, I cannot recommend this iron enough.

Besides asking people whose hairstyle you admire how they do it, you can also find inspiration on Pinterest, Tiktok, and Youtube. As I have long hair, I've followed and learned hacks from YouTuber Alex Gaboury. But if you have short hair, you might prefer to find hacks elsewhere. Brad Mondo is another individual on YouTube. As a hairstylist, he offers a ton of information on how to improve your mane game as well.

As it'll be that much harder to look your best when starting with an unflattering haircut. You could also ask your hairdresser's opinion next time you go in.

If you have a cut or style that you find hard to maintain so it always looks messy, should you switch to a different one that would be easier for you to keep up with? For example, if you dye your hair but are not good about getting touch-ups, would keeping your hair its natural color be easier for you, at least for now? Unless having roots is specifically part of your style, it's not necessarily flattering, especially when dealing with two starkly different colors. If you want to have dyed hair but don't have the time or money to go to the salon as often as you need to, an ombre is a great option. This style helps blend in your growing roots with the colored sections on the bottom.

For other general fashion ideas on all of the above topics, I recommend Shea Whitney and AlexandrasGirlyTalk on Youtube. They share styling tips while keeping things modest and often feminine. They also talk about self-care and self-love.

Body Language

Your body language also plays a role in how you come across to others. Of course, proper posture is good for your body, as it keeps it in natural alignment. But did you know it impacts your mental health as well?

According to the philosophy of embodied cognition, your body is hunched over because you feel unconfident, but you also might be feeling unconfident because you're hunched over. By changing the position of your body you can change how you feel.

This means that by standing up straight, you don't only portray confidence to others, but you also convey confidence to yourself. Standing up straight also makes you appear more attractive, as you're instantly taller and leaner. So if you want to feel and look more attractive and confident, work on your posture. Watch this famous TED Talk about how Your Body Language May Shape Who You Are.

If you tend to be a big sloucher, our boutique offers a great Posture Corrector that helps hold your shoulders back and retrains your body to be in proper form. Even if you're a chronic sloucher like I am, you can instantly see good posture results. I especially appreciate that you can wear this corrector underneath a big comfy sweater and no one will be the wiser.

Posture, gestures, and how we move and interact with objects and others all communicate who we are. Things like a strong, firm handshake and eye contact are important for first impressions, but proper etiquette continues after that first meeting. It's something that we can put into practice daily for the rest of our lives. Knowing how to interact with others in the best way possible is good information to know so that you can continue to put your best self out there. I've enjoyed learning about proper etiquette from

TikToker @sofia.marbella. And TikTokker @patricia.cnr_offers a lot of similar content.

What Matters Most

A lot of the things we went over today are "basic" fashion, like appearing clean, neat, and tidy, but the other things are up to your discretion. Take the suggestions you like and try something new, or keep doing what you've always done if you've found a great style that you love.

Wear clothes and style yourself in a way that makes you feel good about yourself, in a way that expresses your uniqueness and that makes you happy. If you love flats, girl wear those. You don't *have* to wear heels. If you don't like makeup because it makes you feel inauthentic, be true to yourself!

As we went over yesterday, people will judge you based on how you look and what you wear. But here's a little secret, they will judge you *either* way. It's human nature. Our brains are made to draw conclusions from our surroundings so that we can make informed decisions about them.

So while you can follow today's and yesterday's suggestions, I don't recommend doing so at the expense of your personal expression. Don't implement any of these ideas if they're not in alignment with who you are or want to be. After all, appearance isn't everything. "Man looks at the outward appearance... God looks at the heart." 1 Samuel 16:7.

Action Plan

Keeping in mind what we just went over, what can you do to improve how you dress and present yourself?

Are there any clothes that don't fit the best that you could take to be altered this weekend? If so, start a pile. Do your favorite pair of shoes need to be cleaned up? Should you spend some time this evening practicing a quick makeup look or do you need to instead call your hairdresser to schedule a root touchup? How will you work on improving your posture and remember to stand up straight instead of slouching?

DAY 27:
DIGITAL DECLUTTER & TECHNOLOGY TROUBLES

Today, we're quickly going to be covering how to digitally declutter your life, something that could be considered a normal "adulting" behavior. However, I've chosen to place this chapter in the 4th section of this guide as we're going to be mainly focusing on two big problems that I feel plague us hot messes. These include never having enough digital storage and always running low on battery. While I'll only be covering these in regards to your computer and cellphone, <u>follow these suggestions for any other device you have that they apply to</u>.

I'm aware that not everyone understands technology as I'm technologically challenged myself. So if you're struggling to grasp or perform any of the suggestions today, get help from a tech-savvy friend.

Your Computer

Keep It Decluttered & Organized

The jury still seems to be out on whether or not a cluttered desktop slows down your computer. However, I think we can agree that having a screen full of images and files, similar to having a cluttered, messy home, can add to our stress level. Plus, it costs us valuable time when we have to weed through tons of junk whenever we want to find something.

Take some time to go through the contents of your computer, not just the desktop or main screen, but all of its files, and get rid of anything that you can. Organize what you want to keep into folders, and upload things to Google Drive if you need more space or want to back things up.

With Google's stellar services and capabilities, I find the idea of using an external hard drive to back things up rather redundant. But considering that you may run out of free storage on Google Drive at some point and have to transfer things anyway, it's a smart move to <u>keep a backup of your important documents and images</u>. So make sure you are doing so in some sort of fashion, <u>however you prefer to</u>, as you never know when you might spill pickle juice all over your computer (guilty as charged).

Google Drive, as well as Google Keep, will both need to be periodically decluttered and organized as well.

So come up with a plan for when you will regularly address all of these things and do a digital clearout. I suggest you do this monthly, but at *least* once a year. If you save things to your computer a lot, you may want to do this more often.

Email

Empty Your Inbox

Is your inbox overflowing with emails? At one point, mine got up to an insane 40,000+ unread! Can you beat that number? You delete one and receive twenty more by the end of the day. How do we solve this problem?

First, decide if it's worth your time to clear out your mailbox or if you should just start a new one.

It may help you decide one way or the other if I introduce you to this amazing software that will help you quickly declutter your inbox. Sign up for Unroll.me and let it do the hard work for you!

This free software will show you everything you're signed up for so that you can pick and choose what you want to unsubscribe from, and then do so with one click. Then it'll combine all other subscriptions you want to keep into a once-daily "Rollup, " so they won't clog your inbox but will still be accessible.

I decided it would be much faster for me to just start a whole new email. If you're going to be starting over as well, I recommend using Gmail as you already have it set up, and as it connects to Google Calendar and Google Keep.

Make your email address short and sweet. Something like your first and last name, or first initial and last name. We're adults now, so no "hotchic@hotmail.com" or something like that. Keep it professional and easy to spell as you'll most likely need to spell it out to people over the phone at some point.

Create folders to organize your mail. Set up categories for important things you want to keep. For example, I have a folder for "Travel" and then subfolders inside it for different trips I've taken. Other examples could be Health Records, Legal, School with class subfolders, Family, Receipts, Pets, Volunteering, or even Church with conversational exchanges and dates/times of events, etc. Make a folder for every important area of your life in which you receive or send emails.

Next, if you are keeping your old email address, delete, delete, delete, and then organize the remaining important emails into the new folders. Anything you're not sure if you should keep can be archived. This removes it from your inbox and allows you to *still* reference it later. Simply click the "All Mail" button to find the ones that were archived.

If you're starting a new email, sync it to your old one, that way you don't have to worry about switching everything over to the new email address. The new emails will be forwarded to your new email, and then you can just leave your old email as storage in case there is anything in that jumble that you need later. To do this on your old email account if it is Gmail click on "Settings," then "See all Settings", then "Forwarding and POP/IMAP ", and fill out the top section.

Lastly, determine when it will be the best time for you to check your email. Again, add this as a recurring event in your calendar so you can stay on top of it moving forward.

Once you're caught up, you may be tempted to check your email multiple times a day so you don't fall behind again. Or maybe you're already in the habit of checking it often, because you don't want to keep people waiting to hear back from you, or just because you like seeing what emails you got. Be careful not to fall into the trap of checking your email multiple times a day. It's a waste of time.

If someone *has* to get a hold of you, they won't send an email. They'll call you. And if they don't have your phone number, then they aren't someone who needs to be reaching you anyway. Remember what we talked about earlier in this guide, *you* need to determine what you do with *your* time. Don't let others "tell" you by feeling obligated to constantly check your email and instantly respond. That's living a stressful, *reactive* lifestyle.

I'd like to suggest again that if you haven't already turned off your notifications, like I suggested you do back on Day 6, you consider doing so for your desktop *and* phone. It may feel a bit rebellious to no longer know the exact moment when an email comes in, to stop receiving app notifications and news and weather updates, or even stop being notified about messages.

Society expects us to always be available for others. But what if we weren't? What if you checked your emails and messages when it worked for you? We shouldn't be made to feel guilty for being inaccessible during certain times of our day, or dumb or foolish if we decide we don't want to keep "informed" about *everything all* the time, especially when it comes to stuff that doesn't apply to us or that stresses us out.

I found the act of turning off my notifications so freeing and stress-relieving, and I believe you will as well. However, I recommend that you at least keep your calendar notifications on so that you don't miss anything on your schedule. But even if you decide to not cut everything off, be choosy about what notifications you allow to interrupt your life from now on.

Stay On Top of It Moving Forward

With any kind of junk email, you can select them all, click "Report Spam," and then "Report Scam & Unsubscribe." This may be tedious and take a while, especially if you've given out your email a lot in the past. If you tend to enter a lot of giveaways, consider setting up a new email and leaving your old one to serve as a junk mailbox for these sorts of things. This way your new mailbox will stay clearer.

If you want to keep some email subscriptions but don't want to have your inbox bogged down with them, besides getting the "Rollup," you can just create a folder for them to be automatically deposited into. Copy the email address you want to apply this to. In your search bar at the top of the page to the right click the down arrow. Put the email into the "From" field, then click "Create Filter" and mark the appropriate category/s that work for you such as "Skip the Inbox (Archive it)." You can also apply a label on that same screen to make the email easier to find later if you do go looking for it, such as "Beauty Magazine" or whatever name you come up with to match that email address.

You can also put tasks from your emails right into your Calendar and assign them a date and time to be worked on. To do this, look down at the lower right of the screen while you're on your email dashboard. You'll see a "Show Side Panel" button. Click that to pull out your Calendar.

<u>Delete emails when you're done with them or archive them</u>. Leave the inbox space as a representation of items you need to take action on. Do *not* use it as storage.

Your Cellphone

Declutter & Detox

We're about to go over what to do with all of the pictures on your phone. So we won't worry about that just yet. But there are plenty of other things that need to be cleaned out occasionally on your mobile device as well.

Just like what you did with your computer, take some time to go through your phone and get rid of anything you don't use, namely apps. You may have downloaded quite a few having gone through the other chapters, so clear out any that you decided not to use.

File and organize what you can. Put things that you want to access more, like a new budgeting app, towards the front. And put things you might want to access less, like Facebook or Instagram, towards the back, or even inside of a folder so they're harder to get to.

Speaking of, go through all of your social media and unfollow people or things that are no longer relevant or that don't add value to your life. Are you still a part of a bunch of Keto Facebook groups from that one time you tried it a few years ago? Unfollow them. Are you still friends with that one random dude you met at a bar a long time ago who you will never interact with again? Unfollow him. If following a certain boutique will encourage you to break your budget, unfollow them. If someone is always posting pictures that make you feel insecure about your body or unhappy with your life because you don't travel as often as they do, unfollow them. As the young woman mentions in that video I suggested earlier, <u>if you're concerned you'll hurt someone's feelings by unfollowing them, just mute them.</u>

Similarly, go through your phone's contacts and remove any that you no longer need.

Free Up Space

If you have the problem of running out of space on your phone because you love to take a million pictures of your pup or your food, Google Photos can help you. Now, you'll no longer have to make your friends wait to take a selfie with you while you quickly try to delete a few pictures.

Google Photos holds images that are on *and* off your phone, while iCloud only backups those that are on your device. So to accommodate all devices and keep all photos, we're going to be using this specific software.

Download the Google Photos app and use your Gmail account to set it up. Follow the instructions here to then automatically save, backup, and sync your photos as well as videos.

Your photos will now be available anywhere you have Gmail access. For example, if you take pictures on your phone, they'll now be available on your computer without you having to mess with any USB drive or anything!

If you need to, you can pay for additional storage. However, you get a ton of it for free, as in *years* worth of photos (15 GB to be exact).

Now to free up space on your phone for the things that have already been backed up, simply click "Free up space." It's that easy!

Another cool thing you could do, if that was too simple for you, is to designate an Instagram profile or hashtag to a particular thing that you have a lot of photos of.

An example of this would be if you have a million pictures of your dog, you could post them all to a dedicated Instagram profile for her. Or you could use your own profile if you have one, and just upload the excess of pictures you have using a specific hashtag just for her. Then when you look up that hashtag, you'll see all of her pictures.

This is a great option as it can kill two birds with one stone. You'll be able to free up phone space and share the pictures with others who want to stay informed about your life at the same time (like your parents wanting to know how their grandpuppy is). Less work for you!

Another great benefit to freeing up space using Instagram is that there are cool companies out there that can convert your Instagram photos into books!

Shutterfly makes this process simple by connecting right to your Instagram account. (Image from Shutterfly)

The lowest price I was able to find for this was only $9.99 for a hardcover book of twenty pages. But they do offer other options though that go up to sixty pages if you need them. And if you're not artsy, you can have them make the book for you by choosing colors and a theme to go with your images. FYI, <u>this makes an awesome gift!</u>

Google Photos now has its own version of this as well. However, their books are more expensive. Theirs start at $14.99 for a softcover book with twenty pages. But his software already has your photos uploaded to it, so it may require less work. It can also make books much longer, up to 140 pages.

Keep It Charged

Have you ever been in the middle of a conversation that was abruptly ended because your phone died? Have you ever been stranded somewhere because you were using your phone's GPS to get someplace and it shut off?

 I have! There were at least two times in recent years when I had to go to a random gas station, buy a charger, and sit in my car waiting for my phone to turn back on so I could find my way home.

For some reason, keeping our phones charged can be a herculean effort for us hot messes. But we're about to change that.

First, if you have a significant other or a roommate/s, get your own chargers! Don't fight over the cords or share them, because then the chargers will get moved, misplaced, and lost. You'll never know where one is when you need it, so get one for every person in the household. <u>Differentiate between them by getting different colors or by using washi tape.</u>

Second, when you do get your own charger, get one that fits you and your needs. Having your own charger, and a good one at that, will help you be more likely to use it.

Is your phone case too small for your charger so you have to remove the case every time you want to charge it? Get one that fits!

Is the outlet far away? Then find a charger with a long cord. Do you charge your phone in a position that bends the cord and often leads to frayed wires, like charging it while it sits on your chest so you can watch Netflix? Then get a braided nylon one that isn't plastic or that is shaped so it won't bend the cord. This one solves all of those problems as it's ten feet long, braided, and angled.

Do you find that you're too tired at the end of the night to be bothered with plugging in your phone? You're going to have to set it down somewhere, so why not get a charger that you just have to set the phone down on?

This wireless charger leaves you with *no* excuse to not have a charged phone. It has apparently helped a lot of people overcome this issue because it has sold more than 88,000 times. In fact, this is the charger that took me from being a hot mess with a chronically dead cellphone the past eleven years, to a woman who now always has it charged!

This charger won't work if you have any accessories like PopSockets, cardholders, or rings on the back of your phone. But it will work with a thicker case, like OtterBox or the more affordable Incipio, which is a hot mess *necessity* as far as I'm concerned. Side tip, get a super protective case and a screen protector so you can protect your investment and make your expensive phone last as long as possible.

Let's go over some other places you may need a charger.

I recommend you get one for your car. After trying out a few different chargers, I finally landed on this one. I like it because you can move your phone wherever you need it, whether that's on your dashboard, window, or vent. You can view your GPS however you like it by turning it horizontally or vertically. The holder stays plugged in so it too is wireless and requires minimal effort to charge your phone. And it can charge through a thick OtterBox case as well.

Get one for work. I recommend getting another charger for your office that is the same one that you use at home if it works well for you.

Get one for when you're on the move. You can get a cellphone case with a built-in battery. However, these can be large and bulky. You can also just carry around a cord and wall charger in your purse, or get a power bank. Personally, I didn't like taking the time to fumble around and try to find the cord anytime I wanted to charge my bank. That's when I discovered this device that just plugs directly into an outlet.

The key here is that you don't move any of these chargers. <u>Get one for every location and keep them there so that you have them when you need them.</u>

Having a charged phone comes down to *discipline*. All the chargers in the world won't help you if you don't plug in your phone or set it on a wireless charger. But maybe for you, it's not a lack of motivation, but simply that you keep forgetting to plug it in. <u>If your charger is out of sight, it's out of mind</u>.

These little Cord Holders will keep your charging cords up on your bedside table or desk so that you can see them and remember to plug things in.

Finally, make a plan, set a routine, and get in the habit of plugging in your phone. <u>When and how will you charge it</u> ? Will only charging your phone one time a day while you sleep work for you? Or do you use up so much battery that you need to figure out another time and place for a second charge during your day? Do you need all of those different chargers I went over, or will one that works well for your situation suffice?

<u>Add your new mini-goal of plugging in your phone to your Monthly Goal Tracker if you need to.</u> It was this, in combination with the wireless charger I mentioned earlier, that helped me finally kick my bad habit of never charging my phone.

Action Plan

The most important thing you need to focus on today is figuring out how you can keep your phone charged more regularly, in case you ever need it in an emergency.

After that, get started on your email, either clearing it out and organizing, or creating a new one altogether. This way, you'll be more likely to see an important email come in and not miss it.

Lastly, clear out any unwanted files on your desktop, apps you don't use on your mobile, and organize things on both devices. Clear out even more space and back things up by uploading images to Google Photos and files to Google Drive. <u>If you don't complete everything today, as usual, make plans to finish whatever you don't get to another time.</u>

DAY 28:
CHRONICALLY LATE

Us hot messes tend to be chronically late individuals. We're the ones who have to be told an event starts earlier than it does in order for us to show up anywhere near on time.

Whether you're showing up for formal things like work, or informal things like hanging with a friend, showing up at the designated time is a way we can show *respect* to others and ourselves as well.

If you never thought about being late in terms of you disrespecting someone, well, now you can. Think about it this way, if your girlfriend is waiting for you at a coffee shop to chat, and you show up late, you're non-verbally saying that your time and what you chose to do with it is more important than her time and what she chose to do with it, give it to you.

In addition, you've now robbed her of her time in the future as she might feel obliged to chat later than she was planning on to make up for when you weren't there. What if she had other things she needed to do? Now she can't get to them because you thought it was "okay" to show up late.

But even if you don't think that being late is disrespectful, I think we can both agree that it's rude! So to solve this problem, let's figure out why you're always late, so we can nip it in the bud and start showing the people we care about the respect they deserve.

Possible Reasons for Tardiness

You Think You Don't Need as Much Time as You Do

Are you often tardy because you don't account for how long it takes you to get places? Maybe you're going off of your GPS, but that's not accounting for real-world factors like weather, detours, and slow drivers. Or are you often late because of how long it takes you to get ready? You might be basing how much time you need to do these things on how long it's taken you in the past. But considering that you're always late, this is not the right amount of time for you.

Figure out how long it actually takes you to get places, put your makeup on, or do whatever else it is that you're doing that's causing you to be late, and go off of that *personalized* number. If you need to, refer back to the time management chapter where you timed how long certain activities took you. If you timed everything separately, find out the total amount of time you need by adding up how long it took you to do each of the activities that were involved.

And if for some reason you didn't time yourself before, do so now. Next time you're heading somewhere, time yourself moving at a *normal* pace to collect your stuff, get out the door, drive there going the speed limit, gather your stuff to go inside, walk to the door, and get to the room you need to be in. *That's* how long you need to give yourself. Write that number down along with the activity you were doing into your Google Keep for future reference if you need to.

You Don't Realize What Time It Is

You might be tardy because time gets away from you and you don't realize that it is time to leave until it's too late. But there is no excuse for this these days with the technology that we have available to us. You now have your amazing Google Calendar set up, so use it to prevent mishaps like this from happening in the future.

If you haven't already, be sure to start adding multiple alarms to every event in your calendar, or if it's for an event that day, just on your phone. If you need to, go back to the first day of this guide where I talked about setting notifications for events. In a nutshell, I recommend setting an alarm the day before, when you need to start getting ready to leave, and when you need to head out the door. That might seem like a lot, but do what works for you.

You Can't Wake Up

If you're always late because you can't get out of bed in the morning, there's bound to be an alarm clock or app out there that will work for you.

The Sonic Bomb *will* wake you up, I guarantee it. My husband was chronically late for *twenty-two years* of his life. His mom couldn't get him out of bed for school growing up, and I couldn't get him out of bed for work! He started getting in trouble at his job because of this and was given one last warning about showing up late. That same day, he went out and bought this alarm clock. He wasn't late again! This is Amazon's Choice for the "alarm clock for heavy sleepers." So if that sounds like you, consider getting it!

If you don't want to buy an alarm clock, there are plenty of apps that are more compelling to get you out of bed than your traditional phone alarm.

There is the ever-popular Alarmy_app. <u>It offers unique activities or "missions" that will help get your brain active and wake you up. And it doesn't allow you to turn off your alarm until you've completed one of those missions</u>. If you're always hitting the snooze button, maybe having to do a math problem before being able to hit snooze will help you be less likely to keep hitting it. I'm not the best at math, so I'd never be able to hit snooze. But I do find their barcode scanner fun!

There is also the Wakeup_app (only available for Androids) which <u>gradually brightens your room and wakes your body up the natural way</u>. It has peaceful sounds like birds chirping, so you aren't jarred awake by blaring noise (like you would be with the Sonic Bomb). There are lots of other great features that come with this app too, like a Power Nap option.

You Don't Want to Delay Pleasure

If you tend to be late because you want to scroll on your phone for a little bit longer and watch one more TikTok or read one more Instagram post, I totally get it. I'm there with you. What has helped me is remembering that I will still be able to play on my phone *once* I get there, assuming that I get there early enough that I will have a little bit of time to kill. So get there early and *then* scroll on your phone *there*.

You Think It's a Waste of Your Time or That You Have Better Things to Do

You might be late because you feel like being early "wastes" your time. If that is your underlying thought process, let's tweak that just a little bit. Instead of viewing getting someplace early as *throwing away* fifteen minutes of your life, think of it as *giving* you time for reflection, preparation, and relaxation (like to scroll on your phone).

Being early allows us hot messes to get a hold of our chaos in a simple way, by giving us a few moments of peace to collect ourselves and the opportunity to be prepared. For example, if you leave early to drive somewhere and there is a delay, you might not arrive early, but you'll still at least arrive on time. And if you plan to eat out with friends and get to the restaurant early, it gives you time to look over the menu and decide what you want, so others won't have to wait on you a long time if you tend to be indecisive.

You Love Being Stressed

That heading is a joke, but all jokes aside, being late is stressful! Why else would you continue showing up late or rushing to get somewhere if you didn't love the *anxiety* that came with it?

If you start arriving early, you'll be less stressed. Instead of fretting about how late you are or worrying about getting spotted by a cop while you zoom 10 MPH over the speed limit, why not get there with plenty of time left over? <u>You'll be able to relax, take a deep breath, and center yourself. And you'll be more present and in the moment when the event starts or when your friends arrive.</u>

Action Plan

Make the promise to yourself today that you're going to try to be fifteen minutes early everywhere you go from now on.

If you tend to be chronically late, consider which of those reasons for being tardy apply to you. How will you address that reason, or multiple reasons, and change that for yourself so that you can become the kind of woman who is on time? Do you need to spend some time this evening getting a better alarm clock or downloading one of those apps? Do you need to take the time to add alerts to events in your calendar?

Come up with a plan for what you'll do to encourage yourself to leave on time the next time you're tempted to fall back into old tardy habits. Will you remind yourself that you can play on your phone once you get there? Or will it be enough incentive when you remember that being punctual is a way that we can show respect to our loved ones?

DAY 29:
LOSING YOUR KEYS & OTHER STUFF

You finally pry yourself out of bed, rush to dress because you should have left five minutes ago, and then go to grab your keys and run out the door, but wait. Where are your keys?! They aren't where you thought you put them. You tear through your house flipping up cushions and shoving things out of the way. You frantically dump out your whole purse. You were already pushing it and now you're going to be even later!

How many times has this happened to you? For myself, too many to count. I didn't just have this problem with my keys though. I seemed to lose everything!

Keep Track of Your Keys

You may recall Benjamin Franklin's timeless quote, "A place for everything, everything in its place" that I already referenced back in the chapter on decluttering. I've included it here again because I believe that conquering this part of being a hot mess comes down to two points: have a place for your keys (and everything else you're sick of losing) and be disciplined enough to always put them back there. This is key (pun fully intended).

So designate a spot where you'll always leave them from now on. Don't leave them lying on the counter somewhere where they can get pushed off and fall behind something. Not in your pants where you won't remember, where they could get washed and (if you have a fob) broken. Not in your purse if it's a huge, overstuffed one that'll swallow them.

Sometimes, if you're having a hard time getting into the habit of doing something, making the action fun helps!

If you need some incentive to help you get better at putting away your keys, this magnetic cloud might be perfect for you. With it, you may even look forward to hanging them up! The magnets inside of the cloud are so strong that you can toss your keys at it and it catches them. Plus, it's adorable and makes your keys look like rain.

An entryway table with a small drawer is another great option if you can get one or have room. You could also put a pretty, decorative bowl on a table to hold your keys. And if you keep a small, organized purse, then that could work as well. I found that a simple key hook right by my door was all that I needed.

However you decide to keep your keys, <u>find something that works for you so you'll be more likely to use it, and work to build the habit of placing your keys there *first thing* as soon as you get home.</u>

Besides setting up a place to keep them, you also need to make sure you have backups of them. Get duplicate keys for your house, car, and whatever else you have keys for, as you never know when one might become lost indefinitely. <u>I recommend having one for every person in the household plus at least one extra emergency key. If you have a trusted neighbor or friend who watches your home or animals while you're away, get them an extra one too.</u>

Now that we've covered your keys, what about keeping track of other things?

Keep Track of Remotes

The disappearing remote problem can be solved a few different ways.

There are organizers that hang on your couch's arm where you can store not just remotes, but all kinds of stuff that you may want easy access to while sitting there.

You could consider getting a coffee table with a drawer. This way the remotes will be right by the couch for you while being neatly tucked away out of sight.

If your coffee table doesn't have a drawer, here is a creative idea to still keep the remotes close and prevent them from getting lost. Get a strip of velcro. Put the soft side of the velcro on the backside of the remote, and the barbed side underneath your coffee table stuck to the underside. Now your remotes will be able to stick to the bottom of the table!

You also have the option to completely ditch the remote, and use your phone to control your TV instead. It'll be less clutter and less stuff to lose!

If you have a smart TV, look to see if it came with any apps or if you can get any for it. For example, Roku has an app, which among other things, allows you to remotely control it from your phone. There is also this app for those that have a Samsung TV. If you have an iPhone, you can alternatively get the Universal remote tv smart_app which works with many of the big-name brands like Sony, Samsung, LG, and others. And if you have an Android, you can use Universal Remote Control - Lean Remote App as long as your phone has an IR Blaster built into it. To check if it does, just look up your phone model online.

There are lots of other similar apps out there. So if you're interested, check out this list of The Best TV Remote Apps for Android and iPhone.

Keep Track of Your Cell Phone

Now that you're potentially using your phone for your TV remote, as well as everything else, you really need to know how to find it when it's lost! You can use the "Find my Device" service by Google. This technology has improved *so* much in recent years. I just tested mine and it was able to pinpoint the very house that I'm in. This is awesome to know if your phone ever gets stolen (as happened to me when I idiotically left it in a shopping cart and went home). This service allows you to lock your phone and also erase all data remotely ! This is a golden nugget so tuck this information away somewhere in case the worst happens.

But what if you know your phone is somewhere in your house, but don't know which room? You can still use this free service to find your phone. Even if your phone is on silent, you can make it ring for up to five minutes. Just go to your desktop and look up "Find my Device" to access these features.

Get Others On Board

As we discussed, whether you live by yourself or with others, you'll need to practice the discipline of putting things back in their designated place. If however, you live with a significant other or roommate, you'll need to include them and decide together where things will be kept from now on, especially when it comes to things you share.

If things always go missing in your household, this subject may be a bit of a touchy one. To avoid any blaming or finger-pointing, I recommend approaching the topic from the viewpoint that you yourself need to get better at not losing things and ask for their support.

If discussing with your significant other or roommate doesn't prove successful and things still keep getting lost, take a look at yourself first because *you* may be the main culprit!

Second, if you can, get two of the same item that keeps ending up missing, and differentiate between them in some way so that they can be told apart. This way, when the other person misplaces their item, you'll still have yours, and vice versa. This will reveal who the guilty party is without there being any confrontation.

If All Else Fails

Changing your habits would certainly be the most cost-effective option, but if everything else fails, you can always get a Tile. These are great for putting an end to lost things *permanently!*

There are other less expensive versions, but I like this one because it doesn't require an extra remote. Instead, it goes off of your phone. It is thin enough that you can put it in your purse and light enough you can put it on your dog's collar. Plus, it's not limited to short-range, like others that max out at 100ft. It allows you to find the most recent location of things long-distance as well, which is especially handy if your dog ever gets out.

Action Plan

Today, come up with a plan for the things that you lose most often. Where will you keep your keys, your remotes, and any other things that always go missing ? Do you need to get a key hook or designate a key bowl to help you stick to your new plan and make it as easy as possible? Would it be worth it to you to get some Tiles for your most valuable items that often get misplaced? Include your significant other or roommate (if you have one) in these decisions and decide where things will be kept together.

If you don't have a spare or emergency key, should you go out this evening and get one made or add it to your list of errands next time you're out of the house?

DAY 30:
A MESSY CAR & EMPTY TANK

If you have to take five minutes to clean out the passenger side of your car any time someone is going to ride you, or if you've ever pushed the limit to see how far you could drive on empty, today is for you!

The Appearance & State of Your Car Matters

Did you know that if you go for a job interview and the person offers to walk you back to your car afterward, they're secretly doing it just to check out the state of your car? Is it messy inside? That may indicate to them that you're lazy and might be a slob when it comes to work too.

Would you not be hired based on the state of your car right now?

If you're single, did you know that having a filthy car is so much of a turn-off that more than half of people would end a first date over it? It's such a hot topic that for those in a relationship, a whopping 23% of Americans would cut ties over it

People judge you based on the state of your vehicle. If it's littered with fast food bags they may perceive you as being unhealthy. If it's dirty they'll think you're lazy. If there are things that are broken they may deduce that you don't have money. If people often see your vehicle due to the nature of your job, like a realtor, you may scare away clients by coming across as unprofessional or irresponsible.

Putting other people's opinions aside, having a messy car impacts *you* as well!

Remember back in the chapter on eliminating clutter how there was that study I referenced that found out that women who described their living spaces as cluttered were more likely to be fatigued and depressed? While your car may not be your "livi ng space," it's reasonable to apply the same logic, as you spend so many hours of your life in it.

There is also the physical aspect of how unhygienic it is to have all of those food wrappers lying around growing mold. Microbiologists at Queen Mary

University of London, England found that on average <u>the volume of bacteria in your car is 9x more plentiful than on a public toilet seat</u> While that seems a bit extreme to me, I think you get the point.

Keeping your car clean and tidy matters. As I mentioned, you spend a lot of time in your car, so in a way, it is an extension of your home. But it is also a representation of yourself. How do you want to be represented?

How to Keep a Clean Interior

Every time you get out of your car take the trash and your things with you. You might also consider removing the trash whenever you stop somewhere. But when you're on the road, you can throw your little gum wrappers and sticky soda cans in this Carbage.

While there are other more popular car trash cans, I specifically like this one because it clips to plastic floor mats (a hot mess necessity which I'll talk more about shortly), so it doesn't topple over and spill stuff everywhere. It's wide enough that you can toss trash in without being distracted while driving, but still small enough that it doesn't take up a bunch of legroom. It's leak-proof and has a roomy three-gallon capacity, unlike those tiny cup holder trash cans.

If you have other things besides trash, like gym clothes, is there a better option besides letting them fly around loose in your vehicle? Why not leave them in a locker at the gym, or find a gym bag to keep them in so that your vehicle looks organized. Of course, if your gym clothes are old, take them inside to be washed! Don't allow anything that might stink up your car to sit in it longer than necessary!

If your car is really dirty, take it to be vacuumed, or splurge on a one-time detailing so you can start over with a pristine interior.

In between trips, your car will still accumulate lots of dirt and crumbs though. So <u>to make maintaining your vehicle easier, go longer between trips, or even skip the public vacuums altogether, get yourself a</u> car vacuum cleaner. Unlike other designs that are larger and will probably need to be stored in your trunk, this one is small enough that it can fit in your glove box or side door. So you can conveniently grab it whenever you find a minute to spare for quick spot cleaning. This compact, cordless vacuum can be charged right in your car's power outlet. And it can suck up *liquids* as well as crumbs, making it perfect for us klutzy hot messes!

To help reduce the amount of crumbs you need to vacuum, you could always limit yourself to no longer eating in your vehicle as well.

Use these disposable Armor All wipes to keep the interior of your car clean. I swear by these things and use them religiously. I recommend you keep one in every car and within easy reach, like in the center console, just in case you need to quickly clean up a spill. They save you time, as one wipe cleans (almost) all surfaces including any fabric, vinyl, and leather. So you can wipe stuff down and not worry about having to change out rags or products. Just don't use these on glass though, as they leave an oily residue. Armor All makes separate wipes for that purpose.

Pro-tip: maximize your time whenever you're waiting in the car, like when you're waiting for your groceries at Walmart pickup, by cleaning with these wipes and a car vacuum.

For your personal use, I highly recommend you also keep a pack of baby wipes in your car. If you're thinking, "but baby wipes are for babies," don't knock it till you try it. Even though you might not have children, having wet wipes you can safely use on your skin for *any* kind of mess is super helpful! I like to use these if my hands get dirty or sticky while I'm out in public and can't get to a sink. I also like to use these on my face to clean off sweat during the hot summer months and if I eat anything in the car.

Let's not forget about the rule "Preventing a Mess is Always Easier Than Cleaning a Mess" that we learned about back on Day 15. Be prepared for all accidents by using protective covers on anything that you can to make the cleanup easier. Messes are bound to happen, and you never know when coffee might go flying while you zoom around a corner.

Using covers will not just protect your car, but will also protect its value, so you'll get more for it when it's time to sell. This is because a buyer is usually willing to pay more if they think the car's previous owner took care of it, i.e. if it looks clean!

I highly recommend that all the covers you get be easily wipeable and waterproof. There are seat covers, steering wheel covers, and most importantly floor mats. Getting waterproof, plastic floor mats, as opposed to carpet ones, allows you to take them out and quickly hose them down whenever anything happens. Super simple and easy.

For lack of a better place to put this, let's quickly talk about purses. Purses are another form of representation that we bring along with us when we go out.

If you have so many wrappers, receipts, crumbs, and outdated coupons in there that you can't find your keys (like we just went over yesterday), it's not a good thing! <u>Keep it tidy so that you can quickly find important things and so others don't get the wrong impression of you.</u>

If you have a giant tote that's overflowing because it's so easy to toss stuff into, why not downsize to something that restricts you a little more? If you don't want to swap out your beach bag for something smaller, you can always get a purse organizer that divides the inside into compartments. This is a nice option if you're going to be religious about putting things back in their designated place. But if not, I'd caution you against getting this, because you may end up having an even harder time finding things with so many little pockets to lose stuff in.

How to Keep a Clean Exterior

Did you know that the circular swirls you can see on cars, most visible on black ones, are *not* supposed to be there? That is scratch damage in the paint from going through car washes!

When I first heard this, I decided to opt for touchless car washes instead. But then I learned that because these sorts of washes can't rely on a brush to scrub off dirt, they typically use harsh chemicals to help break down any grime. Unfortunately, these chemicals can also break down the wax and clear coat on your vehicle too!

If your car already has swirls in the paint, is a bit older, or if you're not particularly worried about potentially getting wax damage, <u>you may still consider going to a regular car wash for the time-saving convenience.</u> After all, a clean older car is still better than a dirty older car.

If you have a newer car though, or if you would prefer to wash your car yourself, here is how to do it:

<u>The first option is to go to a car wash with wands.</u> While this won't give

you the best cleaning, <u>it is the faster of the two.</u>

First, rinse the car always going from the top down. Next, switch to foam, and let this sit on your car until it has dissolved so it can start breaking down the dirt. Then switch to wash, then rinse, and then wax. You can use a microfiber cloth for spot cleaning. Finish by drying down your car with another microfiber cloth to avoid spots. Alternatively, you can drive immediately afterward and let the moving air do the work for you.

<u>The best option is to handwash your vehicle.</u> You'll need Meguiar's Ultimate Wash and Wax (you can also use Mother's) which is a great 2-in-1 solution that'll help you save time. You'll also need a hose, a clean bucket of water, clean microfiber cloths or microfiber sponges, a nylon scrub brush, and this tire spray.

Follow the directions on the Meguiar's bottle to combine it with the water in your bucket. Next, rinse the car with the hose. Start at the roof, then do the hood, and then move to the trunk, doing all flat surfaces as well as the windows. Remember, always work from the top down. Use a cloth and soap to wash these areas. Rinse these with the hose before the soap dries. After that, do the same thing working from the bottom of the windows down to the bumpers. The last thing you want to do, as it'll be the dirtiest, is the wheel well (the curved part by your wheel).

For the wheels themselves, use a nylon scrub brush for the rubber. Use a separate microfiber cloth for the rim. Then top them off with a nice shiny finish that'll last about a week by using the aforementioned tire spray.

Again, dry down your car to eliminate spots with a separate clean cloth. To save time, you can also just take it for a quick drive immediately after your final rinse to let it blow dry.

To keep your car looking great and go longer in between washes, <u>spot clean your car with this</u> waterless car soap. If you use this, you'll need a clean microfiber cloth as well.

Also, be sure to <u>immediately tackle any bird droppings on your car</u>, as they don't just look unsightly, but are acidic and can cause paint damage.

Legalities

I know that talking about legal stuff isn't fun, but neither is getting a ticket because you're driving with something expired! Plus, all of the different requirements can be a bit confusing.

For this section, I'm going to assume that you already have a license and have been driving for a few years, but maybe your parents helped you fill out the necessary paperwork, so you don't remember how to do it. Or perhaps you've been driving their car, so they did all of the legal stuff themselves. Whatever your situation, let's go over some of the basics now.

First, let's check your license. Why not take this opportunity to verify that it's still good, and then put the expiration date with a set reminder *before* it expires into your Google Calendar. If you let it expire and continue to drive, you could incur fines and receive points on your driving record. If you leave it expired long enough, you'll eventually have to take the driver's test again! It's just easier to stay on top of it and renew it before it goes past due.

If you need to renew your license, you can do so at your local DMV. Some states have different requirements like needing an additional ID, a piece of mail as proof of residence, and will only accept cash or money orders as payment. So look beforehand to see what you need to take with you.

Something to note that is often overlooked is that your place of residence is required to be updated on your license within thirty days of moving, some states as little as ten. Can you just walk into your DMV and update it, or do you need to mail in a written form? Again, verify your state's requirements.

Next, you have your insurance. This is coverage for you and your car if you get into an accident. This often renews automatically. Verify that you have the correct coverage for you. If you don't understand a lot of the things you're paying for, why not talk to someone you trust who can give you good feedback on whether you need certain policies? You can always call your insurer as well.

By discussing my car insurance with my father-in-law, he noticed that I'd been paying twice for body injury coverage. I was able to cut out one of my policies and ended up saving $200. It's worth double-checking to see if you need what you have!

Also, verify with your insurer that you're getting all the discounts you can! There are military discounts, safe-driver discounts, and certain states give you a discount for taking a defensive driver's course. There are also discounts for going paperless.

If you can, I recommend you get Towing and Labor on your policy. This is especially helpful for us hot messes, as it provides emergency roadside service in case we ever need towing, get a flat tire, or *gasp run out of gas!

Most states recognize electronic proof of insurance if you get pulled over. In fact, from my understanding, the only one that doesn't right now is New Mexico. Having electronic proof is nice because you can show the officer your most updated insurance card. However, you may not always have your phone, and if you do, it may not always have service. So ask your insurer to send you a hard copy, or print it if you have a printer, and keep it in your car at all times.

Last, you have registration. This documentation shows that your vehicle is legal to be used on the road. It's how you get your license plate and the little sticker that goes on it. This helps the government link a car to its owner for taxing purposes. Verify that the sticker on your license plate is still good, and again, mark on your calendar when it will be coming due *before* it expires. Keep the registration paperwork in the car at all times as well.

If you need to renew your registration, most states will require you to show that your license and insurance are up to date *first*, so renew those things beforehand if you need to.

Mechanical Care

Make sure you're getting regular checkups. After all, what's the point of having a clean and legal-to-drive car if it can't run?

I know it's easy to put gas in your car and leave it at that, but just because you don't hear any clanking or squealing doesn't mean that something isn't wrong. You could end up paying more to fix your car by letting mechanical checkups slide, than if you have it serviced regularly and catch an issue early.

<u>Your car's servicing needs will vary depending upon how old it is and how much you drive it.</u> Check your car's manual to see what its exact needs are. I know newer vehicles, like my 2014 SUV, only need to be serviced one time a year or every 7,500 miles.

When it's time for a checkup and oil change, the mechanics will do a full inspection of your car to see if there is anything that needs to be fixed. If they recommend that you have something extra done, call your significant other, father, or guy friend, and have them talk to the mechanic on your behalf.

In this study, they proved that <u>women who appear to not be informed about how much a repair should cost will be quoted $20 more on average than if the uninformed individual was a man</u>. You can overcome this gender discrimination by being prepared and knowing the going rates for things. But if you don't understand cars, call a gentleman you trust so they can make sure you don't have anything fixed that doesn't need to be and so you won't be taken advantage of financially.

In the same study, they also found that <u>you as a female are 10% more likely to get a discount than a man. So ask for one!</u> On average, women were able to get their bills knocked down by 13%.

During the checkup, the mechanics will also fill all of your liquids, check your lights, and check your cabin air filters.

Cabin air filters can be about $50 or more for them to install. But the part itself is only about $15-25. So if they say you need a new one, and you want to save a little money, pick one up at an auto parts store and do it yourself. Depending upon your car, this may be as simple as removing a single screw.

All you need to do is tell the clerk at the auto store what you need and the vehicle you drive, and they'll find the exact part. Depending upon the person, you may even be able to get them to go outside and walk you through the process of installing it.

<u>Every time you go in for an oil change, have them rotate your tires as well.</u> Tires can be costly, but you can extend their life by having them rotated.

After your car has been serviced, ask for an oil change sticker if they do not give you one, so you'll know when your car needs to be seen again. If your car keeps track of this for you, ensure the mechanic updates your car's computer before you leave. For added reassurance, add the next due date to your calendar.

I know it might not be the most fun, but we need to know car basics *before* something happens and we get into a pinch.

Set aside some time to learn how to check your tire pressure so you can prevent a flat, and if you do get a flat, how to change the tire. It's also good to know how to check your oil level and fill up your liquids, for the rest of the time when your mechanic isn't doing it for you. For these things and other important topics, check out "Dad, How do I?" on YouTube in his Car Edition playlist. He explains things just as if he were your dad showing you how to do something, simplifying steps and lingo.

Let's not forget about gas. If you've ever pushed the needle on your gas gauge to see how far below empty you could go, STOP! Do you really want to have to wait for someone to bring you gas and come rescue you?

As much of a "hassle" as getting gas is, dealing with a broken-down car along the side of the road is more so, not to mention how *dangerous* it can be for us ladies.

Plus, running your car on empty may even lead to costly damage. Over time, your car's gas tank will collect dirt and sediment which will settle to the bottom. But when you allow your tank to get so empty, the new gas can churn this gunk up, causing it to be sucked through your fuel filter. Once this filter gets clogged, your fuel pump will have to work that much harder to suck in gas, which may lead to it becoming overheated and damaged. How much will it cost to replace it? Up to $1,000! So don't let your tank get empty.

The best practice is to only allow your tank to get down halfway before filling it back up, or at *most* a quarter full.

How can you make getting regular fill-ups a part of your routine? I made a habit of getting gas every time I pick up groceries. By doing this, I usually only need to top off my tank, and it rarely gets near empty.

Maybe you could reward yourself by getting a little treat at the gas station every time you go to fill up. You could also see if there is a gas station with an attendant who could fill up your tank for you to make things easier. But if you're still having a hard time remembering to gas up, why not ask your significant other to be in charge of this if you're married? It's not uncommon for some men to do! I have a girlfriend who has never filled up her tank since she got married as her husband does it for her weekly.

Action Plan

Today, determine how you are going to better maintain your car and the legalities concerning it. Do you need to spend the afternoon at the public vacuums throwing out trash and cleaning the inside? After that, how will you clean the outside? Do you need to schedule some time off work so you can go to the DMV and get your license renewed? When was your car's last oil change and do you need to get its next one scheduled? How will you incorporate filling up your tank into your routine so you never run on empty again?

Make a plan to tackle these challenges, and enlist help if you need it. If you share a car, why not share the responsibilities of getting it cleaned up as well?

Conclusion

Congratulations

OMG girlfriend, you made it through all thirty days! I am so impressed and proud of you. Pat yourself on the back for all of the hard work you did and take some time to celebrate! Hopefully, you feel more in control of your life now than you did at the start of this guide, and are excited to put all of the tools, ideas, and techniques you learned into practice.

How are you feeling now about being a hot mess? Do you feel like a changed woman, or do you feel like something is still amiss?

What if this guide didn't hold the magic "secret" you were hoping it would that would transform you into someone else, someone who is never a hot mess again? You might not see it, because some are good at hiding it, but everyone is a hot mess in some area. No one is perfect. Just like you, everyone is figuring out life as they go.

Whether you still feel like you're riding the hot mess express or not, I believe that <u>you're already well on your way to becoming a refined woman</u>. I have a feeling that life is going to be a wonderful journey for you. It's going to be a ride that you take by the horns, but not as a hot mess, as an adult who adults *well*!

Repeat the Program

You just finished, and now I'm telling you to begin again? Well, not exactly. But I do recommend that after you've had some time to rest and work on the things that you're already doing, you pick this guide back up again.

Go back through it at a later time and see what new things pop out to you, what suggestions you forgot about, and what different ideas you want to apply to your life this time around.

Odds are that you probably didn't do every exercise to its fullest extent or read every single article that I mentioned. Maybe, you only ended up reading through the guide, as I suggested you might have to do back on Day 4. So <u>why not go back through, at a slower pace if you need to, and do the Action Plans and exercises that you didn't do?</u>

I think it would be a worthy goal to spend the month of December going through this guide again. Why not make it a yearly tradition with yourself? That way, you ring in the new year every year with renewed insights and motivation to make the next 365 days as amazing as possible.

Continue Improving

So where do you go from here? Tony Robbins (an American author, coach, speaker, and philanthropist) recommends learning something new every day by spending thirty minutes reading. I recommend you check out any of the books or articles that I mentioned in the past thirty days, and read those to continue learning and improving yourself.

If you're having a hard time remembering which ones I recommended or just want to cut to the best ones, I've listed my all-time favorite books for you here. I believe the following offer practical application, similar to what you experienced in this guide, and will lead to life transformation:

The 7 Habits of Highly Effective Teens by Sean Covey - The original is good, but I got more value out of this version.

 Eat that Frog! By Brian Tracy

Boundaries by Dr. John Townsend and Dr. Henry Cloud

Atomic Habits by James Clear

The 4-Hour Workweek by Timothy Ferriss - This is more for entrepreneurs, but it still has great time-management tips.

Thanks again so much for joining me on this journey to get off the hot mess express!

Woman, live a full life.
Emily Kendall

© Copyright 2021 - All rights reserved.

…………..

The content contained within this book may not be reproduced, duplicated or transmitted without direct written permission from the author or the publisher.

Under no circumstances will any blame or legal responsibility be held against the publisher, or author, for any damages, reparation, or monetary loss due to the information contained within this book. Either directly or indirectly.

Legal Notice:

This book is copyright protected. This book is only for personal use. You cannot amend, distribute, sell, use, quote or paraphrase any part, or the content within this book, without the consent of the author or publisher.

Disclaimer Notice:

Please note the information contained within this document is for educational and entertainment purposes only. All effort has been executed to present accurate, up to date, and reliable, complete information. No warranties of any kind are declared or implied. Readers acknowledge that the author is not engaging in the rendering of legal, financial, medical or professional advice. The content within this book has been derived from various sources. Please consult a licensed professional before attempting any techniques outlined in this book.

By reading this document, the reader agrees that under no circumstances is the author responsible for any losses, direct or indirect, which are incurred as a result of the use of information contained within this document, including, but not limited to, — errors, omissions, or inaccuracies.

....
Thank you for buying this book.

www.ingramcontent.com/pod-product-compliance
Lightning Source LLC
Chambersburg PA
CBHW070505120526
44590CB00013B/751